W9-APG-655

OLTP Handbook

Edited by
Gary R. McClain

Intertext Publications
McGraw-Hill, Inc.

New York San Francisco Washington, D.C. Auckland Bogotá
Caracas Lisbon London Madrid Mexico City Milan Montreal
New Delhi San Juan Singapore Sydney Tokyo Toronto

Library of Congress Catalog Card Number 93-78582

0 9 8 7 6 5 4 3 2 1

ISBN 0-07-044985-6

Intertext Publications/MultiScience, Inc.
One Lincoln Plaza
New York, NY 10023

McGraw-Hill Book Company
1221 Avenue of the Americas
New York, NY 10020

Contents

Foreword

The contents of *OLTP Handbook* illustrates the diverse approaches to on-line transaction processing, and the individuals contributing chapters represent some of the major companies offering products and services in the OLTP market.

I am grateful to each contributor for taking time out from his or her hectic schedule to expand the body of knowledge in this subject area, as well as to provide valuable reference materials for technical professionals. The chapter contributors are all experts in their own right.

—Gary R. McClain, Ph.D.

Preface

On-line transaction processing, as the term implies, is a means of processing large numbers of transactions as they occur—on-line. As a result of recent hardware and software developments, OLTP is moving into the mainstream of corporate computing. IBM's CICS transaction processing monitor, as well as the UNIX operating system, are providing a foundation for OLTP applications. As OLTP becomes more widespread, it will also embrace technologies such as electronic data interchange, so that business-to-business transactions are also processed with the speed and efficiency of customer applications.

Hardware and software vendors are communicating their OLTP solutions, offering diverse approaches, and the MIS manager is left with a plethora of options and stated directions from which to choose. To further complicate matters are the increasing demands for OLTP from users and management, and an already installed base of hardware and software resources that represents a large financial and manpower investment.

The overall purpose of *OLTP Handbook* is to provide both a technical and practical reference book for anyone involved with the justification and implementation of an OLTP system. The reader will be able to look to this book when evaluating OLTP options, justifying the decision and subsequently implementing and managing the OLTP system.

The intended audience for this book is networking and systems professionals in the MIS departments of large- and medium-sized organizations.

OLTP Handbook is organized in five parts. The introduction in Part 1 is written by Gerald Held of Tandem Computers, the company viewed by many as a pioneer in the field of OLTP. Part 2 focuses on database and application development issues, including program design concerns, the role of fourth-generation languages, managing OLTP on diverse hardware platforms, and system reliability. UNIX concerns are the focus of Part 3, with a focus on understanding the role of UNIX and enhancing UNIX-based OLTP, as well as the role of OSF/DCE as illustrated through a discussion of Transarc's Encina product. Part 4 focuses on CICS issues from both application design and CICS management perspectives. And Part 5 looks at related issues, including on-line complex processing, as well as a discussion of smartsizing as conceived by Integris Corporation and its business partners.

Chapters in each part focus not only on specific technical concerns and guidelines, but also discuss OLTP in relation to the "real world."

Contributors

Scott Dietzen
Transarc Corporation

John Enck
Forest Computer Incorporated

Jeffrey Gui
Sequoia Systems, Inc.

Gerald Held
Senior Vice-President
Strategy and Corporate Development
Tandem Computers Incorporated

Roland N. Luk
Hewlett-Packard Corporation
General Systems Division

David McGoveran
Alternative Technologies

Nancy K. Mullen
Andersen Consulting

Nicolas C. Nierenberg
Chief Technology Officer and Co-Founder
Unify Corporation

Alan Paller
Computer Associates

James Peterson
Landmark Systems Corporation

Michael Snyder
Kaiser Foundation Health Plan, Inc.

The Strategic Planning Group
Integris Corporation

Colin J. White
DataBase Associates

Part 1

Introduction

Chapter

1

On-Line Transaction Processing Systems

Two Decades of Challenge and Innovation

Gerald Held
Senior Vice-President
Strategy and Corporate Development
Tandem Computers Incorporated

During the past 25 years, companies around the globe have embraced on-line transaction processing (OLTP) as an integral part of doing business. This technology, which has evolved into a $60-billion-a-year market while spurring extensive innovation, is particularly vital to business-critical applications conducted by a wide variety of industries, including banking, securities, telecommunications, retail, transportation, manufacturing, and health care.

Prior to the development of OLTP systems, companies generally limited the commercial application of computers to automated record-keeping and off-line batch processing. In the 1950s and 1960s, many users found computers to be too expensive and unreliable to connect them directly to their businesses. Instead, the big mainframe machines were placed in a back room or basement, where each night they processed the day's receipts and generated reports for the following morning.

Starting in the early 1970s, different industries began to adopt OLTP strategies by tying their computer systems directly to business transactions. The airline industry was the first to make a massive investment in OLTP technology, spending hundreds of millions of dollars on large mainframes to develop on-line customized reservation systems. This novel approach made booking reservations much more efficient by connecting an airline's most valuable asset—seat inventory—to an on-line system.

Nevertheless, any company that decided to run its business electronically rather than on paper took a huge risk. Early OLTP systems were technically difficult to build, expensive to operate, and unreliable. Banks, manufacturers, and other companies attempted to convert batch mainframe computers by painstakingly programming them to perform jobs they were never designed to do. These pioneers recognized the important benefits of collecting and managing information about customers, inventory, and orders in a timely manner, but also feared losing transactions or access to the data completely if a computer failed. To bolster system reliability, therefore, designers typically bolted two machines together to provide system redundancy, or backup capability. Much like trying to fit a square peg in a round hole, these contrived OLTP systems were awkward, short-term fixes to important, complex business problems.

Tandem Computers Incorporated was formed in 1974 to find a better answer. In less than 18 months, the startup company introduced the world's first fault-tolerant computer system, designed specifically to handle OLTP applications for the business-critical market. Called the NonStop system, the machine eliminated the pain from OLTP by offering a technological solution that industries such as the airlines and the financial world had struggled to achieve. In essence, Tandem created a new computer market.

Designing Critical OLTP Features

From a business point of view, moving from a paper-based to on-line business represented a tremendous leap of faith. System requirements for OLTP were quite different than those for batch processing modes. With so much at stake, OLTP computers needed to combine high availability, a smooth upgrade path, flexible connectivity with other systems, and the ability to maintain the highest possible data integrity.

In the manufacturing industry, for example, the need for higher shop floor efficiency, better responsiveness to customer demands, and cost-effective inventory control drove the trend toward OLTP systems. Manufacturers typically scheduled their entire production operations by paper, which followed the product—whether a car, computer, or toy—through the factory cycle. Once warehouse inventory was checked out to the shop floor, no efficient way existed to track individual components. This lack of immediate, on-line information from the factory had severe cost consequences; companies routinely ordered too much inventory, did not schedule workers efficiently, and often failed to identify quality-control problems until after products left the plant.

On-line information allowed manufacturers to implement just-in-time (JIT) inventory control with bar code tracking. This capability permitted tighter management of raw material purchases and enabled companies to monitor the movement of components as they flowed through production. The key to success was that properly designed OLTP systems minimized the risk and maximized the benefits of replacing paper-based processes with computer-driven applications.

To meet business requirements in a wide range of industries, Tandem designed a number of key fundamental features into its systems which the developers regarded as critical to any true OLTP environment. These included fault tolerance to ensure continuous system availability, linear expandability, distributed databases, networking, data integrity, and system security.

First and foremost, computers processing transactions in real time could not fail or corrupt data. Banks routinely send wire transfers worth billions of dollars between corporate accounts, and the financial consequences of losing a large transaction due to a system crash would be disastrous. In manufacturing, a large French automobile maker that produces more than two million vehicles per year calculates it would cost $4,000 each minute the company's production line is down. Simply stated, industries that run their operations on-line need to have their computer systems up and running.

A parallel processing architecture solved this availability problem by providing the first fault-tolerant design which prevented any single hardware or software malfunction from disrupting system operations. The computer systems divide the workload among loosely coupled processors that perform multiple tasks simultaneously. If a processor fails, its functions are automatically taken over by the other central processing units (CPUs).

In addition, a fault-tolerant operating system further protects the computer by enabling users to run primary and backup software processes in separate CPUs for all applications. Development of a pioneering requester/server software structure also divided applications into client/server components. The client portion was dedicated to capturing the on-line transaction, while the server handled the database part of the transactions. Introduced in the mid-1970s, this fundamental OLTP concept emerged as an early precursor to the client/server software strategies touted today.

Moving from a batch environment to on-line processing also required linear expandability. In the 1960s, IBM, DEC, and other computer manufacturers had introduced the model concept, where customers could initially purchase a small computer, then replace it with larger models from a compatible family of products. Although this concept protected businesses to a certain degree as processing needs grew, pulling out one machine and wheeling in another also caused system downtime and disrupted operations.

With their businesses tied tightly to computer systems in an on-line environment, many companies could not afford the downtime required to bring in a new model. Training and software reprogramming issues presented additional obstacles. Moreover, planners had trouble predicting how fast transaction volumes might grow as customers reacted to on-line services, making it difficult to select which size model to install. Therefore, enterprises faced a dilemma: If business was good and transaction volumes high, they still might run into problems if an undersized computer could not provide enough power to handle the processing load; If they purchased an oversized system and business volumes did not grow, their service could become too expensive.

The concept of modular expandability for commercial OLTP computing solved this dilemma by enabling companies to add processors and disk storage on-line, without any reprogramming. This also allowed users to increase the size of their system configuration over many years by simply plugging in additional processing capacity. If business increased dramatically, companies could seamlessly upgrade to more powerful computers without disruption to on-line services.

The need for distributed computing represented another important difference between OLTP and batch processing environments. As a network application, OLTP involves many different sources of business transactions. Enterprises therefore need to provide a common view of their service to customers at various network locations, such as automated teller machine (ATM) sites or worldwide branch offices that handle local order entry.

A parallel processing architecture allows centralized or distributed processing. Data can either reside on a single computer or be distributed across multiple systems around the world. This design enables companies to link different transaction locations via a transparent network, where the distributed database appears to all users as a single system. Moreover, the introduction of a fault-tolerant structured query language (SQL) implementation of the American National Standards Institute (ANSI)–standard SQL provided software programmers with the ability to design applications capable of managing highly complex distributed databases.

The Rush to Build OLTP Systems

Despite these innovations, the computer industry was slow to react to the business-critical OLTP market during the 1970s. From 1980 to 1985, however, the trend toward OLTP systems exploded.

During this period, many companies attempted to build business-critical OLTP systems. Venture capitalists poured several hundred million dollars into more than a dozen startups, including Parallel, Tolerant, Stratus, and Auragen. Aside from Stratus, which competes today in this market, most of these entrepreneurs failed for two reasons. One, none of the companies offered products that improved on the pioneering OLTP computers' unique technical design, and two, although some manufacturers developed computers with technically comparable architectures, they lacked an established reputation and installed base of systems, which made it more difficult to attract customers. In general, these unsuccessful companies failed to provide refinements that made them better than OLTP technology.

Large computer giants such as IBM, DEC, and Siemens also saw an opportunity in the OLTP market. These enterprises collectively spent more than $1 billion on research and development to build business-critical systems in the 1980s. Despite this huge investment, many projects either failed or were canceled. The companies instead developed their own form of OLTP solutions which did not include fault-tolerant architectures.

Today, OLTP has become pervasive throughout the business world. From factories to gas stations to stock exchanges, high-availability on-line computer systems play a key role in capturing and processing transactions, as well as enhancing customer services and enabling industries to offer new products. In the future, OLTP will continue to evolve and promote innovation as banking, retail, telecommunications, manufacturing, and other industries venture into new areas of endeavor.

OLTP in the Banking Industry

Prior to deregulation, the banking industry was much like a slow-paced country club, where every member had their own franchise. Open weekdays from 10:00 A.M. to 3:00 P.M., most bank branches maintained hours that often made it inconvenient for customers to conduct financial transactions. Although increased competition led banks to distinguish their service levels by extending branch hours and offering other incentives, it also resulted in higher staff costs.

The need to offer customers better, more diverse services without significantly increasing operating costs drove the banking industry to look for alternative delivery platforms which did not require adding more employees. This key objective marked the advent of automated teller machines (ATMs).

However, early ATMs were off-line, which required the bank to either take the risk that some customers might withdraw unavailable funds, or place limits on the sessions, thus offsetting the increased convenience of the machines. Card holders could only receive up to $50 in cash, and accounts were settled after hours via batch processing on a mainframe computer. Even though a few financial institutions went through the expensive task of placing their ATMs on-line, the machines typically still remained operational only while the bank was open.

The introduction of the NonStop system helped solve this problem. Banks needed reliable, up-to-date, instantaneous information about account balances to offer ATM services, and the computers provided the timely transaction data required.

In California, for example, Wells Fargo Bank has developed a highly successful, cost-effective ATM network that takes full advantage of OLTP fundamentals. Headquartered in San Francisco, the bank has expanded its network from 10 ATMs in 1978 to 1,700 machines today. This growth included a merger with the former Crocker Bank, during which Wells Fargo was able to easily expand its Tandem-based OLTP system and smoothly incorporate Crocker's ATM machines into its own network, without any downtime.

To support this network, Wells Fargo operates two data centers—one in San Francisco, the other in Los Angeles—that simultaneously communicate with each other whenever an ATM transaction takes place. As a result, if a customer withdraws $100 cash from an ATM connected to the San Francisco facility, then immediately places his or her card in one linked to Los Angeles, the account will show the updated balance.

One unique configuration aspect that has attracted officials from other U.S. and European banks is that Wells Fargo's network features a "disaster-proof" design, which provides full and immediate business resumption. The bank has configured each branch with a minimum of two ATMs: One machine is connected via phone lines to the San Francisco data center, while its partner is linked to the Los Angeles facility. If an earthquake, flood, fire, or other disaster should knock out one data center, Wells Fargo customers would not lose service because the other center would pick up the workload. By taking advantage of key OLTP fundamentals such as continuous availability, expandability, and distributed processing capabilities, Wells Fargo has developed a unique ATM network which serves as both a marketing tool and a competitive edge in providing extremely reliable OLTP services.

Expanding the Use of OLTP Systems

With the initial success of on-line ATMs as cash disbursement machines, banks moved to expand use of their OLTP systems into other areas. Efficient, highly reliable OLTP technology made the evolution painless. In addition, information systems managers were eager to find new uses for the on-line computers to justify spending millions of dollars on a computer system designed for a new, one-market application.

As a result, financial institutions began using OLTP networks to support new types of electronic payment methods, including the wire transfer systems that moved billions of dollars between banks on a daily basis. The high availability, reliability, and data security provided by OLTP systems ensured that the funds would not be lost or routed incorrectly. Moreover, banks also developed corporate cash management products for their customers that recognized the need for timely, efficient funds transfer. Home banking systems were introduced, such as Pronto from Chemical Bank, which allowed customers to pay bills, make balance inquiries, and transfer funds between different accounts.

Although home banking was limited in the United States due to the relatively high investment users needed to make in equipment, the service achieved high success in France, Japan, and other nations where governments provided subsidies to develop the market. More recently, new kinds of voice-activated delivery systems such as smart telephones, pager technologies, and 800-number call centers have reduced the cost to the point where home banking is more attractive to a wider audience in the United States.

Redefining OLTP

Today, the banking industry is redefining OLTP. Until recently, OLTP primarily involved on-line credit and debit processing, where the system applied simple logic to business transactions and provided an answer. For example, when a customer used an ATM to withdraw $200, the OLTP system checked the account for available funds, dispensed the money, and debited the account. If the account did not contain at least $200, the system routinely denied the withdrawal, often resulting in an unhappy customer.

With competition increasing thoughout the banking industry, institutions must further differentiate their services to attract and maintain customers. In fact, customer service is the primary battleground in finance today. Providing basic transaction processing through an ATM network is no longer enough. Innovative banks instead are seeking a competitive edge by changing their focus from account-oriented transaction processing to information processing, which places greater emphasis on customer service and satisfaction.

The move toward information processing is the next significant step in the evolution from account-driven to customer-oriented banking. It enables institutions to consider the sum total of an individual's banking relationship—including how long he or she has been a customer and the amount of money kept in savings, certificates of deposit (CDs), or other accounts—when making a decision to dispense cash, approve loans, or grant lines of credit. By capturing information on-line, a bank may allow the customer to withdraw $200 cash from an ATM even if his or her checking account lacks sufficient funds. In lieu of making a decision based on one account, the bank can use its computer network to quickly review multiple accounts, leading to better service and, ultimately, satisfied customers.

Achieving information processing will not be easy. Unlike other industries, large banks deal one-on-one with millions of customers, each of whom averages about 30 checking account transactions per month. These active business relationships often last 5 years or longer. With such a large amount of data to capture, banks today face great difficulty in linking diverse accounts and computer systems located in different geographic areas. For example, a bank may maintain its checking account information on a host system in one city, its savings accounts on a minicomputer in another city, and CDs on a workstation in a third city. Historically, it has not been feasible either technologically or economically to capture business relationship data for millions of individual customers.

Furthermore, to move from transaction to information processing, the complexity of application software and investment required by banks will increase significantly. This software investment makes system scalability and expandability critical issues. If a company spends $100 million in software, it cannot afford to run out of processing power or bring in an incompatible larger system which would require rewriting millions of lines of application code. By starting out on a seamless OLTP system that enables the business to add CPUs and disk storage in a linear fashion, the users do not need to alter the application software when upgrading systems.

The third step in the OLTP evolution will be knowledge processing, whereby banks will incorporate artificial intelligence into their systems. Still in its conceptual stage, knowledge processing will allow the computer network to make informed business decisions based on behavorial knowledge of the bank's customers—much like a person does—rather than only account information.

Take the example mentioned above. A customer requests $200 from an ATM but does not have enough money in her checking account. However, for the past 5 years on the same day each month, this particular customer has withdrawn $200 and deposited her payroll check that night. By knowing this behavorial pattern and combining it with account information, the bank may decide to approve the transaction despite the current insufficient funds. Moreover, the system may know that this customer recently called the bank's service center to complain about a mistake on her monthly account statement. If the customer has been profitable and the bank fears losing her business if it makes her unhappy again, it may decide to take the risk and dispense the money based on that knowledge, rather than simply checking to see if she has enough money in multiple accounts to cover the withdrawal. In contrast, a bank could deny the cash to unprofitable customers.

The trend toward knowledge processing presents significant challenges for the technology needed to drive banking systems. According to an annual technology survey conducted by Ernst and Young for the American Bankers Association, the amount of data storage required by the U.S. banking industry will skyrocket as institutions move toward knowledge processing. Furthermore, if a company needs 5 million instructions per second (MIPS) to conduct simple OLTP, it will require approximately 50 MIPS to provide information processing, and 500 MIPS to handle knowledge processing.

Clearly, the new emphasis on knowledge-based customer services requires the support of key OLTP fundamentals: 24-hour-a-day system availability, modular expandability, advanced networking capabilities, superior relational database management systems, and strong data security. Knowledge processing will also demand that OLTP systems incorporate highly flexible open systems connectivity and client/server strategies. Requests for knowledge may come from many different sources, and the OLTP network must interplay with multiple environments to access or supply needed data.

A client/server environment that provides database interoperability will enable systems to extract information from a wide variety of sources, quickly assemble the data into knowledge, apply logic to it, and formulate an answer. Some banks today are already combining multimedia capabilities on a limited scale to handle compound transactions. In processing loan applications, for example, they may use imaging technology to capture pictures of documents or customer information, then add voice notes and circulate the entire data package via electronic mail to various bank officials for approval. Future advances and innovations such as these will rely heavily upon the ability of OLTP systems to keep pace.

Bringing Stock Exchanges On-Line

In addition to playing a key role in the evolution of banking, OLTP has made a dramatic impact on another sector of the finance industry—stock exchanges. In the 1970s, many financial markets were notoriously unreliable due to frequent system outages. Computers were primarily used to report the day's trades, but they did not handle transactions on-line. Volume was also very limited; major exchanges traded less than 20 million shares per day on average.

Seeking constant availability and timeliness in reporting trades, the New York Stock Exchange automated with OLTP systems, followed by NASDAQ and scores of other markets. The payoff has been tremendous; today the combination of OLTP technology and disaster backup sites has all but eliminated computer downtime and reporting delays. With modular expandability, the systems can also easily handle huge trading volumes, which routinely reach more than 200 million shares per day. And although some exchanges still require large amounts of paper to settle trades, a growing number have moved to totally electronic trading, where OLTP computers match a sell request with a buy order or process the entire transaction.

In addition, at the Chicago Board of Trade (CBOT), the oldest and largest futures exchange in the world, each year OLTP technology smoothly and accurately handles price reporting for more than 140 million contracts for a variety of grain products and interest-sensitive financial instruments, representing billions of dollars in investments. With fast, efficient electronic order entry and delivery, CBOT will help member firms increase productivity and reduce costs through elimination of labor-intensive practices. The fundamental features of OLTP technology also have allowed CBOT to introduce after-hours trading, the initial step toward its ultimate goal of an electronically supported, 24-hour trade capability.

OLTP in Point-of-Sale and Retail Applications

Closely linked to banking, credit and debit point-of-sale (POS) transactions today represent a major trend for the retail market. As early as 1919, Filene's Department Stores of Boston offered the first credit card. Major retailers such as Sears and Montgomery Wards followed with their own proprietary cards, which consisted of metal plates with a notch on the side to identify the issuing store.

With the advent of computers, the first plastic bank credit card was introduced in the 1950s. Called BankAmericard®, it marked an important new trend by providing consumers with revolving bank credit while promoting shopping convenience.

Other banks soon joined forces to bring credit-acceptance capabilities to merchants not offering proprietary cards. Introduced as the Interbank card, this popular plastic payment method soon became known as MasterCard®. To conduct a business transaction, the merchant placed the customer's imprinted card in a special device and pulled down the handle to capture the data on a receipt. The pieces of paper were bundled at the end of the day and taken to a bank, which processed the sales slips in a batch environment.

Along with this new payment method came different forms of abuse. Fraud and misuse forced banks to print a Pick-Up bulletin, which listed the account numbers of bad credit cards. Unfortunately, the catalog was often out of date by the time it reached the stores. Merchants also found it cumbersome and time consuming to read the small print when checking account numbers, which detained and inconvenienced shoppers. The need for a better way to identify bad or illegal cards spurred the effort to initiate electronic credit authorization in the mid-1960s. Despite this advance, the day's receipts were still sent to the bank for batch processing.

By the late 1970s, the combination of OLTP-based POS systems and magnetic stripe technology allowed banks and retailers to electronically authorize credit purchases while also capturing transaction data at the same time. This move toward electronic draft capture significantly reduced the need for paper; banks received sales slips from merchants only for archival purposes, not processing.

With the proliferation of ATM networks, banks and retailers evolved the idea of using ATM cards at the point-of-sale by directly debiting the amount of purchase from customers' checking accounts. Hundreds of thousands of terminals—and millions of cards—now exist where cardholders can use stand-alone POS devices or upgraded cash registers with magnetic stripe readers and personal identification number (PIN) pads. By adding value to this single piece of plastic, ATM cards have emerged as the key for customers to access their money from nearly any place in the world, ranging from local gas stations to foreign retailers.

For example, Lucky Stores, a Northern California supermarket chain, invested in an on-line POS debit system that enables shoppers to receive cash back. Randall's Stores in Texas has also implemented a highly successful system. With security risks a problem at outdoor machines, indoor debit systems can also help prevent theft by now allowing customers to withdraw up to $300 at 24-hour retailers linked to an ATM network. Moreover, ATM cards are accepted today in Canada, Mexico, New Zealand, and many European countries, decreasing the need for cumbersome paper or travelers checks.

The use of debit cards offers several important benefits to retailers and customers. One, it lowers the cost of operations by reducing bad checks (a major concern of the supermarket industry) and cutting bank processing charges. Food industry studies suggest that paper checks cost supermarkets approximately twice as much to process as a typical debit card transaction. Two, debit cards reduce float and enable merchants to collect their money faster from the banks. And three, shoppers are provided with another payment choice, which does not require keeping cash on hand or paying interest on credit card purchases.

Both credit and debit transactions at the point-of-sale are dependent on key features provided by business-critical OLTP systems. As electronic funds transfer (EFT) transactions skyrocket, the need for "7-day by 24-hour by forever" continuous availability and system expandability to handle rising volumes has become essential to business growth. If an on-line system is down, the store may lose customers, and retailers will no longer tolerate unreliable networks that do not allow patrons to use plastic payment cards.

To avoid these problems, 67 of the top 100 EFT networks in the world today run on fault-tolerant OLTP systems, including STAR in California, PULSE in Texas, HONOR in Florida, and NYCE in New York. The computer systems provide device handlers for every terminal on the market, and they can communicate without restriction to any host mainframe computer. In addition, network providers can bolt on additional capacity as workloads increase, which preserves their substantial software investment and insulates them from worrying about which model to install.

On-Line Electronic Benefits

POS has also helped bring a wide range of electronic benefits on-line, such as food stamps, aid to families with dependent children (AFDC), unemployment insurance, social security payments, and supplemental social income. Many federal and state agencies now issue benefit recipients a plastic card with a magnetic stripe and PIN, much like an ATM card. Along with removing the stigma of purchasing groceries with food stamps, it reduces the time required for the government to reimburse stores from 2 weeks to 2 days. Card-based electronic transactions also substantially help cut fraud, protect against stolen food stamps, and nearly eliminate the ability of recipients to trade benefits for nonfood items, including drugs or alcohol.

Furthermore, POS technology is being widely employed for non-payment transactions. For example, California Motor Vehicle licenses now include a magnetic stripe, which contains an individual's name, expiration date, and license number. Supermarkets and other retailers can use the license for identification and check guarantee purposes by running the stripe through an on-line POS terminal at the cash register. Pharmacies also now accept plastic cards that verify customer prescriptions and co-payments. By passing the card through the on-line POS terminal, the system transmits the information to the insurance carrier, who reimburses the pharmacist for the prescription.

The Smart Card Evolution

Another recent innovation that relies on OLTP systems is the smart card, a plastic debit device containing an integrated microchip capable of holding 2 to 4 megabytes of data. This stored data, such as credit amount and personal identification information, can be captured at the terminal and transmitted to an on-line or off-line system. Although today's ATM and POS infrastructure cannot read smart cards, this combination identification/payment device is carving a niche where magnetic stripe cards have not yet penetrated.

Among its many current uses, the smart card replaces coins needed to make calls from public phones or buy time on parking meters. Some college campuses also sell cards to students, who use them in vending machines, at laundromats, in the school cafeteria, or at local retailers who have installed terminals. Stored on the chip, the amount of credit paid for by the user is reduced each time he or she makes a purchase. When the credit runs out, the user can replace the card or replenish the credit line.

By storing individual identification data, including fingerprints, voice prints, and retinal information, smart cards can also significantly reduce fraud. In contrast, banks that issue credit cards with magnetic stripes and customers who use them still lose billions of dollars each year to counterfeiters and con artists. In contrast, both ATM debit transactions and smart cards make it much more difficult to defraud.

In the future, use of plastic cards will continue to proliferate. Banks will place both credit and debit capabilities on a single card, which will require enhanced intelligence on the part of ATM and POS terminals. To keep pace, retailers have already started installing "smart" personal computer (PC)–type cash registers that can accommodate new applications. In addition, strong growth is predicted in self-service technologies, such as kiosks where consumers will be able to purchase airline tickets and register at hotels without talking to a desk clerk, terminals where customers can purchase personally designed greeting cards, order food selections at fast food restaurants, or pick up and return rental cars automatically. As 24-hour-a-day on-line transactions continue to grow, the next generation of OLTP systems is being developed to take advantage of these innovative applications.

OLTP in Telecommunications

Spurred by increased competition resulting from the breakup of AT&T in 1983, business-critical OLTP systems have proliferated throughout the telecommunications industry. Today, on-line technology is positioned to facilitate and support a wide variety of emerging customer services, ranging from smart phones and private virtual networks to wireless communications and universal numbers.

Much like banking institutions, telephone companies (telcos) were often slow paced and reluctant to change prior to deregulation. Telcos took great care to protect their networks, which provided highly reliable basic service. In many cases, technical managers shunned innovations that required changing the network. Although some telcos attempted to automate their cumbersome billing and paper-handling functions with batch processing, the systems primarily impacted labor requirements rather than the way in which industry conducted its business.

Business-critical OLTP systems today are making a tremendous impact throughout the telco industry by providing enhanced network intelligence that facilitates new services and improves productivity. More and more, phone companies are demonstrating how OLTP fundamentals fit hand-in-glove with telecommunications' philosophy and standards.

One key example is that telcos now routinely serve as billing agents for retailers. OLTP networks provide the physical resources necessary to handle a wide range of electronic transactions, including catalog shopping or ordering home-delivered restaurant meals, which currently account for more than 20 percent of all retail sales. Moreover, consumers can use their touchtone pads to pay monthly bills, including phone service charges. In addition to enhancing customer convenience, this capability benefits telcos and banks by eliminating millions of paper invoices and checks, which reduces costs and enables both industries to serve more customers with fewer people.

During the past several years, improvements in basic network intelligence have also advanced many customer services, including 800 numbers and number translation capabilities. When a caller dials an 800 number, the network quickly translates it into the actual business number and routes the call to its proper destination. A popular option, 800 service accounts for a sizable portion of AT&T's annual revenues and has grown rapidly among major phone companies. Telcos, for example, now also offer customers residential 800 numbers. As a result, frequent callers, such as children away at college, can use the 800 service to phone home without being charged.

Enhanced Customer and Operator Services

As exciting new products and network services become available, however, consumers must be able to order them efficiently. In the past, customer service representatives at many phone companies relied on large arrays of catalogs and a calculator to determine phone installation costs or handle requests for new options. This manual method proved extremely inaccurate: Representatives could not tell customers their new phone numbers, the exact monthly costs, whether or not specific options were available at a location, or even when service would commence. With on-line, electronic information, the representative of today can precisely calculate costs, instantly provide new phone numbers (or schedule service within a 2-hour window if a phone company employee must visit the site), and offer a list of options available on the network. Phone companies can also handle customer billing inquiries much more effectively, thanks to on-line data.

OLTP has also paved the way for a wave of new and enhanced operator services. Volt Delta Resources Inc., of New York City, is working to rekindle the industry's tradition of superior directory services through the development and integration of large-scale, cost-effective information solutions for telephone companies and interexchange carriers. By combining its Delta Operator Services System (DOSS) software with OLTP computers, Volt Delta has enabled phone companies to increase revenues and complement traditional directory assistance by positioning them to offer new creative operator services, including electronic yellow pages, call completion with message delivery, special name and address listings, third-party calls, and billing options.

Unlike products limited by fixed functionality, the DOSS platform incorporates key OLTP fundamentals: a fault-tolerant architecture, modular expandability allowing the addition of future applications and services, and a relational database management system (RDBMS) capable of handling tens of millions of listings. The system also features advanced retrieval technology, which provides subsecond response time when an operator looks up a phone number.

The DOSS system is designed to implement the concept of a universal operator who can provide callers with a wide range of community information. For example, if a customer wants to know the location of the nearest drug store that accepts credit cards or a gas station within one mile of his home, DOSS can enable operators to find that specific information within milliseconds. In the past, operators were not allowed, by regulations, to provide the data, plus no effective way existed to search for it.

Reducing Business Costs

Faced with fierce competitive pressures, many companies are turning to OLTP-based private virtual telephone networks in order to lower costs and enhance service. Until recently, businesses that operated dedicated private networks paid ownership costs 24 hours a day, even when the phone service was not in use. With a private virtual network, companies borrow a portion of a telco's public network, but pay only for the amount of time that they use it. Users receive the same excellent service provided by a private network, while companies benefit through lower costs of doing business. Providing this service requires intelligent OLTP networking systems that can identify callers, translate numbers, route calls properly, and handle billing procedures.

An additional cost-effective benefit is that U.S. businesses can set up time-of-day and date parameters within their phone networks which will automatically route customer service calls made on holidays, such as Independence Day and Thanksgiving, to Canadian affiliates, and vice versa. This system flexibility eliminates the need to bring workers in on their holidays. Likewise, companies can route East Coast evening calls to time zones where facilities remain open for business.

Another significant business service on the horizon will involve associating a phone number with an individual employee rather than an instrument. Customers will receive a single, universal number and the network will track the person, transferring calls and messages as he or she moves from location to location. This innovation will eliminate the need for customers to remember multiple numbers, such as home, office, and car telephones, and voice mail. To support this and other advanced features, telcos will require information processing in an OLTP environment.

An exciting new technology beginning to shape the future of telecommunications around the globe is wireless. These facilities will allow workers to move relative to the communications infrastructure, whose components will be monitored and controlled by highly sophisticated OLTP switching networks. Using a pocket device that indicates incoming calls by vibration or tone, users can receive messages anywhere in the world, including ships or airplanes. The communicator will display the identifier of the person trying to contact them—much as with today's pagers—giving users the choice of whether or not to take a call. OLTP systems will support wireless communications by providing the high-performance database necessary to keep track of mobile telephones and billing information.

Limited wireless communications are currently being offered at high premiums in the commercial voice telephone marketplace. Today's cellular telephone environments, which operate on a bounded set of radio frequencies, usually encompass large areas that range for many miles. By limiting the physical range of communicators, however, telco service providers can reduce wireless environments to microcells approximately 100 to 200 yards in size, permitting them to reuse the same radio spectrum frequencies in multiple locations and in very small packages. Once available, this technology will enhance communication between employees while eliminating rewiring costs often incurred by companies when relocating individuals or entire departments from building to building.

Future Trends in OLTP

With digital technology exploding in all facets of business, two key breakthroughs will create a tremendous need for advanced OLTP systems. Companies are developing smaller, more powerful, cost-effective devices, such as screen-based smart phones, personal digital assistants (PDAs), notebook computers, pen-based computers, and specialized industry hand-held devices (commonly used today by express delivery companies) for information processing. In addition, these devices need to interface with larger computer systems over broadband or wireless communication networks, providing users with the ability to transmit massive amounts of voice and data. To meet this challenge, OLTP providers must design more powerful products capable of handling a wide range of new, innovative applications.

Today's growth in digital transactions represents only the tip of the iceberg. By the year 2000, three emerging markets are expected to generate more than $1 trillion in annual revenues by taking advantage of interactive multimedia: business applications, home entertainment, and health care networks.

During the past decade, many young people have grown up as "video junkies," accustomed to interactive relationships with electronic devices. This mindset will fuel a trend toward two-way, information-on-demand capabilities in home and business applications. The home entertainment market will initially drive the advance toward interactive multimedia systems, followed by business, education, and health care.

In the home, consumers will soon be able to select videos at their convenience from a large electronic database library, access electronic games, or talk with family members across the country over smart high-definition TV screens or video terminals. Videoconferencing technology will also allow business colleagues to interact electronically, as increasing numbers of employees work at home. OLTP systems will be a vital part of this evolution, providing the complex infrastructure and relational databases needed to handle service requests and customer billing, while offering seamless system expansion capable of satisfying the high growth expected in the entertainment market.

Still in its early phases, interactive multimedia information is today being transmitted in crude form via PCs and screen-based smart telephones, which represent a major trend in how customers will use phone services during the next decade. Designed to maximize ease-of-use, these units contain both a processor and memory to store information, accumulate messages, identify callers by name, and provide ready access to new network services.

Bolstered by a court decision permiting telephone companies to provide video dial-tone services, pilot programs are now available that allow customers to dial up programming on demand, eliminating the need to go to a video store. Moreover, home users will soon access data and simple graphics via the two-way telephone screen to conduct personal business, such as purchasing tickets, filling eyeglass orders, and obtaining information.

As interactive multimedia becomes widespread in office environments during the 1990s, emerging technologies such as digital transmission of television, video compression, and high-definition graphic devices will allow workers to create and manipulate on-screen images, statistics, and other data during videoconferencing sessions. Beyond the year 2000, electronic appliances will be embedded throughout many businesses. Instead of PCs, offices will provide workers with flat-screen computers built into desks. Today's white boards will be replaced by devices that translate a person's handwriting into digital code and transmit it immediately to co-workers down the hall or across the country. Moreover, offices will be equipped with sensing devices that recognize individual employee badges containing smart chips—much like those worn by Enterprise crew members on *Star Trek: The Next Generation*. The sensors will keep track of employees as they move around the corporate campus. Even today, companies have begun to design electronics into their building structures to prepare for the future. As these and other technologies become pervasive, they will require transmission of huge amounts of on-line transactions over sophisticated networks to highly reliable OLTP computers.

Controlling Medical Costs with Technological Solutions

By the mid-1990s, health networks will become more important for medical care, enabling physicians to administer services to patients in their homes. Some medical companies today make house calls to provide patients with injections, medications, or other services, such as changing kidney dialysis equipment. The next step will involve monitoring patients at home electronically. Staff personnel at nurses' stations will watch patients via video screens, checking vital signs and talking to patients as if they were in a hospital room down the hall. In addition, electronic video technology will enable physicians with specialized training to treat patients located in other clinics or hospitals.

Achieving remote health care and other new services will require large communication networks capable of reducing high administrative costs. Today, the health care industry remains extremely paper intensive, with manual handling of medical records and payment processes. Insurance companies currently process approximately ten million claims per day using traditional paper billing methods. To handle this massive amount of data more reliably and accurately, the industry needs to create a national infrastructure which will automate all health care information services, billing procedures, and payment processes.

Advanced OLTP systems can provide this infrastructure. Within 3 to 5 years, the technology will allow the health care and insurance industries to handle payments electronically. Instead of being sent a bill from a doctor or submitting paper forms, patients will receive monthly credit card-type statements from payment associations which will itemize visits, detail what portion of the bill was paid by insurance, and indicate the balance due.

Although today's fault-tolerant OLTP systems are well suited to credit card billing procedures, health care payment processes present a challenge that will require more sophisticated databases. Payment adjudication often involves transactions that include technical information, such as family histories, lab services, and treatment data, as well as large dollar amounts. OLTP solutions have already been developed to handle claims and payment processes, while new systems are being planned to process complex information and perform the adjudication function on-line.

Once the structure is in place, the technology will permit the industry to do a much better job of managing and reducing costs. All procedures, tests, and operations performed by hospitals and individual physicians will be stored in large interactive multimedia databases, enabling insurance providers or employers who pay claims to closely track the average cost for specific methods and scrutinize the actual utilization of practices. For example, if a certain medical procedure usually requires two follow-up visits and a patient comes in for ten treatments, payers and clinicians can ask questions based on comprehensive records and other data to better control use of services. By using this prospective utilization capability, insurance plans can also establish conditions in advance that define what costs will be paid. Moreover, on-line claims handling will support faster payments to physicians. Medical offices can use the network to verify patient coverages and co-payments efficiently, reducing the time required to receive fees from several months to 10 days.

Conclusion

During the past two decades, OLTP technology has provided a flexible platform for many innovative applications, ranging from ATM networks to computerized stock exchanges to shop floor automation. Today, creative developments in banking, telecommunications, health care, home entertainment, and other industries have increased the need for more intelligent networks with greater functionality. Therefore, business-critical OLTP technologies must continue to offer new features, including permanent availability providing zero outage minutes, open systems connectivity, more complex relational databases, and even easier seamless expansion.

The future also holds great promise for many bold new applications, as OLTP systems become more powerful, sophisticated, and user friendly. With client/server strategies, networks will manage critical data more efficiently in a distributed fashion, while also linking previously stand-alone PCs, workstations, and systems into a single, comprehensive environment. Finally, by providing the flexibility and reliability needed to compete in today's global market, evolving OLTP fundamentals will enhance business enterprises' ability to use their computer systems as strategic weapons offering customers high quality and dependable services when they need them any time day or night.

About the Author

As Senior Vice-President of Strategy and Corporate Development, Gerald Held, Ph.D., is responsible for Tandem Computers' overall strategic planning. He started the company's New Ventures program and also directs Tandem's merger and investment activities. During his 17-year career at Tandem, Mr. Held has served as the principal designer and development manager for the company's relational database system and has held the key position of Director of Research. Prior to joining Tandem, Mr. Held worked at RCA, where he developed CAD and database software.

Mr. Held received a Ph.D. in computer science from the University of California at Berkeley, where he was a principal designer of the INGRES relational database management system. He also earned a B.S. from Purdue University and an M.S. from the University of Pennsylvania. He is a graduate of the Executive Program of Stanford University's School of Business and has authored several technical articles on database management.

Tandem Computers Incorporated

Tandem Computers Incorporated is a leading supplier of online transaction processing (OLTP) systems and networks for critical processing requirements. A wide variety of Fortune 1000 companies and other large organizations worldwide—including financial institutions, telecommunications providers, manufacturers, retailers, and stock exchanges—use Tandem systems in applications where high volumes of business transactions must be processed each second and recorded instantly.

As the originator of fault-tolerant OLTP technolgy, Tandem manufactures and markets two versatile families of systems designed to operate continuously despite any single point of failure. Tandem offers the NonStop systems family with the company's Guardian operating system software and the Integrity line of UNIX-based computer systems. All Tandem systems also incorporate modular expandability, distributed processing, networking capabilities, data integrity, security, and other key OLTP fundamentals required to support on-line applications. The company employs 10,700 people and generated revenues of more than $2 billion during 1992.

Part 2

Database and Application Development Issues

Chapter

OLTP Program Design

Nancy K. Mullen
Andersen Consulting

Introduction

On-line transaction processing (OLTP) systems are typically the lifelines of a company's computer systems. They tend to be the operational systems that are critical to the fulfillment of the mission of the company. This is true whether the "company" is a commercial enterprise, a government agency, or a voluntary organization. Thus, the operations of the company are often linked to the successful operation of the major OLTP systems.

Operational systems have made a major transition in the last two decades. Systems that once were well served by batch processing now need the rapid responsiveness that can only be found with on-line systems. The customers and suppliers of most businesses demand faster responses—more timely information. Many systems now provide this kind of ready response by putting OLTP systems directly in the hands of customers, suppliers, and employees.

OLTP computing is fundamentally different from the batch computing that preceded it. It requires different approaches to the design of programs. Failure to create suitable designs directly limits the ability of a business to operate and to achieve its mission. Unfortunately, the principles needed for good OLTP design are not intuitively obvious. "Common sense," to designers used to batch systems, dictates solutions that cannot be tuned and cannot deliver the responsiveness the company seeks. An OLTP system built on traditional batch principles is like a house built on sand; neither is solid and neither will withstand the test of time.

The major OLTP design characteristics are these:

- Single function programs
- Recoverable units of work
- Small, discrete units of work
- Independent units of work
- Work flow management

This chapter will describe these design principles in detail.

Foundation

Before describing OLTP design principles, it is useful to lay some foundation regarding the three most common styles of computing. This will help to place OLTP computing in the broader context of contrasting computing styles.

There are today three primary computing styles:

- File-oriented batch
- Record-oriented OLTP
- Event-driven interactive

Let us explore each of these styles in turn.

File-oriented batch computing was the dominant style of the 1960s and 1970s. It was characterized by the concept of "old master in–new master out," as shown in Figure 2.1. The approach was to scan the entire file to complete all processing needed for the period—typically a day but often a week, month, or year. Recovery from computer failure was simple; rerun the job.

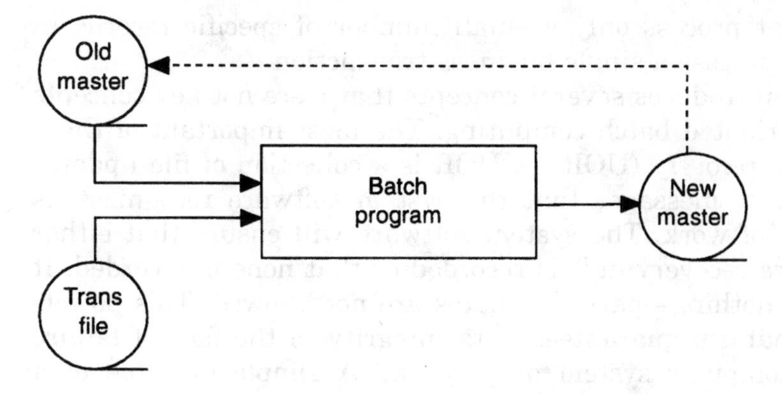

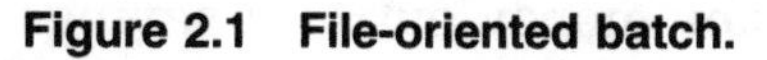
Figure 2.1 File-oriented batch.

In the 1980s, this style of computing became increasingly unacceptable, even for batch processing. Today, batch windows are shrinking. Many companies cannot complete their batch processing while the on-line system is down. Therefore, the batch processing needs to run in the background while on-line systems are running concurrently. This invalidates the overall file-oriented style. Today, batch systems need to be designed according to the principles of OLTP so they can run in the background cooperatively with OLTP running at the same time; however, further discussion of batch processing is beyond the scope of this book.

Record-oriented OLTP might better be called unit-of-work computing, as illustrated in Figure 2.2. It was the dominant style of the 1980s, and continues in the 1990s as the dominant style for operational systems. It is characterized by units of

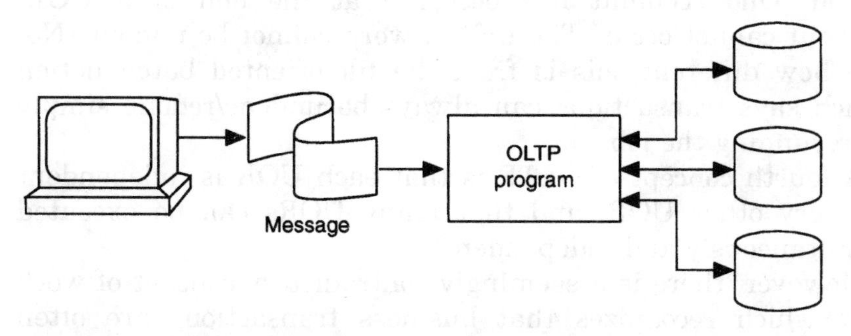

Figure 2.2 Record-oriented OLTP.

work that process only a small number of specific records in order to process a single business transaction.

OLTP introduces several concepts that were not key concepts for file-oriented batch computing. The most important of these is *unit of recovery* (UOR). A UOR is a collection of file updates and system messages that the system software recognizes as one unit of work. The system software will ensure that either the entire recovery unit is recorded or that none is recorded. It is all or nothing—partial updates are not allowed. This powerful mechanism guarantees data integrity in the face of failure of the computer system or program. A simple example of a UOR is a bank transaction to transfer money out of a savings account into a checking account. If the system should suffer a power outage after the savings account had been decreased but before the checking account had been increased, the system software would undo the updates to the savings account as soon as power was restored, before any new processing would be permitted; but all earlier recovery units that had completed successfully before the power outage would not be affected.

Another concept that was introduced by OLTP computing can be called *dynamic transaction backout*. This process is invoked after a failure occurs, to undo partial updates. It may be invoked as part of the recovery from a power failure, as described earlier, or as part of the recovery from a program which terminated abnormally due to a program bug. Dynamic transaction backout is the mechanism that guarantees that partial updates are undone.

A third concept introduced by OLTP is the notion of a *commit*. A commit is the seal that says a recovery unit is completed. Once commit has occurred at the end of a UOR, backout cannot occur. The unit of work cannot be undone. Notice how different this is from the file-oriented batch notion which says transactions can always be undone/redone simply by rerunning the job.

A fourth concept of OLTP is that each UOR is independent of every other UOR, and that many UORs can be executed simultaneously and independently.

However, there is a seemingly contradictory concept of work flow which recognizes that business transactions are often large, complex, and composed of many steps. Although one

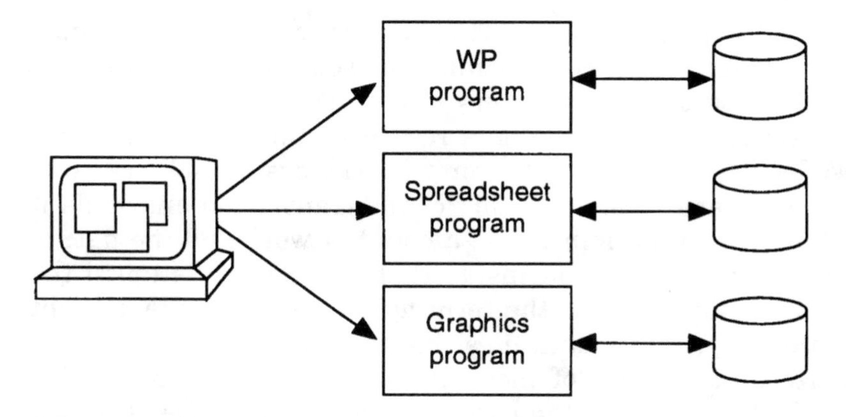

Figure 2.3 Event-driven interactive computing.

user's work is independent of other users, the sequence of steps within one user's work may be highly significant. Therefore, there needs to be a technique for managing the work flow of individual users. This technique is called *context data*. Through context data, the work of an individual user can be controlled and sustained through a series of transactions to help the user complete the work efficiently and effectively.

The third style of computing is **event-driven interactive** computing, as illustrated in Figure 2.3. This is the style that takes maximum advantage of the power of workstations. It provides interactive, unstructured support for knowledge workers. There is no predefined work flow, no constraints on the user's ability to invoke many independent processes. The system reacts to a single command like a mouse click or pen selection. The notion of *recovery unit* is much more difficult to define, since the work is inherently unstructured. Further discussion of event-driven interactive computing is outside the scope of this chapter.

OLTP Design Principles

Let us start the discussion of OLTP design by setting forth some principles that I have found to be useful as guides to good OLTP program design. Once those principles have been set forth, I will describe techniques that can be used to improve the quality of your program designs.

There are nine principles. They are centered on the concepts of transaction and recovery unit, but some additional discussion of transaction and recovery unit is needed first.

A transaction is defined as a recovery unit; the system software defines what a recovery unit is. The system software creates a marker at the beginning of the transaction and seals it at the end with a commit. The amount of work and the nature of the work that goes on inside that transaction is up to the program designer. I use the term *work* to refer to the amount of processing against data files that is done by the program or the size and number of messages being shipped around the network. Compared to the cost of these two activities, the cost of all other computing in normal OLTP programs is immaterial. One program may be designed to update only one record of one local file within the transaction. Another program may be designed to update hundreds of records, spanning many remote files, within the transaction. Clearly, the second program is doing much more "work" in one transaction.

How much work should a transaction do? Ideally, if technology were not an inhibitor, one transaction would complete a logical unit of work. Phrased another way, one transaction would complete all work that the business user views as one unit of work. Unfortunately, technology *is* an inhibitor and logical units of work are often very large. Therefore, it is an axiom of OLTP that a business unit of work will often span many transactions. However, the system software can only guarantee to undo a single UOR. This creates a design problem for the application designer. The designer must recognize when failure has caused part of a logical unit of work to be undone, leaving the logical unit only partially completed. The designer must design processes to correct incomplete logical units of work.

Principle 1: A logical unit of work should be structured across discrete recovery units according to the demands and limitations of the technology.

This principle recognizes the limitations imposed by technology. Figure 2.4 illustrates a typical organization for a cus-

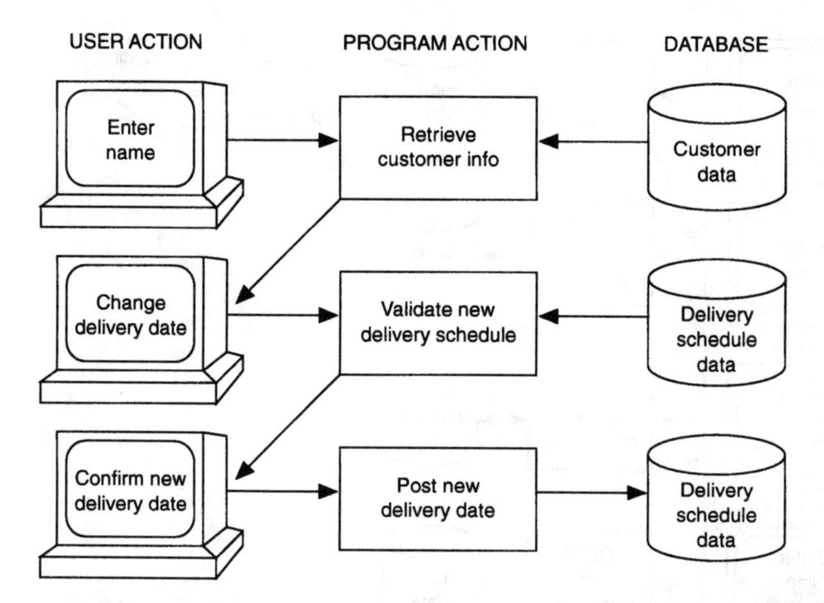

Figure 2.4 Customer service dialog showing three UORs to complete one logical unit of work.

tomer service function using CICS/VSAM. The capabilities of the technology must dictate acceptable sizes for the UORs. This will allow you to take full advantage of the technology to deliver a powerful system that works well. Any attempt to make one technology behave like another is fraught with danger. Take advantage of the strengths of the technology you are using. Learn its strengths and weaknesses. Design with full recognition of those strengths and weaknesses. Later, some techniques to help you do this will be discussed.

Principle 2: A logical unit of work should be split across the fewest UORs possible, considering the technology.

Each UOR that is only a partial logical unit of work means more work for the program designer. The designer must design a solution to the problem that failure in any of the UORs may leave the logical unit of work in an incomplete state. The fewer the number of UORs for a single logical unit of work, the less work for the designer.

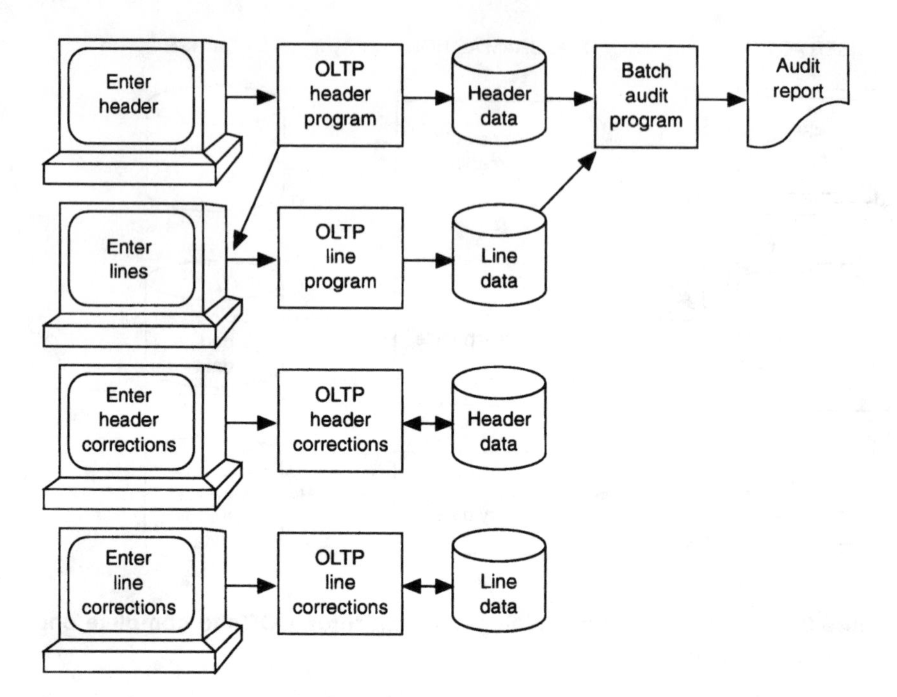

Figure 2.5 Processing flow showing two OLTP data entry programs, two error-correction programs, and one batch audit program that scans data looking for disintegrity caused by UOR failure.

Principle 3: An OLTP application must provide whatever processing is necessary to recover a complete logical unit of work.

When a logical unit of work is built as a single UOR, the system software provides full assurance that the logical unit of work will be fully processed, or not processed at all. However, when the logical unit of work spans several UORs, the application must consider the effect of failure in one of the UORs, and must provide the recovery scenario. This often means error reports and error-correction programs must be specially written, as illustrated in Figure 2.5.

Principle 4: An OLTP program should be simple and modular, reflecting one simple business function.

Whereas batch programs tend to be large, complex structures that perform many functions, OLTP programs should be simple structures that complete only one business function. This makes OLTP programs simpler to design and test. A good on-line program is difficult to break into modules because it is already restricted to a single atomic function.

Principle 5: An OLTP program should be small.

OLTP programs should perform a small amount of work. Limiting OLTP programs to one simple function naturally leads to small programs. The natural question to ask is, "What is a small amount of work?" The answer depends on the technology in use, but a useful guideline is to limit the number of physical reads or writes in any UOR to a maximum of 50 and to limit the messages crossing the network to two (one in, one out), comprising no more than 2KB each. This is, in fact, a high limit. Most OLTP transactions should do much less work than 50 physical reads or writes and most messages should be much smaller than 2KB. But as a maximum, these are limits that work well until you understand your own environment fully and can develop a more refined limit.

Principle 6: All OLTP programs that run on the same CPU should be of the same size.

A CPU can be pictured as an hourglass with a small waist, as in Figure 2.6. Above the waist are the OLTP programs waiting their turn to pass through the waist of the hourglass, where

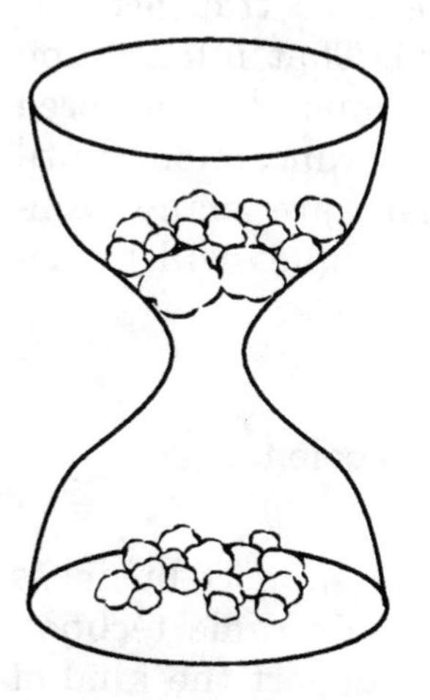

Figure 2.6 OLTP programs should be of uniform size for maximum efficiency.

they can be processed. The most efficient way to complete the processing for many programs is to have them all of uniform size, like the grains of sand in a traditional hourglass. If some of the grains are very small while others are large, the programs may become jammed as they enter the waist, and no programs will be processed at all. The large grains interfere with the processing of the entire system.

Principle 7: The UORs that comprise one logical unit of work should be connected through context data.

When a logical unit of work must span several UORs, it is important to manage the flow of work through the successive transactions. A common example is an order entry function that spans four transaction types:

- Order header
- Order lines (may generate multiple transactions to process multiple order lines)
- Shipping instructions
- Pricing and discounting

The business function will not be complete until the pricing transaction is complete, as shown in Figure 2.7. The pricing transaction needs information from the earlier transactions, which have been completed and committed. That information is called *context data.* This context data must be gathered along the way and passed on to successive transactions until the logical unit of work is complete. There are many techniques for passing context data. Those techniques will be described later in this chapter.

Principle 8: The use of workstations does not negate the importance of UORs.

Workstations offer powerful opportunities to support business processing that was never served well by mainframe technology. However, when using workstations to support the kind of OLTP processing that was well served by mainframes, the

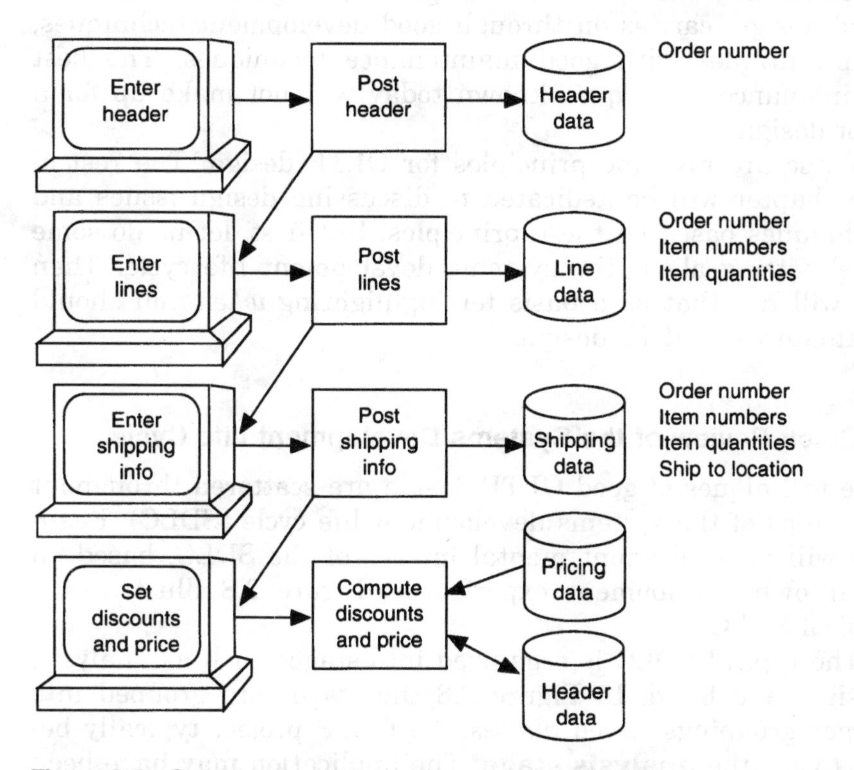

Figure 2.7 Order entry dialog with context data that must be "remembered" to compute discounts and pricing.

principles of good OLTP design still apply, despite the use of workstations. The work that comprises a UOR needs to be organized in such a way that it will all be committed together, or not at all.

Principle 9: It is not possible to tune a bad design.

I have occasionally heard database administrators (DBAs) or systems administrators advise application designers that they do not need to worry about performance, because performance is the job of the DBAs or system administrators. I would most emphatically argue that performance is everyone's job. No person within the IT community who is involved in building or maintaining applications can dismiss performance as being the responsibility of someone else. A good application starts with a good design, carries on through good development techniques, and continues with good maintenance techniques. The best maintenance techniques known today will not make up for a poor design.

These are my nine principles for OLTP design. The rest of the chapter will be dedicated to discussing design issues and techniques based on these principles. But first, let us do some level setting about the systems development life cycle. Then we will use that as a basis for highlighting *when* you should evaluate your OLTP design.

A Quick Review of the Systems Development Life Cycle

The techniques of good OLTP design are scattered throughout the steps of the systems development life cycle (SDLC). Readers will have different mental images of the SDLC, based on their own development experiences. Figure 2.8 illustrates a typical SDLC.

The typical SDLC is organized into stages such as analysis, design, and build. In Figure 2.8 the stages are grouped into larger groupings called *phases*. An OLTP project typically begins with the **analysis stage**. The application may have been defined during an information planning effort. It will be assumed that you completed such a plan before initiating a specific OLTP project, as discussion of information planning is beyond the scope of this book. The analysis stage of a development project normally consists of the analysis of business requirements and the development of models for the system: data models, process models, and event models. For OLTP systems, data models and process models are more useful than event models.

Following the analysis stage there is a **design stage**. During the design stage, databases are designed, the user interface is designed, and program modules are identified. This is where good OLTP design begins.

Following the design stage, the **system installation**, or construction phase, begins. During system installation, the build stage requires that each program be designed in detail and that the program code be generated and tested. During the

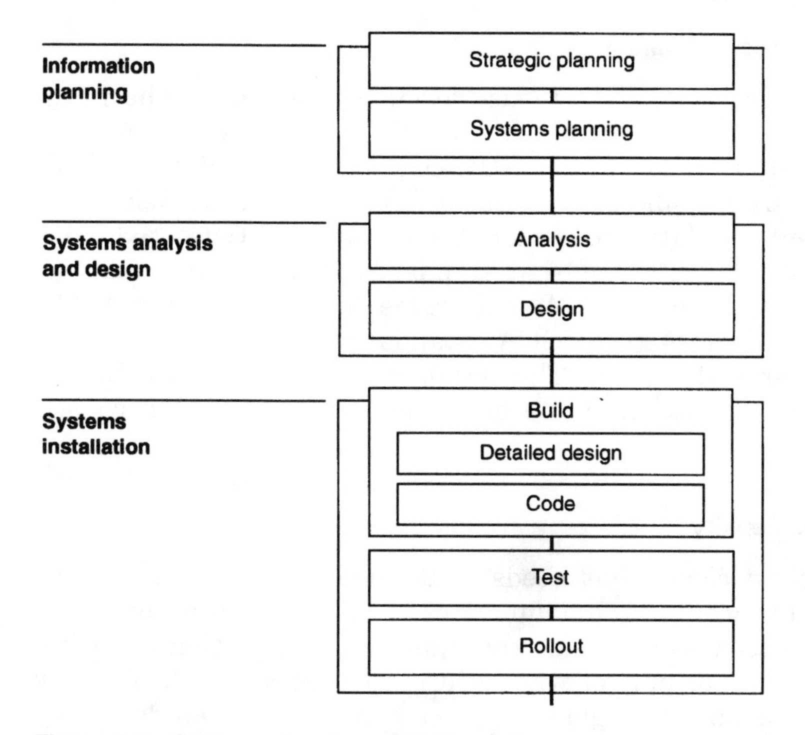

Figure 2.8 Systems development life cycle.

subsequent test stage, system testing is completed. The rollout stage moves the application into production, typically through phased delivery. These stages of the installation phase must be completed with a diligent eye for good OLTP design if an effective system is to be delivered.

The balance of this chapter will discuss the use of various techniques and will position them at the stages of the SDLC described above. I leave it to the reader to translate my names for the SDLC stages into the names used at your company.

OLTP Design Alternatives

During the design stage of the SDLC, you will have to make several design decisions that will affect the way your OLTP application behaves. It is important to make these decisions early. Establish standards to ensure that all similar parts of the application behave the same way. The following section discusses some design choices.

Window Design Standards

OLTP processing tends to use formatted windows. The hardware may be dumb terminals like 3270 terminals; they may be graphical user interface (GUI)–based workstations. In both cases, OLTP applications tend to format fixed data fields that represent the data needed for the transaction. Today there are a variety of window design standards from which to choose. Companies with an IBM mainframe bias tend to use IBM's Common User Access (CUA) standard. Others use Motif or Macintosh style guides. The standard you choose is less important than the fact that you have chosen one and use it consistently.

Window Density

An early decision that needs to be made while designing the user interface is the amount of data to be placed on one window. A desire to minimize the number of UORs that comprise a single logical unit of work will encourage you to load many data fields onto a single window so one program can do all the work of the logical unit of work. However, a desire to build uniformly small UORs will encourage you to design windows with very little data on them. The most important consideration is your user.

Users who are operating in "heads-down" fashion, pounding data into windows without distraction, need subsecond response time after each entry. Subsecond response time can only be delivered for transactions that do very little work. This suggests that such users should have windows that contain very little data. For example, for users doing order entry where typical orders contain many order lines, entering one order line per window will provide better response time than a window that accepts 15 order lines in a single window. One order line per window would generate many more transactions, but each transaction could respond very quickly.

Management of Context Data

Context data can be passed in many ways. For small amounts of data, it may be possible to store the data in the window, perhaps as “nondisplay” data. Nondisplay data is data that travels back and forth to the terminal with the window message, but is not displayed for the user to read. The window can only hold nondisplay data if there are unused white spaces on the window where the data can hide. This is a simple technique, but it has the disadvantage of increasing the size of the messages going to and from the user.

Context data can be stored in the database in records that are especially designed to hold the context data. The advantage of this design is that all context data from completed UORs will be saved, making recovery easier. The disadvantages are that it creates extra physical I/O for every transaction and that you must be sure to delete the context data whenever a logical unit of work is completed.

Specific system software may offer additional options. CICS provides a special program-to-program communications area called COMMAREA. It also provides a feature called *temporary storage*, which is commonly used for context data.

Update Strategies

You must decide how and when programs should update the database. Your decision will affect the robustness your application.

One simple update strategy is to allow each UOR to update the database with the part of the logical unit of work that it has completed. For example, in Figure 2.7, the “Post header” UOR would insert the order header data into the database. The second UOR, “Post lines,” would insert the order lines.

While this is a simple update strategy, it creates a complex recovery scenario. Imagine that you have designed an order entry application to update the database in each UOR. In the example of Figure 2.7, you must design the order line program so that it recognizes that it could fail before completing the order lines, leaving an order header in the database with no order lines. How will you recover? You may simply want the user to continue by re-entering order lines when the system is available again. But have you designed the order entry programs to allow a user to begin in the middle of the order entry dialog? Or did you design it to require that the user always begins by entering the order header? You can certainly design it either way. The critical idea here is that you have to recognize the possibility of failure in the middle of the dialog, and design the recovery scenario into the dialog.

An alternative design is to defer all updates until the dialog is complete, storing the information in some temporary database until the logical unit of work is complete. This has the definite advantage in that recovery is simple; throw away the temporary database record and tell the user to start over. It also makes it easy to design *Cancel* logic. Cancel logic allows the user to undo all processing back to the beginning of the logical unit of work. This is a difficult process under the earlier scenario, but very easy under this scenario. There are two disadvantages to this end-of-dialog scenario. First, the end-of-dialog UOR may have serious performance problems because it is doing so much work. Second, it violates the principle of uniform small UORs and may slow down the entire system. However, for applications of moderate transaction volumes, this is an effective design technique.

Design Reviews

Now we are ready to discuss techniques for ensuring that the OLTP designs you are creating will work well. The following techniques will help you deliver the kind of operational system your company needs if it is to reap the full potential of OLTP systems.

Design reviews of your OLTP application focus attention on how your design will perform. That attention must be provided at several critical points during the design-and-build stages of development. The rest of this chapter will describe techniques for evaluating how your application will perform.

There are five points in the SDLC where you need to evaluate the design. These five points are highlighted in Figure 2.9.

1. In the design stage, part of the task of identifying programs requires some high-level calculations of the work performed by each critical program.
2. In the installation phase, as the detailed design is completed for each program, a detailed calculation needs to be developed for the program.

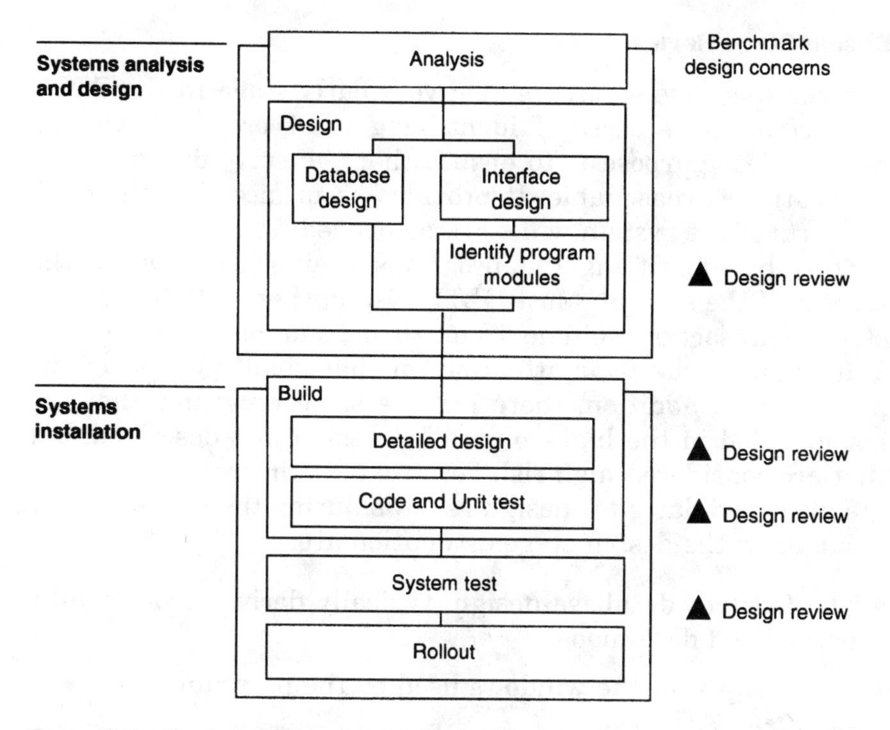

Figure 2.9 Design reviews and the SDLC.

3. During code generation, the unit test of the code needs to ensure that the access paths being used by the program are the access paths which the program designer expected the program to use. This is particularly critical with relational systems, as the relational database management system (RDBMS) has an optimizer which selects the access path, rather than the programmer specifying the access path in the program.
4. This point occurs during system testing, when volume testing ensures that the application can actually work under real life demands.
5. This point occurs at any point along the design/installation continuum: The fifth point is to benchmark the actual execution of critical, high-risk parts of the system in a timely fashion to provide assurance that the programs will work as required.

Each of these five points is discussed below.

Design Stage Review

Design stage review occurs at a very early stage in the SDLC as part of the process of identifying what programs will be required. Its purpose is to ensure that the early design of the application is reasonable. It provides assurance that the critical parts of the system will work as needed.

Start by identifying the programs that are critical to the success of the system. Most OLTP systems generate 80 percent of the transaction volume from 20 percent of the programs. You should focus your attention on that small portion of the programs. In addition, there may be some programs that are not included in the high-volume processing just described, but that are considered high risk because of their processing; those are also candidates for design reviews during the design stage.

Inputs to the design stage estimation are:

- The first-cut database design, typically derived from a fully normalized data model
- The designs for the windows used by the program
- The definition of the program function
- Program design guidelines that put limits on the number of physical I/Os per program permitted in the on-line environment

The outputs of the design stage review are estimates of the number of physical I/Os that can be expected for the major application programs. Along the way, you can expect to revise some program definitions, some window designs, and the database design. When you are finished, you will have confidence that the database design and program designs will support all the major application functions. The less critical application functions do not have that assurance, but they can be accommodated during the later stages of development. Because they are noncritical, problems with them will not jeopardize the entire application.

The steps of the process are:

1. Identify all the critical and complex programs in the application (about 20 percent of all programs)

2. For each critical or complex program:
   a. Define the call pattern
   b. Compute the number of logical I/Os for a typical execution of the program
   c. Compute the number of physical I/Os for a typical execution of the program
   d. Change the design as needed to meet the maximum limits defined

The design stage review starts with the assumption that a fully normalized database design is desirable, but may not be possible, depending on application needs. If acceptable application performance can only be provided by denormalizing the database design, then the database design must be denormalized, but this technique provides the guidance you need to determine when that is necessary.

Define the Call Pattern The first step for reviewing the design of a critical or complex program is to define the call pattern. A call pattern is the pattern of database and file calls that the program would issue on a typical execution of the program. There may be several paths through a program, all of which describe critical transactions. In such a case, you should develop separate call patterns for each transaction, treating each one as if there were separate programs supporting each call pattern. Because you are only looking for the 20 percent of the paths that produce 80 percent of the transaction volume, you can ignore all the less-used paths through the program, such as error handling and exception processing.

Structured query language (SQL) can make the call pattern confusing. I recommend during the design stage that you pretend that SQL does not exist, at least for the purposes of this design review. Write the call pattern as you would do if you were developing this application against flat files. For example, a join between an order header and its 15 order lines would produce a call pattern of one logical read against the header file and 15 logical reads against the line file.

You may think it is difficult to develop a call pattern for a program that has not even been designed yet, but the purpose of this process is to determine whether or not such a program should be designed. That is why the windows are important inputs. Looking at the window and the first-cut database design, ask yourself what database activity is needed to perform the business function of the window. How many table lookups will be needed to validate the data being entered? Make some assumptions about how the data should be organized for validation purposes, if that data is not already in the first-cut database design. Then add it to the database design. Thus, the database design will evolve rather quickly to support any critical functions that might have been omitted from the first-cut design.

Figure 2.10 shows a typical design review worksheet for an order entry dialog. Note that each window is analyzed separately. The call pattern is the list of tables or files accessed by each window.

Compute Logical I/Os For the order header window, 15 validating reads are shown. I have not bothered to specify which tables or files would be read to do the validations. It is sufficient for our purposes here to note that there are 15 validations. The trick to successful reviews at this point in the design stage is to do only what is necessary to identify the work that will be done by these critical processes in a single UOR.

Compute Physical I/Os Notice in Figure 2.10 that the ratio column shows a ratio of 2. This represents an assumption that the data is accessed by an index, that the upper levels of the index are already in memory, and that one logical read will trigger two physical I/Os (one read for the lowest level of the index, one for the data); this is a good starting assumption for an OLTP application. But you have the responsibility of ensuring that the program design will allow access of the data by an index. You may observe that we are so early in the design process that we cannot know what indexes will exist on the tables (assuming an RDBMS). This is quite true, but at this point you can assume that every relational table will have an index on the primary key. One of the important contributions that this review will make to your database design is that it

Sample design phase estimating							
Dialog	Window	Table/file	Access	Access path	Log. I/Os	Ratio	Phy. I/Os
Order entry	Header	Validations	Read	Primary key	15	2	30
		Header	Insert		1	2	2
		Total PI/Os					32
	Lines	Validations	Read	Primary key	3	2	6
		Line	Insert		1	2	2
		Total PI/Os					8
	Shipping	Validations	Read	Primary key	2	2	4
		Ship_instr	Insert		4	2	8
		Total PI/Os					12
	Pricing	Price rules	Read	Primary key	16	2	32
		Header	Update	p	1	2	2
		Total PI/Os					34

Figure 2.10 Sample design phase estimating.

will identify for you the places where you need more indexes to support your major programs.

There is one primary case when your OLTP program will not use a ratio of 2; when you will be retrieving a set of related rows. For example, an order inquiry window might show as many as 15 order lines for the requested order. If you are using a DBMS that supports physical sequencing of the data, then it may be reasonable to assume that all 15 rows for the same order will be physically stored together on the same data page. Then you might get all 15 order lines for a cost of just two physical I/Os, not 30 I/Os. That is a determination you will make based on your data.

One more simplifying assumption: I always assume at this stage of design that all my tables will be sequenced in the order of the primary key. This design review will help you identify tables that need to be stored in some other sequence.

Figure 2.10 shows that the validation on the header window will trigger 30 physical I/Os, which makes that pretty busy window. At the detailed design phase you may want to tune the design to generate less I/O activity. But for our purposes at this early stage, it looks OK—the design looks reasonable. If this review had shown that one window would generate several hundred physical I/Os, then I would start redesigning the application, since hundreds of I/Os should not be part of an OLTP window. The total physical I/Os is computed for each window. No grand total is shown; a grand total would be a meaningless hash.

Change the Design as Needed Suppose that one of the windows just reviewed did show more than 50 I/Os. What options are available for redesigning the application? You may choose to redesign the window to do less work; you may redesign the program to reduce the work it needs to do; you may denormalize the database design to allow the same functional processing to occur with less database activity. This review technique does not help you design a solution to your performance problem—that is where your creativity and experience must be used. This technique will help you to decide when you have a problem. It will also help you decide when you have fixed the problem.

One final remark about this review technique. There are many things that this technique is not:

- It is not the basis for capacity planning
- It is not the basis for determining response time
- It is not a guarantee that your application will perform well

What this technique *is* is a technique for finding the design problems that may jeopardize the entire application. It is looking for the big hitters, the major problems. Other problems will be found during the system installation phase and will be solved there. This technique focuses on the major issues early, leaving minor issues to be settled in due course.

Installation Phase Detailed Design

During the installation phase, it is possible to complete a much more thorough analysis of the design. While the design stage only examined the high-priority programs, the installation phase should examine every program as a design is developed. This is the most critical time for each program. The design that is developed here will determine how well it performs in production. Before any code is generated, the design needs to be evaluated for its effectiveness and efficiency. Design reviews are critical. Design reviews ensure that the program is designed to deliver the functionality it should deliver. They also ensure that the program is designed to access data efficiently and to work efficiently in the context of the entire software environment.

Each program designer needs to accept the responsibility for the effective and efficient performance of his or her designs. No one else can be held responsible for the functionality of the program. No one else can be held responsible for the efficiency of the design.

Design reviews at this point give the designers confidence that their designs will work well, or they highlight problems with the designs. Often the designer is not in a position to solve performance problems. That is why technical staff review the designs and help the designer find a better design.

The design review of each program is similar to the design review developed earlier. The differences lie in the deeper understanding now available about what each program will do and a more refined database design. It is my experience that the programs that are analyzed first during the installation phase are the easy, less important programs. This is a natural outcome of the fact that the important, critical programs always have difficult design issues that take a long time to resolve. The programs that have no issues and can be completed quickly are the less important ones. Thus, the needs of less important programs are used to validate the database design before the needs of the most important programs are known. If the important programs were not reviewed during the design stage, even superficially, there is a very strong probability during the installation phase that it will be discovered that the database design will not work for these programs. At this time, the cost of rework to the database design and to completed program designs is high. This makes rework at this late stage a very unpleasant task.

The process for design reviews during the installation phase is similar to that described above for the design stage. The inputs to estimating are:

- The completed action diagram or program design specification
- The most current database design
- Program design guidelines that put limits on the number of physical I/Os per program permitted in your on-line environment

The outputs of the installation phase review are estimates of the number of physical I/Os that can be expected for all application programs. Along the way, you will revise some program designs and some database designs. When you are finished, you will have confidence that the database design and the program designs will support all the application functions.

The steps of the process (applied to every program in the system) are:

1. Complete the action diagram or detailed program specification
2. Define the call pattern
3. Compute the number of logical I/Os for a typical execution of the program
4. Compute the number of physical I/Os for a typical execution of the program
5. Change the design as needed to meet the program design standards

This detailed design task begins with the designs for the tables and indexes as defined after the design stage, after the design reviews for critical programs were completed, and any necessary database modifications had been included in the database design. Thus, the starting point uses database designs that have, at some cursory level, been deemed appropriate for the most critical programs. As further modifications are proposed, the demands of the critical programs must be remembered, so that those critical requirements will remain at the forefront of database design decisions.

As performance estimates are developed, remember the importance of the UOR; this is the unit that must be analyzed. On-line programs are not normally modularized, since each program performs only one small function, but if you should find yourself designing in a modular environment, recognize that you must identify all the I/Os that occur in the recovery unit. If you are working in a computer-aided software engineering (CASE) environment where the CASE tool will generate physical I/Os on your behalf, then you need to understand the behavior of the CASE tool well enough to predict those I/Os. The most common example is automatic validation of data. If the CASE tool will generate table lookups to validate data, you need to include those table lookups in your call pattern.

Beware of analyzing single modules if those modules are part of a larger recovery unit. It is the performance of the entire recovery unit that is important, not the performance of individual components.

Unit Test

Relational database management systems have optimizers that select access paths into the data. Some RDBMSs make the selection as part of the compile and link process for the program. Others make the selection at execution time. In either event you must examine the decision as part of unit testing, to ensure that the RDBMS is selecting the access path chosen by the designer. Be sure that you test the access path selection while using databases that are similar in size and composition to the production databases. Most RDBMSs choose different access paths for small databases than for large databases. Because most unit testing is conducted against small databases, you need to arrange to have production-size databases for this part of unit testing.

If the RDBMS is not choosing the most desirable access path, examine the SQL in the program to ensure that the SQL is optimal. All RDBMSs choose their access paths based on the SQL in the program. Each RDBMS is different. Some will not choose indexes if the SQL uses host variables that have different sizes defined than the size of the columns in the tables. Some are more efficient when joins are specified; others are more efficient when embedded subselects are specified. It is critical to know the SQL for your RDBMS vendor, and to use those forms of SQL that will encourage the RDBMS to make the access path selections you need.

If performance problems cannot be fixed by changing the SQL, then examine whether or not it is possible to modify the program to use the data differently and get design improvements that way. If program design changes are not enough to do job, then denormalize the database design as needed to get the results needed.

System Test Volume Testing

The proof is in the pudding, and system test is dessert time. Once all the functionality and integration requirements of the system have been validated, it is time to try to break the system. Transaction loads that exceed planned production volumes need to be pushed through the system, database volumes that exceed planned production volumes need to be stuffed into the databases, and the application needs to be tested under more load than you expect the production system to undergo.

If you have done the other levels of design reviews well, this test should simply confirm that the system performs as designed; it is too late to discover that it does not work. Never leave performance management until system test. Remember, you cannot tune a poor design. This is the time to receive assurance that all your earlier hard work was worth it; this is not the time to begin the analysis.

Benchmarking

I use the term benchmarking to refer to testing you do during the course of development to test and stress any parts of the system that you consider high risk for performance. This has nothing to do with the benchmark wars between vendors that receive so much coverage in the press. Rather, these are specific tests you run to convince yourself that high-risk parts of the system are feasible. You may begin benchmarking during the design stage to see how a CASE tool generates SQL calls, or you may begin benchmarking during the design stage to see how a few specific functions will work under various design alternatives.

The key to successful benchmarking is to keep the test narrow, focused on some specific question. It is not necessary to reproduce the business function in question; rather, the challenge is to reproduce the CPU consumption and I/O activity of the business function. This means you only need program skeletons that omit all the exception handling that fills most programs. Once the benchmark has proven that the main function in question will work technically, then the remaining logic can be added during normal build tasks.

Entire books have been written on benchmarking. I will not attempt to present equivalent detail here. Suffice it to say that any high-risk component of the system should be benchmarked. Parts of the system that will be reused by many other parts of the system need to be benchmarked very early to guarantee that the design is solid, before other parts of the system begin to rely on the design.

Conclusion

OLTP program design is critical to the success of any OLTP system. Programs need to be simple, single-function programs that complete one recovery unit. Transactions need to be designed to be independent and simple. The database needs to be designed to support critical transactions, to ensure that they do the work of the business efficiently. Finding the proper balance between the flexibility of normalized designs versus meeting the processing needs of the business requires analysis and creativity. This chapter has presented some techniques to support your analysis. The creative solutions are up to you.

About the Author

Nancy K. Mullen is Director of the Multi-user Systems Group within Andersen Consulting's headquarters in Chicago. The group provides specialized expertise in data architecture and application architecture issues to Andersen Consulting clients worldwide. Mrs. Mullen's technical expertise includes UNIX DBMSs like Informix, Oracle, and Sybase, as well as mainframe technologies like IMS DB/DC and CICS/DB2.

Chapter

3

The Role of Fourth-Generation Languages in OLTP Environments

Nicolas C. Nierenberg
Chief Technology Officer and Co-Founder
Unify Corporation

Within the category of transaction processing there is actually a broad range of application types. These range from a small Intel-based personal computer (PC) with five users all the way up to geographically distributed environments involving dozens of computers and thousands of users. A useful discussion of the use of fourth-generation languages (4GLs) in transaction processing needs to be segmented according to the size and complexity of the application environment. As you will see, 4GLs can have a role across the entire spectrum, but the implications and considerations vary widely.

The clear reason for using 4GLs versus other approaches is speed of development and ease of adaptation. Because most on-line transaction processing (OLTP) applications involve application development that is specific to an organization, a key factor in their viability is the cost of that development. In general, 4GL solutions take less time to implement, are easier to modify, and provide simpler migration paths to new technologies and configurations.

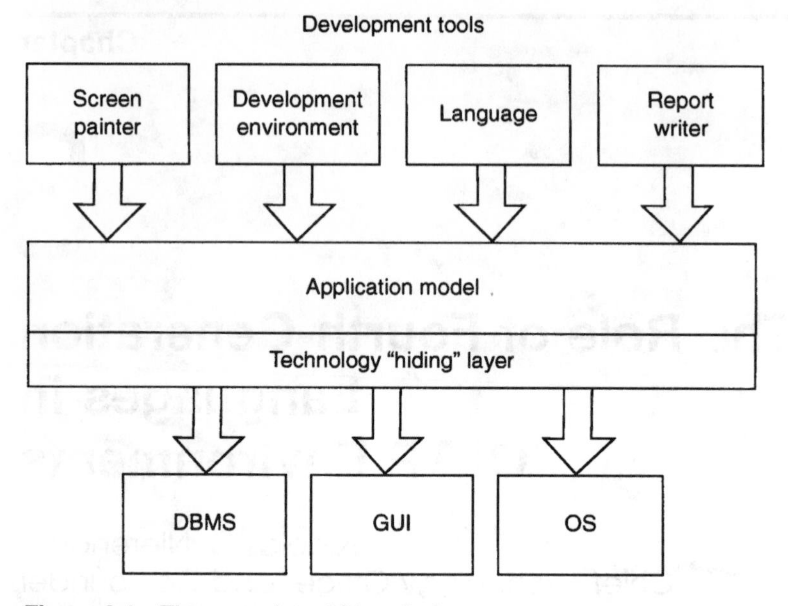

Figure 3.1 The complete 4GL solution.

The key features that make a 4GL more productive when compared to third-generation languages (3GLs) such as C, C++, and COBOL are an application model, an integrated set of development tools, and technology hiding (Figure 3.1).

The application model is an extremely important feature of a 4GL environment. The 4GL has an idea of the transaction application environment even before the first screen is defined and the first line of code is written. The 4GL has an inherent understanding of user interface processing and of database interaction. In many cases, simple data entry forms can be developed without writing any procedural code. This can replace literally hundreds or thousands of lines of 3GL code using WYSIWYG techniques. But the benefits are also large when the procedural language of the 4GL is used, as its language has a specific knowledge of things like structured query language (SQL). This makes the coding process much simpler and direct. The contrast between an SQL search in the "C" language with a search in a typical 4GL language is shown below.

In "C" SQL is not truly a part of the language, and in fact it is integrated with a preprocessing step. Sections of the program that are going to use SQL have to be specially delimited for the preprocessor. For example, when declaring variables that can be embedded, the preprocessor has to be informed as follows:

```
BEGIN SQL DECLARATIONS
char name[20], address[30];
long custid, custlow,  custhigh;
int custidind, nameind, addressind;
END SQL
```

Then the SQL statement has to be associated with a cursor, which will later be used to perform the actual query. The statement does not actually do anything at the point where it is declared. The values of the variables custlow and custhigh only become important when the cursor, c1, is opened.

```
BEGIN SQL
DECLARE c1 CURSOR FOR SELECT customer_id, name, address
FROMcustomer
    WHERE customer_id BETWEEN :custlow and :custhigh;
END SQL
```

Later, when the program wants to actually perform the query, it sets the values of custlow and custhigh to the appropriate values and opens the cursor.

```
custlow = 21;
custhigh = 55;
BEGIN SQL
OPEN c1
END SQL
```

But this does not actually return any data; it just "points" c1 to the first row in the set of records. A fetch statement has to be run in a loop to actually retrieve the rows. Note that since "C" does not have the SQL concept of a Null value, the indicator variables (custind, nameind, and addressind) are set to 0 if the value in the associated column was actually null.

```
do{
BEGIN SQL
    FETCH c1 INTO :custid :custidind, :name :nameind,
:address :addressind
```

```
END SQL
    if(sqlstatus != 0)
    break; /* No more records to retrieve */
....process the data...
}while(TRUE); /* go until the break happens */
```

In contrast, Accell/SQL achieves the same result with:

```
SET custlow to 21
SET custhigh to 56
SET custid, name, address TO SELECT custid, name, address
FROM customer
    WHERE custid BETWEEN :custlow AND :custhigh
    EXECUTING   BEGIN
    ....code to process the row
    END
```

The developer does not have to deal with declaring and managing cursors or variables, as the language takes care of that itself. In addition, the executing portion of the select statement replaces results testing to see when the last row is retrieved. Finally, because Accell/SQL variables can have the Null value, there is no need for separate indicator variables.

The second key feature of a 4GL is its integrated development environment. Generally, a 4GL is actually an integration of a set of specialized tools designed for different parts of the development process. A forms generator is used to develop the user interface portions of the application and can frequently be used to generate default applications. A high-level language is used to supplement the processing logic of the forms generator and to write the batch processing portions of the application. Because report generation generally has a different model than user input processing, a separate report generator is provided with a specialized model for that portion of the application. In this way the developer is always working with a tool that has an idea of what he or she is trying to do. This is a large contrast with third-generation approaches, where a single language is applied to all tasks.

The third key to developer productivity is technology hiding. Today, the application developer is faced with rapidly increasing complexity in the surrounding environment. Technologies like client/ server, graphical user interface (GUI), and relational database are, of course, very beneficial to the overall power of the computing environment. To the application developer, however, they represent a tremendous increase in the difficulty of developing and testing applications. 4GL environments provide a tremendous benefit by hiding this complexity from the developer and allowing him or her to focus on the specific needs of an application. Issues such as the 300 MS/Windows interface functions do not concern the developer, as the 4GL deals with translating the functionality of the application into the appropriate interface calls.

Figure 3.2 shows the architecture of a typical 4GL development system. An application generator is used to provide WYSIWYG development of user interface screens. In addition to layout, the developer uses the generator to specify a number of processing options such as the database table(s) which the form will operate against, the particular columns which the input areas relate to, and the display and input formatting options, such as any special sorting criteria. The output of the generator is then sent to a special resource file. In many sys-

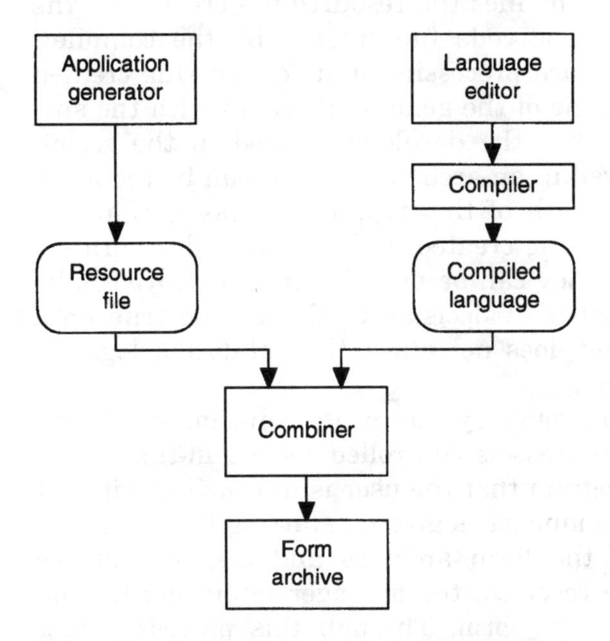

Figure 3.2 4GL development system architecture.

tems the run-time component can take the information created in the generator and execute an application without any further development. This application is able to find, add, modify, and delete records. It can also coordinate the actions of multiple forms, display help messages, and perform a variety of edit checks.

In parallel with designing the user interface screen, the developer can also create a script file which contains the processing logic for the screen. This logic is generally written in an event-driven manner. Events consist of things like the user pressing a particular function key or completing input on a field. The developer puts programming logic in the script file for each one of the events that he wants to handle in a special way; for example, going on to another form when a function key is pressed or validating a field after input is completed. The script file is passed through a compiler which converts it into a pseudocode file for faster execution at run time. The script files can deal with anything from computing an extended price by multiplying two fields, all the way up to a complex batch posting process for an accounting application.

A separate process combines the resource file created by the generator with the pseudocode file created by the compiler. This way a user interface processing unit (or form) is created which combines the logic of the generated screen with the special processing logic that the developer placed in the script. The form is then stored in an archive where it can be retrieved at run time. The strength of this type of process is that, because the user interface is created and maintained separately from the logic script, they can be modified and improved independently of one another. A decision to change the trim on a screen or move a field does not affect the validation logic on that field and vice versa.

Figure 3.3 shows the same system in its run-time configuration. The execution process is controlled by a run-time manager, which is the program that the user is interacting with. At startup the run-time manager is given a starting form which it reads out of one of the form archives and displays on the screen. As events are received, the manager interprets the appropriate logic out of the form. Through this process a new form may be requested, which the manager retrieves from the appropriate archive, and the process continues. The run-time

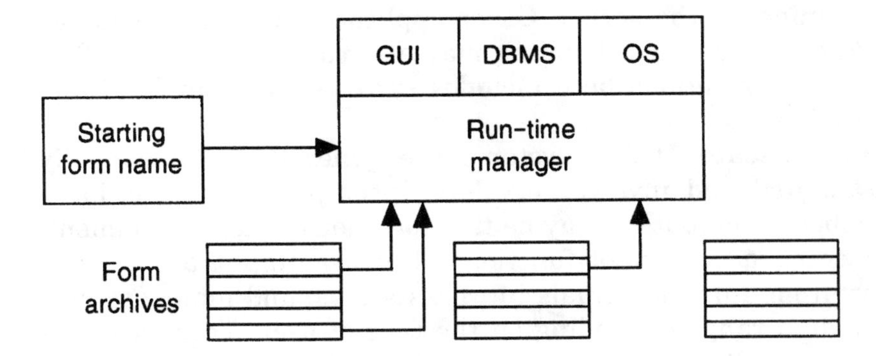

Figure 3.3 Run-time configuration.

manager is responsible for displaying and executing the implied logic of the generated forms, interpreting the associated logic scripts, and interfacing with the user and the variety of system resources needed by the application in its particular environment.

In looking at the use of 4GLs in transaction processing, it is first necessary to define three broad areas of OLTP. Almost all on-line systems fit fairly well into one of these three categories.

1. OLTP light
2. Client/server OLTP
3. Large-scale OLTP

The **OLTP light** category is the classic small company or departmental computing solution. It involves a single computer with generally fewer than 200 users. Today, dumb terminals are the most widely used interface devices and they are generally connected to the computer with serial connections. MS/Windows and 'X' terminals are starting to be used in these applications, but that is in a relatively small percentage of the cases.

Client/server OLTP involves the use of intelligent workstations connected over a network to one or more server computers. In most cases there are fewer than 50 users and only one server machine, but this can vary quite a bit. The classic configuration is to have the user interface application programs running on the workstations, while the database engine is running on the server. Other application programs such as reporting and batch updating may also run on the server. The use of workstations here includes systems that run DOS and MS/Windows.

Large-scale OLTP systems are generally geographically distributed and involve very large user populations. A large number of computers may be tied together in the environment, providing a variety of functions. The user input devices can vary from dumb terminals to workstations, and many systems include a range depending on the type of user. These systems also generally require much larger databases than the other two environments.

Obviously, there are very large differences between these environments. They involve different types of applications, computing resources, and networks. In addition, the systems management and performance management tasks are completely different. In the case of OLTP light, updating the application is a relatively simple task of testing it and then installing it on the operational machine. In the large-scale OLTP case, there could be dozens of systems changes to coordinate. The requirements for development tools in these environments are quite different.

So what do these systems have in common? First of all, they are intimately tied to the operations of the organizations that utilize them. In today's environment the business processes and the applications that support them are inseparable. As a result, in many cases it is difficult to find off-the-shelf solutions, and so custom development is required. Flexibility is also required, so that the applications can evolve as the needs of the users change. In addition to this, performance and reliability are critical to success across the whole range. The systems need to keep up with an organization's transactions, and they need to be available virtually all of the time.

The following sections will look at the use of 4GLs in each type of transaction-processing environment.

OLTP Light

In this environment a single computer handles most of the processing load. The users interface with the computer using

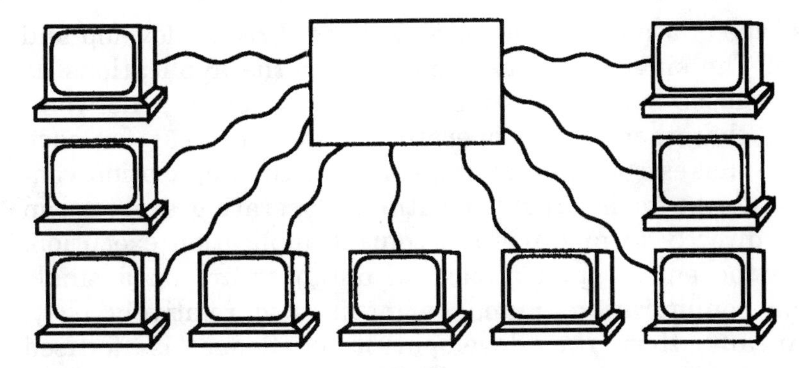

Figure 3.4 OLTP light configuration.

mainly character terminals. The terminals are typically connected to the computer using a serial interface. Figure 3.4 shows a typical OLTP light configuration.

The application architecture mimics the system architecture in this case. Both the applications and the database engine run on the single computing resource. In most cases there is an application process for each active user. Most current database systems also create a second process for each active user to handle the database processing in addition to their own background processes. These database processes communicate with each other through shared memory. Figure 3.5 shows the application architecture of a typical OLTP light environment.

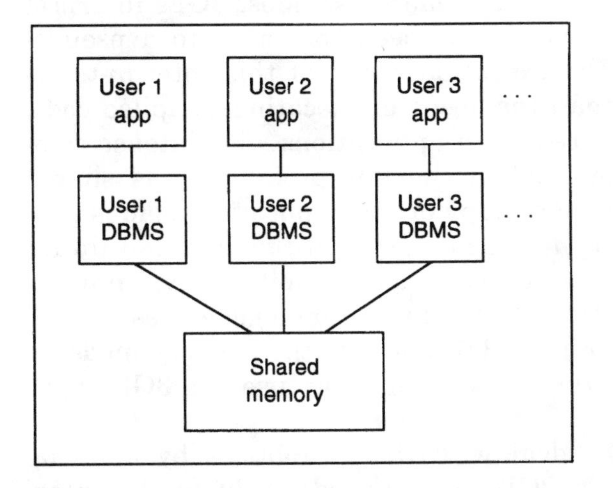

Figure 3.5 Architecture of an OLTP light environment.

This type of system is the easiest of the three to develop and manage. The single computer means that the applications do not have to be split into component pieces across a network. The fact that there is an operating system process for each user also makes run-time management of the application convenient, as the tools provided with the operating system can be used directly to monitor and control application execution. Because the entire application and database are on a single machine configuration, management is also relatively easy. This means that the development challenge is focused squarely on developing the application logic and making sure the resulting system performs adequately.

As a result of these characteristics, most 4GLs work well in OLTP light environments. They allow for rapid development and ease of database programming. The lack of environment complexity means that the 4GL's focus on application logic rather than systems logic works very well. In addition, the vast majority of 4GL systems were designed for character terminals, and this characteristic of the OLTP light environment also fits. As will be seen in the following discussion, the burdens on the 4GL increase in the other types of environments. As a result of the fit between 4GLs and the OLTP light environment, effective applications can be developed in a fraction of the time of 3GL solutions.

The biggest drawbacks for a 4GL in the OLTP light–type system are performance and memory use. Most 4GLs interpret the application logic, which has been converted to a pseudocode, at run time. The execution speed of this interpreter is many times slower than the speed of executing compiled code. This can be quite noticeable in applications with intense computation requirements. While the interpreter code is shared among all of the users, one copy of the application logic is generally kept in memory for each user, and this can add up for large user populations. In contrast, compiled environments generally share one copy of the application logic across the entire user population. Figure 3.6 contrasts the memory model of a typical 4GL application with the memory use of a 3GL application.

Most modern 4GLs deal with these problems by allowing functions written in a 3GL to be added easily to the inter-

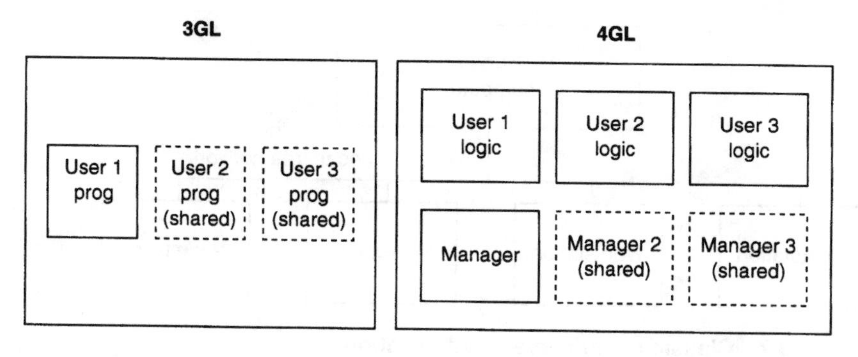

Figure 3.6 4GL and 3GL memory use compared.

preter environment and by doing clever memory management. The 3GL functions extend the interpreter environment and allow intense computation to take place at compiled speeds, without losing the overall development speed and convenience of the 4GL. The memory management functions ensure that only needed application logic is kept in memory and overall usage is minimized. As a result of these features, the rapid improvement of price performance and the plummeting prices of memory, 4GLs represent a highly attractive solution for OLTP light development despite the trade-offs.

At a certain level of user counts, and certainly when other types of display devices are required, OLTP light configurations no longer make sense. Most experts feel that the process-per-user architecture begins to involve too much overhead, and the single computer solution lacks flexibility. At this point a different configuration generally is used regardless of the development tools.

Client/Server OLTP

In client/server OLTP a set of computers are combined using a network to perform the processing tasks. In most cases client/server networks are not spread over a wide geographic area and the number of users is generally less than 250. In general, the user interface is graphical with anything from a personal computer to a powerful workstation dedicated to each person on the network. Figure 3.7 shows a classic client/server configuration.

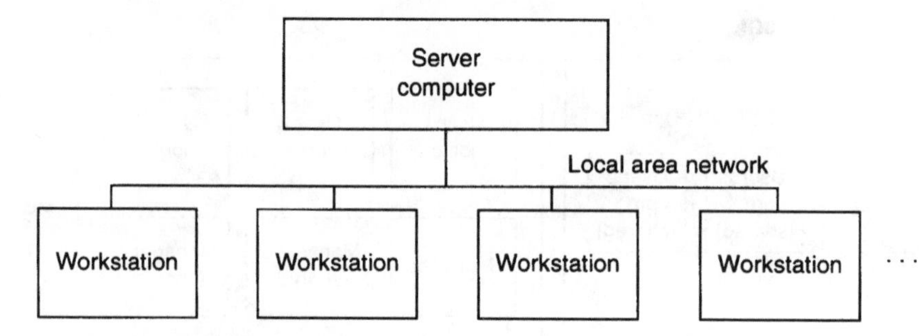

Figure 3.7 Classic client/server configuration.

The typical application configuration in this environment is for each of the client workstations to have the application programs executing locally, communicating via SQL to a database management system running on a larger server computer. In many cases, however, the server computer can be performing many other tasks for the workstations including printing, file serving, and communication to outside environments.

This type of system has several advantages over the OLTP light system. First of all it is highly configurable, and the amount of computing power expands more gracefully as the user population increases. Instead of running out of steam on a single computer, which has to perform all of the tasks, new application processing power is added with each user's workstation, and additional server machines can be put on-line as needed to keep up with the centralized tasks. Another benefit, and often the primary reason for implementing this system, is that the users receive a graphical presentation of their application. This increases acceptance and reduces training costs. Some applications, such as those that employ multimedia, are not even possible to implement in the OLTP light configuration.

Of course, with those advantages come some significant disadvantages. The client/server system is significantly more difficult to configure and administer than the single computer in the light environment. Probably the most significant factor is that applications are much more difficult to write. The key factors that cause the increased difficulty in applications development are graphical user interface programming, connecting to a database server, and coordinating the portions of the system that will run on the client with the portions that will run on the server.

As is typical of many things in computing, a graphical user interface makes things much easier on the end user while it increases the difficulty of the developer's job. Instead of a simple world of characters on an 80 by 24 grid, the developer is faced with a complex world of fonts, images, controls, pixels, colors, and mice. In a character-oriented program, input will arrive through the keyboard with a limited set of possibilities. A graphical program can receive input from the keyboard or the mouse, and there are literally hundreds of possible events it needs to be ready to respond to. The result of this is that writing a program with a graphical interface is in general many times more difficult than writing a similar program with a character user interface.

Database interfaces also pose their own challenges in the client/server world. Many of the databases have features like stored procedures and binary large objects (BLOBS). Support for these features requires more expertise on the part of the programmer, and even though the network connection to the database server is theoretically transparent, it generally requires effort to deal with things like performance and possible errors in connection.

Finally, many applications are best served by dividing their tasks between the client and server. The simple mechanism for doing this is with a database server, but many other tasks like batch processing and reporting are more suited to running on the larger server machines. Unfortunately, this often involves developing portions of an application on two different operating systems at the same time. For example, the client software might be running on Windows while the server software might be running on UNIX. This can involve two different knowledge bases for the developers. In addition to this problem, the different portions of the application need to communicate, and implementing this type of communication can be difficult and error prone.

As a result of the increased complexity of this, environment organizations can find themselves spending a significant portion of their development resources dealing with technology issues instead of application issues. Also, they often find that their applications lack robustness since it may be difficult to find the time to tie down all of the loose ends and complete the application functionality in time. For these reasons the promise of the client/server architecture has, in many cases, not been fulfilled.

Many organizations are finding that the solution to these problems can be found in fourth-generation environments. The key benefit of "technology hiding" allows developers to focus on the application rather than the technology. An appropriate 4GL can deal with the issues of graphical user interface, database interface, and multiplatform development. Figure 3.8 shows the architecture of a typical 4GL, which has built-in support for several GUIs and client/server databases. In addition, because of technology hiding it can be used to create applications for different operating systems and computers without the developer having to focus on the differences between those systems. The 4GL translates the application model that is created into the appropriate calls to the underlying resources, such as the GUI and the database management system (DBMS), automatically.

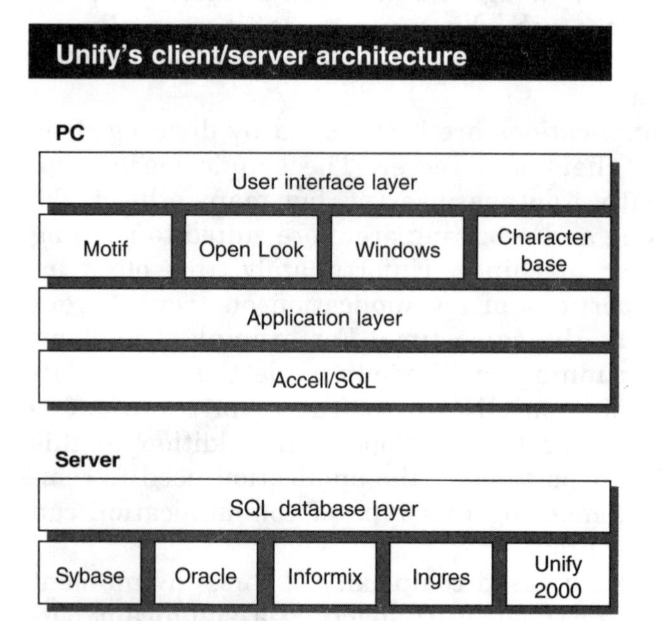

Figure 3.8 Accell/SQL applications run transparently across hardware, operating systems, networks, and user interfaces.

The key disadvantages for a 4GL in the client/server environment are performance and lack of complete developer control. Much as in the OLTP light area, the 4GL uses more memory and central processing unit (CPU) to achieve the same result. This can be particularly significant in the server portion of the application, which has to serve many users. Developer control over the specifics of the application is caused by the technology hiding of the 4GL. In some cases, the 4GL may not have in its application model the specific look and feel that the developer wants.

The performance trade-off is generally considered less significant in the client/server environment due to the immense amount of inexpensive resource that can be thrown at the problem. In many cases each user has on his or her desk a powerful computer with significant amounts of memory. Because these resources are dedicated to that particular user, it is not particularly important that a large percentage of them are used up to run the client portion of the application. In addition, because the client systems are doing a large portion of the work, it frees up the centralized system resources and makes it more feasible to write larger programs to achieve a purpose.

Likewise, while the developer may prefer to have more control over the final application, this type of technology hiding may be the enabler that even makes the development possible. Large portions of the application work exactly as desired and they can be completed within the allowable time frames and budget, even if small portions of the application have to work somewhat differently than the ideal. In cases where this is not acceptable, developers decide to use a combination of 4GL for the bulk of the application while using a 3GL to implement the few areas where a specific effect is critical.

For these reasons 4GLs are being most rapidly accepted in the client/server area. A large number of tools are appearing and having significant success filling the gap between the desire of organizations to develop these types of applications and the technology mountain that they face in doing so. It is only through the use of these high-level technologies that significant numbers of client/server applications are beginning to appear.

Large-Scale OLTP

The large-scale OLTP system involves many coordinated computer systems, potential distribution over a large geographic area, and large user populations. These systems are often key central processing functions for large organizations. Classic examples are hotel and airline reservations, production and ordering systems, and automated teller machine (ATM) networks. Key requirements for these systems are high availability, transaction integrity, and predictable response time.

Figure 3.9 shows the classic architecture that has been used to implement large-scale OLTP. The users work at relatively dumb block mode devices which accept a screen full of data. This data is then packaged up into a transaction, sent through concentrators, and routed to a large centralized mainframe. The mainframe handles the bulk of the work using transaction-processing monitors like Customer Information Control System (CICS). These programs route the transactions from thousands of users to the processes on the mainframe, which execute the transactions and send the results back to the users. The mainframe programs have to be written in low-level languages and carefully tuned to achieve the necessary system performance. The systems are not highly interactive, as each round trip to the centralized system is very expensive.

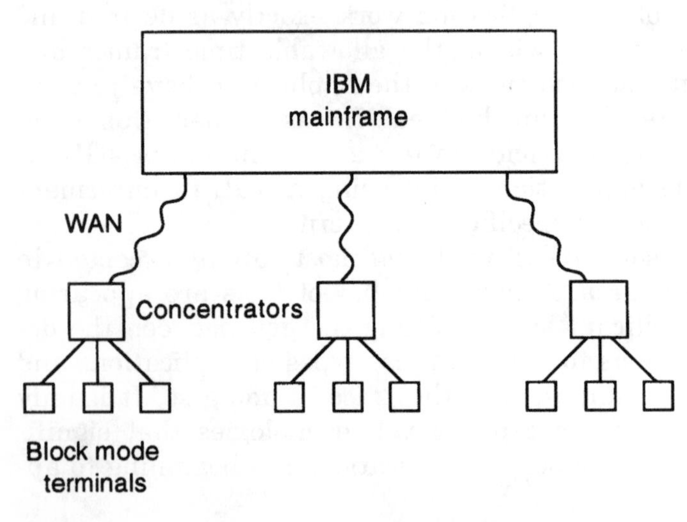

Figure 3.9 Classic architecture for large-scale OLTP.

This architecture has been highly successful in the past. The systems have met the requirements of availability and performance and served their roles well. Travel agents from all over the world can rapidly check the status of flights and make reservations on virtually any airline. General Motors dealerships can check on the availability of particular parts and order new supplies if necessary.

Many organizations want to develop new large-scale OLTP systems using a more distributed processing model. They want to take advantage of the new hardware and software environments to make these systems less expensive, more responsive, and more user friendly. In many cases this will make large-scale systems possible which were previously prohibited by one of these factors.

In order to do this, the development techniques are going to have to change from the classic model. Instead of having a highly tuned, hugely powerful, central system there will be a network of smaller computers which will have to be well coordinated in carrying out the tasks. In addition, the user interface will be much more interactive with the definition of a round trip getting a lot fuzzier.

Figure 3.10 shows the architecture of a large-scale OLTP system of the future. It is made up of a hierarchy of systems, from desktop PCs to large-scale database server computers. For reasons of cost the user input devices may range from character terminals to powerful workstations. The trip that a particular transaction takes can vary from a completely local interaction on the user's desktop, all the way to a multimachine journey to one of the largest-scale machines located a continent away.

The interesting thing about this type of environment is that it contains elements of each of the other two types of OLTP systems. A single computer can be supporting a set of dumb terminals with local application and database support. Elsewhere there can be a local client/server configuration with applications located on workstations communicating with a database server machine. Each of these local environments would function like its small-scale counterpart until it would become necessary to do something that required interaction with the broader environment; then it would package up a transaction and send it to the appropriate place.

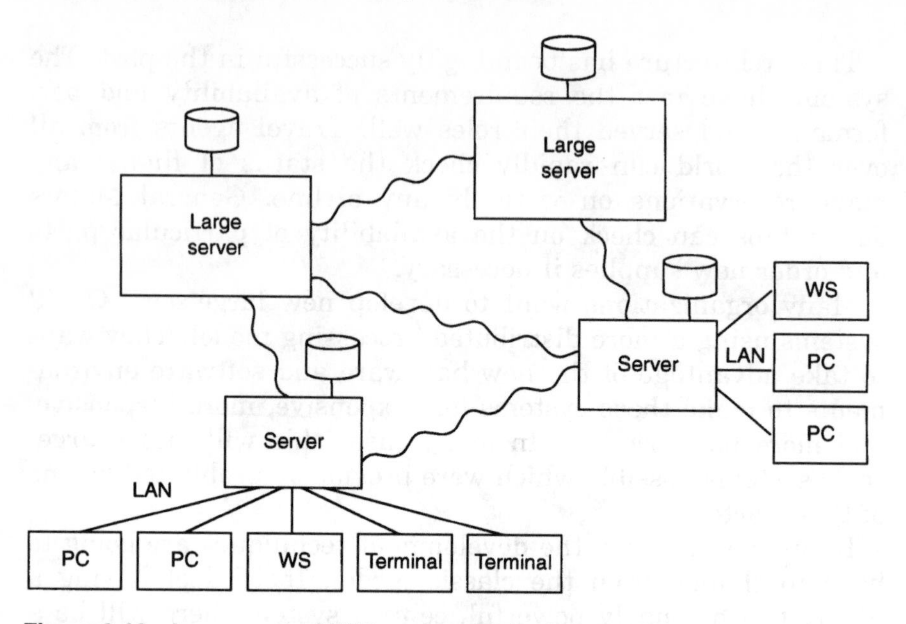

Figure 3.10 Large-scale OLTP system of the future.

For example, a bank branch might have a local environment that contains all of the information about the customers at the branch. It would have local loan and deposit information, as well as records relating to the sales activity of the branch personnel. If a customer were to walk in who belonged to that branch, then most of the activity would look like either an OLTP light environment or a client/server environment, depending on the specific configuration. If, however, a customer from a different branch came in, then a transaction would be sent out over the network to get the necessary information on the customer from the appropriate branch. The reply to the transaction would be loaded into the local database and the branch employee would be ready to work with the customer. Of course, a given corporate customer might have information stored with several branches and a money transfer operation might need to be coordinated between all of them.

To carry out these types of tasks it is necessary to use a distributed transaction monitor. These systems are designed to route transactions generated by a process on one machine to the appropriate process that provides the service. Figure 3.11 shows the architecture of this type of transaction monitor. The

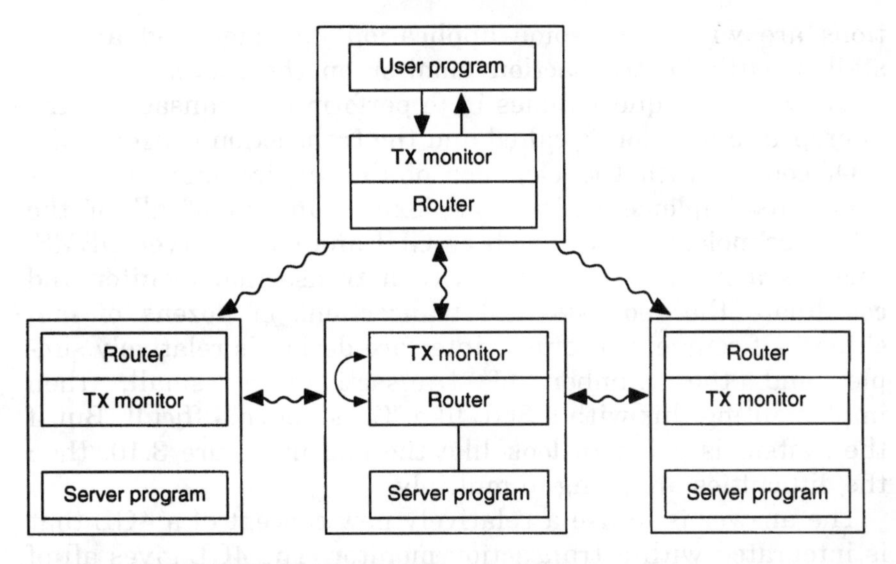

Figure 3.11 A distributed transaction monitor.

monitor is responsible for taking the transaction request, validating it, and then sending it over the network to the appropriate server machine. On the server machine the monitor accepts the request and then queues it for processing by a server process, which has been designated for that task. When the transaction is completed, the response is sent back by reversing the process.

There are many advantages to using a transaction monitor. First of all, it provides the mechanism for routing a transaction over a potentially complex network environment. Second, it makes sure that transactions arrive at their destination and that appropriate results are returned. Third, it provides optimum performance on the server systems by queuing the requests from potentially thousands of requesters into just a few server processes. Finally, it provides reliability by coordinating multiple smaller transactions into one larger transaction that either completes or has no effect.

Of course, this means that the specific transactions that the system will provide have to be decided in advance. For example, there might be a transaction to retrieve the account history for a particular customer. A separate transaction might update a customer's account balance. Still another might update the customer's address information. All of these transactions are written in some application language and are installed with the transaction monitor on the server machine. Then, when a request comes in to perform the transaction, the appropriate function is called and the transaction is executed.

Of course, with the elegance of this environment there is enormous implementation complexity. On top of all of the other technology issues, such as GUI and client/server DBMS, there is a need to integrate with a transaction monitor and coordinate the requests and transactions of dozens of machines. Of course, if the user interface design is relatively simple and the number of transactions is small, then implementing this with a 3GL like "C" is not so difficult. But if the system is going to look like the one in Figure 3.10, then the difficulties are going to multiply.

The answer is to use a relatively new concept of a 4GL that is integrated with a transaction monitor. The 4GL gives all of its previously defined benefits in the local environments, but adds a whole new dimension. It also provides the ability to work with the transaction monitor to implement both the requests for services and the services themselves. The result is a major reduction in both development time and technology training.

Figure 3.12 shows the architecture of an integrated 4GL and transaction monitor. Notice that the 4GL run-time environment is present on the server machines to execute the transaction services. When a request comes in to the transaction monitor, it asks the 4GL run-time environment to execute a specific task and passes in the parameters. The 4GL developer is insulated from the complexities of both issuing the transaction request and receiving it; he or she can focus on the application logic on both sides of the communication without being burdened by the systems technology.

The following example is based on an ATM environment. This is a relatively simple example, which is designed to show how a 4GL can be integrated with a transaction monitor in order to implement large-scale OLTP applications. In this application, accounts are stored at two different branches. The records for these branches are stored on computers at the branch locations. Updates involving both branches have to be coordinated. For example, when money is transferred from one

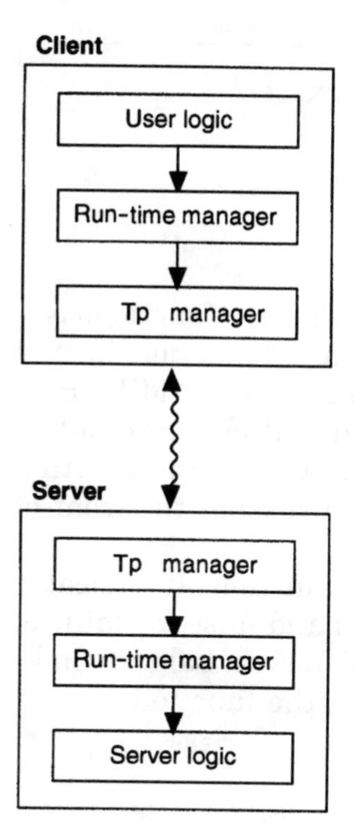

Figure 3.12 An integrated 4GL and transaction monitor.

branch to another, both the withdrawal from one branch and the deposit to the other branch have to be completed.

In this system only a few transactions are implemented. A customer can ask for his account balance, withdraw money from either branch, deposit money to either branch, or transfer money between the branches. The user interface is provided on a graphical device so that the customer can point to what he wants.

The client program running on a workstation (substituting for an ATM machine) gathers up the user's request by responding to button presses and numerical entries on the keypad. When a complete request is entered, it passes the transaction to the transaction monitor, which forwards it to the appropriate branch machine. On the branch machine the transaction monitor queues the request to the appropriate 4GL function that will perform the transaction. The 4GL functions are the same on both machines.

```
BOOL FUNCTION DEPOSIT ( ACCOUNT_ID, TX_AMOUNT, RESULT BALANCE,
RESULT STATLIN  )
BEGIN
```

Figure 3.13 Source code for the deposit function.

Figure 3.13 is the source code for the deposit function. Notice that its structure looks like an ordinary function in any high-level programming language. This function could be running directly inside a local application without changes, but in this case the transaction monitor is going to call the function when a request for this type of transaction reaches the front of the queue.

This is the declaration for the deposit function. It indicates that it returns a Boolean (true for success and false for failure) and the arguments. The result keyword before balance indicates that this value will be returned from the function.

First the account number is validated.

```
IF ( ACCOUNT_ID < MINACCT  OR ACCOUNT_ID > MAXACCT ) THEN
  BEGIN
    SET $STATLIN to 'Invalid account number';
    return (FALSE)
END /* if */
/* convert string to float amount */
set $amt to $TX_AMOUNT;
```

Then the deposit amount is validated to be greater than 0.

```
/* must have valid amount to deposit */
IF ( $amt <= 0.0 ) THEN
  BEGIN
    SET $STATLIN to 'Deposit amount must be greater than $0.00'
    return (FALSE)
END
```

This declaration starts a local transaction. If this request is part of a group of requests to other servers it will be coordinated using two-phase commit logic.

```
BEGIN_TRANSACTION_CODE_SECTION
    /* get account balance */
```

The actual body of the function performs the necessary database operations to update the bank records.

```
SET $acct_bal TO SELECT BALANCE
      FROM ACCOUNT
      WHERE ACCOUNT_ID = $ACCOUNT_ID
    EXECUTING BEGIN
      /* Get teller balance */
      SET $branch_id, $tlr_bal  TO
        SELECT BRANCH_ID, BALANCE from TELLER
        WHERE TELLER_ID = $teller_id
      EXECUTING BEGIN
        SET $branch_bal TO
          SELECT BALANCE from BRANCH
          WHERE BRANCH_ID = $branch_id
        EXECUTING BEGIN
          SET $branch_bal to $branch_bal + $amt;
          UPDATE SELECTED ROW set BALANCE = $branch_bal;
```

The Exit Transaction statement checks the status function for an error and, if there is one, it aborts the current transaction.

```
          EXIT_TRANSACTION_CODE_SECTION_ON_ERROR( status$() )
          END    /* select BRANCH */
          EXIT_TRANSACTION_CODE_SECTION_ON_ERROR( status$() )
          /* update teller record with new BALANCE */
          SET $tlr_bal to $tlr_bal + $amt;
        UPDATE SELECTED ROW set BALANCE = $tlr_bal;
        EXIT_TRANSACTION_CODE_SECTION_ON_ERROR( status$() )
        END    /* select TELLER */
      EXIT_TRANSACTION_CODE_SECTION_ON_ERROR( status$() )
      SET $acct_bal to $acct_bal + $amt;
      /* Update account record with new BALANCE */
            UPDATE SELECTED ROW set BALANCE = $acct_bal;
            EXIT_TRANSACTION_CODE_SECTION_ON_ERROR( status$() )
     END    /* select ACCOUNT */
     EXIT_TRANSACTION_CODE_SECTION_ON_ERROR( status$() )
```

```
        insert into HISTORY (ACCOUNT_ID, TELLER_ID, BRANCH_ID, AMOUNT,
        TIME_STAMP, DATE_STAMP)
        values ($ACCOUNT_ID, $teller_id, $branch_id, $amt, 0, 0);
        EXIT_TRANSACTION_CODE_SECTION_ON_ERROR( status$() )

        set $STATLIN to 'SUCCESS'
        set $BALANCE to $acct_bal
    END_TRANSACTION_CODE_SECTION
```

If the transaction fails for any reason, then the following section is called automatically to clean up.

```
    BEGIN_ABORT_TRANSACTION_CODE_SECTION
        set $STATLIN to 'FAILED'
        set $BALANCE to UNDEFINED
        If( $fail_reason = SS_USSER OR $fail_reason =  SS_DBINT )
    THEN
        SET $fail_reason to dbms_status$()
        LOG_MSG( 'DEPOSIT TX failed at point '+val_to_str$(
    $fail_point )+
    ' for reason '+ val_to_str$( $fail_reason) )
    END_ABORT_TRANSACTION_CODE_SECTION

    END /* deposit */
```

Notice that the function did not have to deal with typical activities like unpacking the arguments or packing the results. It also did not have to make low-level calls to coordinate its activities with the transaction manager or indicate completion. These types of things are handled by the 4GL layer, which integrates with the transaction monitor. The developer was able to spend all of his or her time focusing on the logic of the transaction itself.

Figure 3.14 shows a portion of the source code in the client program that deals with calling the deposit function. Notice in the declaration of the function that it was declared as an Accell TP function. This tells the 4GL environment that it needs to pack up the arguments for this function and then make the appropriate transaction monitor calls to pass this to one of the servers. The client program actually has no idea where the transaction monitor will pass this transaction to; it could be a

```
EXTERN ACCELL_TP BOOL FUNCTION DEPOSIT( account_id, tx_amount,
                        RESULT balance, RESULT statlin );
FORM txsummary
```

Figure 3.14 A portion of client program source code.

program on the local machine or a mainframe computer on the other side of the world. Likewise, the developer does not have to handle issues such as connecting to a particular server or packing the data.

The calling program declares deposit as an external Accell Transaction Processing (TP) function. This signals the run-time environment the need to coordinate with the transaction monitor to carry out this function.

This declaration puts an OK button on the screen, and says that, when it is pushed, this form will terminate.

```
DEFINE COMMAND ok ACTION IS 'ENABLED' BUTTON at (7,34)
LABEL is 'OK '
NEXT ACTION IS PREVIOUS_FORM

BEFORE FORM
```

This declaration starts a global transaction with the transaction monitor. All of the service requests will be coordinated until the transaction is terminated.

```
BEGIN_GLOBAL_TX
```

Depending on the user action, call the appropriate service routine.

```
switch( atm:$user_action )
begin
    case DEPOSIT_ACT:
    SET $account_id to atm:$account_id
    SET $tx_amount to atm:$tx_amount
```

Here is the actual call to the deposit function from the client side.

```
IF( NOT DEPOSIT($account_id, $tx_amount, $balance,
$statlin) ) THEN
BEGIN
    display 'Deposit service failed' for fyi_message wait
    ABORT_GLOBAL_TX
    END ELSE BEGIN
    SET $tx_type to 'DEPOSIT'
    SET $bal1 to 'Balance: '+val_to_str$( $balance )
```

This commits the global transaction.

```
    COMMIT_GLOBAL_TX
END

    SET $bal1 to 'Balance: '+val_to_str$( $balance )
    COMMIT_GLOBAL_TX
END
```

The transaction monitor integration also handles issues like commit coordination between servers. One important function of a transaction monitor is to provide two-phase commit between different services. This is a protocol that assures the developer that, regardless of system failures at run time, a transaction will either be completely executed, or have no effect. The classic example is the transfer of funds between two branches. It would be undesirable if, due to a system failure, just the withdrawal from the first branch was recorded but not the deposit. Likewise, it would be bad for the bank if the deposit was recorded but not the withdrawal. By coordinating a two-phase commit the transaction monitor prevents these types of problems.

Figure 3.15 shows the server code involved in the funds transfer. A service called transfer is called to move money between two accounts. Behind the scenes the server 4GL is coordinating with the transaction monitor to perform the withdrawal and deposit functions as part of a single global transaction. This shows how a service routine can call other service routines to carry out its function. If the systems were to go down before the commit was completed, then there would be no effect on either local bank machine. Once the commit is

```
EXTERN ACCELL BOOL FUNCTION DEPOSIT( account_id, tx_amount,
                  RESULT balance, RESULT statlin );
EXTERN ACCELL BOOL FUNCTION WITHDRAW(account_id, tx_amount,
                  RESULT balance, RESULT statlin );
BOOL FUNCTION TRANSFER( DB_ACCOUNT, CR_ACCOUNT, TX_AMOUNT,
                  RESULT DB_BAL, RESULT CR_BAL, RESULT STATLIN )
BEGIN
    LOG_MSG( 'TRANSFER CALLED' )
    IF(  NOT WITHDRAW( $DB_ACCOUNT, $TX_AMOUNT, $DB_BAL,
$STATLIN ) ) THEN
        BEGIN
#     set $STATLIN TO 'TRANSFER: WITHDRAW service failed'
    LOG_MSG( $STATLIN )
    return( FALSE )
    END
    IF( NOT DEPOSIT( $CR_ACCOUNT, $TX_AMOUNT, $CR_BAL,
$STATLIN) ) THEN
    BEGIN
    set $STATLIN TO 'TRANSFER: DEPOSIT service failed'
    LOG_MSG( $STATLIN )
    return( FALSE )
    END
    return( TRUE )
END
```

Figure 3.15 Server code involved in funds transfer.

completed the developer is assured that all of the updates will go through.

The withdrawal service routine declares the deposit and withdrawal functions as external local functions.

About the Author

Nicolas Nierenberg, 35, co-founded Unify Corporation in August of 1980. In his current position as Unify's CTO, Mr. Nierenberg is a major contributor to the company's product strategy and technological direction.

Active within the UNIX industry, Mr. Nierenberg is a board member of UniForum, a position that allows him to help define industry standards and to solve UNIX-related issues.

At Unify, he led the design of the company's first product, the UNIFY RDBMS. Mr. Nierenberg helped establish and develop the product's initial markets. His positions within the company have included chairman of the board, president, and vice president of engineering.

Prior to founding Unify, Mr. Nierenberg was the head of systems software for Rogers, Kirkman, and Associates, Inc. (RKA). During his tenure at RKA, he was responsible for selecting, developing, and implementing new products. Additionally, he was the lead analyst on a variety of application development projects.

He attended the University of California, Los Angeles, and the University of California, San Diego, where he studied economics and computer science.

Mr. Nierenberg has made his home in Sacramento, California, for the past 14 years. He resides with his wife Caroline, his daughter, Anna, 6, and son, William, 3.

Chapter

4

OLTP in a Multivendor Environment

John Enck
Forest Computer Incorporated

Introduction

When you think of a multivendor on-line transaction processing (OLTP) implementation, you might picture a set of processing threads perfectly woven together to create an intricate and beautiful application tapestry. Chances are pretty slim that this vision reveals the paths the individual threads take to compose the tapestry; the details of where threads start, end, and the route they take in between are often lost in the big picture.

Unfortunately, implementing or managing an OLTP solution in a multivendor environment requires attention to detail at all levels of processing. In most cases, a multivendor OLTP implementation presents a much broader range of processing issues than a single vendor OLTP implementation. Technical considerations range from high-level headaches like trying to interface Digital C programs with IBM RPG programs, to low-level details like translating between ASCII and EBCDIC storage formats. And in between these extremes are a number of other technical traps waiting to be sprung.

Despite the technical challenges, multivendor OLTP implementation is one of the most promising paths for the future of data processing. The application possibilities are vast. For example:

- Data generated and stored on Digital or Hewlett-Packard computers in third-party databases such as Oracle or Ingres can be linked to data generated and stored on IBM systems in proprietary IBM databases. A single user transaction can retrieve data from or post data to all of the involved databases.
- Duplication of data on separate platforms can be eliminated by creating one or more central database servers accessible to applications on all other platforms. Thus, the point of origin for a user transaction does not inherently limit access to information.
- Laboratory and process control applications can interface with technical or analog equipment and with administrative computers. An administrative transaction can query the state of the real-time technical environment, or a technical transaction can exchange information with the administrative environment.

Implementing these types of OLTP solutions requires an underlying mechanism to facilitate intersystem communication between the different platforms. This interface may be a well-defined, high-level interface or a down-and-dirty, low-level interface; but either way, an interface must be present.

Simple program-to-program interfaces are available that provide synchronized one-in-one-out communications, and so are complex interfaces that facilitate asynchronous queue-oriented communications. Interfaces may be implemented via high-level language hooks available to all programs or through low-level server programs that funnel communications within a platform. The choice of an intersystem interface is driven by available technology, staff expertise, and application requirements; the choice is yours to make.

However, the program-to-program communication interface is only one aspect of implementing a well-integrated OLTP solution in a multivendor environment. For example, file transfer may be needed to move source code or test files from one platform to another. Terminal access can be used to give the technical staff a "user's view" of the application, regardless of what terminal the user is using and what terminal the technician is currently using. Other services, such as device sharing or electronic mail exchange, provide similar benefits.

Given the complexity of the environment, the trick to implementing a powerful and flexible multivendor OLTP environment rests not only in the selection of the intersystem interface, but also in the selection of all of the ancillary services around the interface. With this in mind, this chapter will explore popular strategies used to implement full-featured interoperability environments.

Interoperability Products

The spectrum of interoperability products is broad. At the low end of the spectrum you can find simple, low-performance products providing American National Standards Institute (ANSI) or TTY terminal emulation and Kermit, X-, Y-, or Z-modem file transfer. These products are reasonable solutions for casual usage or low-volume environments, but they lack the power and flexibility to be considered fully functional interoperability solutions.

In the middle of the spectrum are proprietary architectures which have gained sufficient popularity to be force fitted into foreign platforms. Here we find products like systems network architecture (SNA), remote job entry (RJE) file transfer, SNA 3270 workstation emulation (both native to IBM mainframe networks), and VT220 terminal emulation (indigenous to the Digital environment). Being force fitted does not mean these solutions are ineffective or "bad"; rather, they are introducing foreign protocols into a system, and these protocols are a far cry from any of the defined international standards.

At the high end of the spectrum are full-featured products that cater to the best features of all the systems that they are interconnecting. Two different types of products fall into this category:

1. Products that implement international interoperability standards (defined or de facto). For the purpose of this dis-

cussion, this includes OSI, TCP/IP, and DCE protocols and services.

2. Gateways that act as intermediaries between proprietary protocols and services.

The common element between the two types of products is that they both provide a rich array of services without crowbarring proprietary architectures into foreign machines. Standards-based products rely on the international community to define acceptable interoperability services. Gateways translate between existing proprietary protocols and services to deliver the functions of interoperability. Both approaches utilize well-understood and widely established technologies, and both strive to optimize performance by tightly integrating interoperability services with the operating system of the host system.

In the current market, products that fall into the high-end classification are "hot." With this in mind, this chapter will focus on the interoperability strategies of:

- Gateways
- Open Systems Interconnect (OSI) Reference Model standards
- Transmission Control Protocol/Internet Protocol (TCP/IP) suite of protocols and services
- Distributed Computing Environment (DCE) suite of protocols and services

Interoperability Services

Before discussing these interoperability strategies in detail, we must first examine the purpose and value of interoperability services. Clearly implementing OLTP in a multivendor environment requires interoperability services. These services may be as basic as program-to-program communications, or they may be more sophisticated services such as global structured query language (SQL) access or record-level access to flat files across platforms. The specific service selected is a function of the OLTP design; for example, flat file access is obviously of little value in a distributed database environment.

In brief, the following interoperability services should be considered as valuable tools in a multivendor OLTP environment:

- Program-to-program communications
- Remote file access
- SQL passageway
- Terminal access
- Device sharing
- Command/job submission
- Electronic mail exchange
- Network management

The exact "spin" to each of these services is dependent on the computer platforms involved. For example, implementing terminal access between DEC and UNIX systems is a quite different problem than implementing terminal access between DEC and IBM systems. To make matters interesting, IBM and DEC are most frequently the two types of systems that require this degree of integration. Because the DEC and IBM architectures are so often targets for interoperability, the following discussion of services will use the Digital Equipment Corporation DECnet architecture and the IBM Systems Network Architecture (SNA) to illustrate the functions of each interoperability service.

Program-to-Program Communication

Program-to-program communication has a distinctive flavor based on its environment. For many OLTP solutions, the program-to-program methodology is often the underlying technology that enables information to flow between platforms. With program-to-program communications, programs can set up peer or master/slave relationships with one another.

Program-to-program communication can be performed on a synchronous or asynchronous basis. Synchronous communication requires each program to "talk" or "listen" at the appropriate time. In many implementations of synchronous communications, a program that is in a "listen" state must request to "change direction" in order to move into a "talk" state. This is the architecture used by IBM's Advanced Program-to-Program Communications (APPC).

Under IBM's APPC architecture, a program has a set of "verbs" that it can use to establish links with other programs to receive data, request to send data, actually send data, terminate links, and more. These verbs are part of IBM's SNA Logical Unit 6.2 (LU 6.2) definition, and are also considered a key element of the Common Program Interface for Communications (CPI-C) specification, which is part of IBM's Systems Application Architecture (SAA).

Alternatively, in an asynchronous environment, programs may "talk" or "listen" when they so desire. This architecture depends on message queues to hold on to messages until programs are ready to pick them up. As an adjunct to this approach, message queues may also be recoverable, allowing the OLTP environment to survive program and minor system crashes without the loss of all messages currently in the system.

Asynchronous message delivery is the standard practice of Digital's task-to-task facility within DECnet. Two styles of DECnet task-to-task access are available: transparent communication, which allows a program to write and read to a logical file to send and receive messages, and nontransparent communication, which uses a "mailbox" facility to forward and receive communications with other programs.

Digital's transparent communication was designed for quick and easy network applications. Nontransparent communication, on the other hand, has greater sophistication. For example, nontransparent communication allows a program to send and receive interrupt messages, to accept or reject link requests, and to easily handle concurrent communications with multiple programs. Nontransparent programs can communicate with transparent programs.

IBM has also moved toward an asynchronous architecture with its Message Queue Interface (MQI). Unlike APPC, MQI provides asynchronous communication and recoverable message queues and is intended for use in multivendor environments.

Remote File Access

Remote file access can take on a number of appearances. From a broad perspective, remote file access can be broken down into three categories:

1. **File transfer.** This is the traditional implementation of remote file access, born from the days of tape transport and IBM RJE. In this case, a file is physically copied over the network to another location where it can be manipulated and, if necessary, copied back to the original location. File transfer is a traditional and widely implemented means of moving files around in an interoperability environment.
2. **Record-level access to specific files.** This mechanism allows an application to directly access one or more specific files on a remote system, providing it has proper name and ownership information. Once the remote file is open, the application can perform record-level reads and writes on the file. Record-level access is normally available between similar platforms (e.g., between two DEC VAXes or two AS/400s), but is difficult to find as an interoperability service between dissimilar platforms.
3. **Network file server.** Personal computer local area networks (PC LANs) and intelligent workstations have popularized the concept of a network file server as a repository of files that can be shared by systems on the network. In reality, this concept breaks down into two styles of implementations.
   a. **File set services.** File set services make a group of designated files available to the network. These files may be accessed by the sponsoring host as well as the other systems in the network. For example, a PC could mount the files in a Digital VAX directory as a virtual disk, and both the VAX and the PC could access those files.
   b. **Virtual disk services.** In this scenario, a portion of a disk on a host system is used as a virtual disk for other systems in the network. Generally speaking, this approach is used to allow a larger system (e.g., a Digital VAX or an IBM AS/400) to act as a server in a PC

LAN. The key factor in this approach is that the host actually emulates a PC network drive, and the physical files on that drive may or may not be accessible to the host itself.

In Digital DECnet networks, file transfer and record-level services are handled by the File Access Listener (FAL) utility. In the IBM mainframe environment, file transfer services are performed by the RJE facility associated with the mainframe operating system (e.g., POWER for VSE, RSCS for VM, and JES for MVS). In the IBM midrange environment, file transfer services can be handled by the Distributed Data Manager (DDM) facility or SNA Distribution Services (SNADS). Record-level access in the IBM midrange environment is handled by DDM. Finally, in both the IBM and Digital environments, network file system services are focused on PC integration, and not peer-to-peer access.

Regardless of the type of service, most file access implementations handle conversion between different character codes and support binary access. Less available is support for field-level conversion; for example, being able to take a signed, packed, decimal field on one system and write it as a signed, packed, decimal field on another system. The internal representation of numeric data is wildly different from system to system.

SQL Passageway

While file-oriented services solve a variety of problems in interoperability environments, they do not provide much value in environments using sophisticated database structures. The problem of multivendor database access is further complicated by third-party implementations of databases. The end result is that two different database products may not be able to interface with one another, even if they are implemented on the same vendor platform in a network.

IBM's solution to this problem was the development of the Structured Query Language (SQL). SQL has gone on to have meaning beyond the IBM environment and is now an established standard for accessing every major database. The basic function of SQL is to define a series of command statements that can be used to open, manipulate, and access databases. The commands necessary to perform a specific operation (i.e., open a database) are applicable to all databases supporting SQL access.

Since SQL provided a "universal" interface to databases, the necessary ingredient to implement SQL access on a network-wide basis is a means of feeding SQL commands into a platform and receiving the responses back. Thus far this aspect of SQL access is lacking in most major platforms, including IBM and Digital, but it can be provided by client/server programs using program-to-program services.

Terminal Access

Terminal or workstation access to applications remains an important factor in Digital, IBM, and many other environments. In these cases, terminals of varying levels of intelligence provide the primary means of access for the user community. The way in which terminals interface with the application hosts varies from vendor to vendor.

- In the IBM environment, groups of workstations are attached to workstation controllers which, in turn, interface to a central system or a front-end processor. This creates a structured, hierarchical environment.
- In the DEC environment, terminals are normally attached to terminal servers which, in turn, are directly attached to a LAN. This allows any terminal to access any host over the network and creates a distributed, free-form environment.

The primary concern of interoperability is not the attachment architecture; instead, it is the way these devices operate. Specifically, terminals and workstations normally fall into two different categories:

- **Block mode** devices collect keyboard strokes locally and then transmit them to the host when an Enter or function key is pressed. Applications interacting with block mode devices usually present a data entry form and then wait for the data within the form to be transmitted back. The keystrokes required to enter the data in each field, or to move from one field to another, are not received by the host or host application. This is how IBM mainframe (3270 class) and midrange (5250 class) workstations operate.

- **Character mode** devices transmit each character as it is typed on the keyboard. The key travels over the data communications (or LAN) link to the host for processing. Applications interacting with character mode devices can choose to receive (and possibly act on) each keystroke as it is pressed, or they can have the operating system collect them and present them when a termination key (i.e., Return, Tab, or Enter) is pressed. This is how Digital VT terminals (100/200/300/400 series) operate.

Some manufacturers (Hewlett-Packard to name one) have implemented other variations of character and block mode operations. This includes, for example, line mode, where each line is transmitted, and page mode, where an entire display page is transmitted, regardless of field delimiters. These implementations, however, should be considered unusual.

To facilitate interoperability between both types of terminals and both types of applications, two levels of translation must be performed. The most straightforward level involves the translation of character codes (ASCII/EBCDIC), cursor movement directives, video highlight commands, and special keyboard keys. For example, if an IBM workstation is accessing a Digital application, the interoperability service must translate the Digital bold, blink, and underline sequences into the appropriate sequences for the IBM workstation.

The more complex level of translation involves making a character mode device look like a block mode device and vice versa. Of the two, making a character mode device look like a block mode device is a relatively easy task; the interoperability service simply buffers up the keystrokes until a transmit function is requested.

Making a block mode device look like a character mode device, however, is more difficult. In this case, the interoperability service must receive a block transmission from the workstation and feed it to the host as individual characters or as a stream of characters. In this environment, the interoperability service must be able to determine when it is appropriate to terminate a stream with a Return, what to do with remaining characters in the buffer if the application accepts one character and enters a new mode, and so forth.

Device Sharing

Device sharing allows expensive devices such as printers and tape drives to be shared by multiple systems in a network.

Tape drives are extremely specialized devices that have a close relationship to the hosting operating system and hardware. This specialization makes it difficult to share a tape drive in a multivendor environment. Some interoperability vendors provide basic file backup and restore capabilities by using file set access to read and write files to a tape device, or by using bulk file transfer techniques to copy files directly to the tape device. Unfortunately, using tape drive interoperability services for operating systems loads or native backup/restore operations is nearly impossible, because these operations assume a tight relationship between the operating system and the tape drive hardware. This restricts tape sharing to custom backup and restore operations.

Print sharing, on the other hand, is not as highly specialized. In the majority of connectivity environments, print sharing is implemented as part of a file transfer solution. However, unlike physical file transfers, print file transfers involve moving data from one output queue to another. Additional considerations for print sharing include making sure that the output being generated matches the printer where it is ultimately printed, and making sure carriage control directives travel along intact. All things considered, print sharing is relatively easy to implement and can represent large cost savings over duplicating printers for different systems.

Command/Job Submission

Remote command and/or job submission allows one system to submit a command or job for execution on another system.

The concept of job submission has its roots in the IBM mainframe RJE environment, where distributed processors could submit jobs to the mainframe for processing and then receive the results back. Processing for this style of job is typically done as a background task, independent of terminal activities. RJE-style batch processing remains an important component of the IBM mainframe environment.

This same style of processing is also available in Digital systems and IBM midrange systems. Digital systems accommodate jobs through batch queues; for example, each user has a SYS$BATCH queue. Similarly, IBM midrange systems have batch processing queues to receive job input.

A similar facility is command submission. In this case, a single interactive command is passed to a remote system and the results of that command are forwarded back to the initiated system. Although this facility is available on IBM midrange systems (via the submit remote command directive), it is not common on IBM mainframe or Digital systems.

Electronic Mail Exchange

Electronic mail is an application distinctive to the type of host it runs on. Furthermore, the functions of electronic mail differ from one implementation to the next. At the basic level, electronic mail allows for ad-hoc messages to be sent from one user to another. On the high end of the spectrum, an electronic mail implementation may include support for word processing to compose or edit mail, a calendar capability for scheduling, assorted desktop tools (calculator, "to do" list management, etc.), a filing system to organize information, and, of course, the fundamental capability of being able to send mail (notes or documents) to other people in the network.

In the IBM mainframe environments, electronic mail is typically handled by the IBM's PROFS or NOTES software. In the IBM midrange environment, electronic mail is handled by AS/400 Office. In the Digital environment, mail services are available through VMS Mail, which offers basic electronic mail services only, or through ALL-IN-1, Digital's high-end package, which provides additional functionality.

Network Management

As the size of networks grows, the need for sophisticated network management tools also grows dramatically. Unfortunately, the availability of products that implement network management or participate with existing network management services has not grown in proportion with the need.

The IBM solution to network management is NetView. NetView uses SNA LU 6.2 services to receive network statistics, alerts, and configuration information from devices in an SNA network. Non-SNA devices may be accommodated though NetView/PC, a gateway device that allows non-SNA devices to feed information into the NetView environment. Unfortunately, the central component of NetView currently only runs on mainframe systems, which greatly limits its usefulness in midrange environments.

Digital uses the network management facilities inherent to the DECnet suite of protocols to perform network management. The administration and management of the network is performed by a Digital product named DECmcc Director.

Both IBM and Digital have recognized the inherent weakness of using proprietary services to perform network administration and management. With this in mind, both companies have taken steps to embrace the Simple Network Management Protocol (SNMP). This protocol will be discussed further under the TCP/IP heading.

Interoperability Strategies

Given this set of environments and potential services, the task becomes finding a solution that implements the services you require to implement or supplement your OLTP environment. The following four strategies provide different approaches for implementing robust interoperability:

- Gateways that interconnect networks by translating between proprietary and/or open protocols and services
- Standards from the International Standards Organization's (ISO) Open Systems Interconnect (OSI) Reference Model
- The TCP/IP and its suite of related protocols and services
- The Open Software Foundation's (OSF) DCE suite of protocols and services

Although each of these strategies provides its own solutions to the problems presented by interoperability, a single strategy may perfectly address a series of requirements. Therefore, it is not unusual to find interoperability environments that include mixtures of different strategies.

Gateways

Gateways provide interoperability between different network architectures by translating between network-level protocols and services (Figure 4.1). For example, a gateway between an IBM SNA network and a Digital DECnet network could:

- Facilitate program-to-program communications by translating between SNA APPC and DECnet task-to-task conversation formats.
- Implement file transfer by interfacing SNA RJE traffic into the DECnet File Access Listener (FAL) environment (and vice versa).
- Provide terminal access by translating between Digital VT and IBM 3270 data streams and device operations.

Gateways have been a traditional component in the construction of networks for quite some time. Gateways evolved from single-purpose—and relatively unintelligent—protocol converters to provide a suite of services for a given set of network architectures. The multipurpose orientation and higher level of digital intelligence set gateways apart from protocol converters. For example, gateways are usually implemented using general-purpose processors like 80386, 80486, or RISC processors, whereas protocol converters are often implemented using device processors such as the Z80 or 80186.

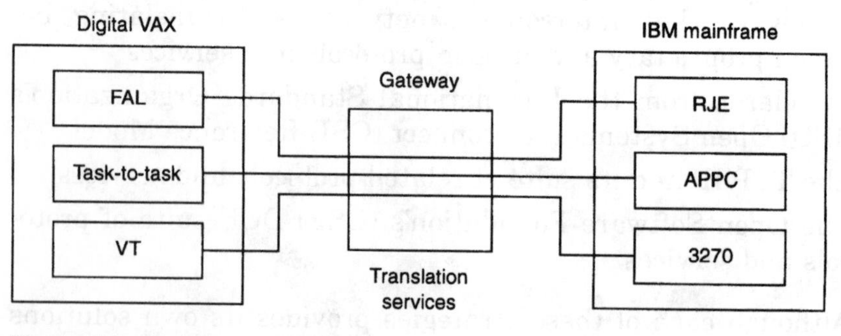

Figure 4.1 Gateway strategy.

Because gateways originally served to interconnect proprietary networks, the advent of open and de facto standards have had an effect on their purpose and usage. Interestingly enough, rather than restricting their use, standards have increased the gateway market, because gateway vendors were quick to integrate support for the new standards in their products. Thus, while yesterday's gateway might have only served SNA and DECnet networks, today's (and tomorrow's) gateways serve combinations of SNA, DECnet, TCP/IP, OSI, and DCE networks.

This flexibility allows gateways to be used as stand-alone solutions or as supplements to other interoperability solutions. For example, TCP/IP may have been chosen as the overall standard architecture, but one type of platform does not support TCP/IP or its services. In this case, a gateway could be used to tie the proprietary architecture into the "standard" architecture.

The OSI Reference Model

The OSI Reference Model was designed by the ISO to serve as a model for the development of a set of international standards to address the various aspects of interoperability (Figure 4.2). Input for the model and its related standards came from a number of standards organizations, including the American

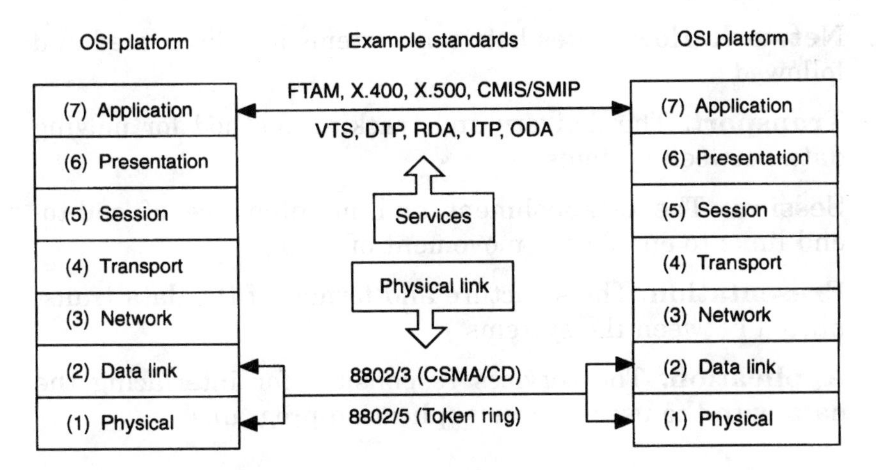

Figure 4.2 OSI strategy.

National Standards Institute (ANSI) and the International Telegraph and Telephone Consultative Committee (Comité Consultatif Internationale de Télégraphique et Téléphonique [CCITT]). These organizations also received input from smaller standards organizations such as the Institute of Electrical and Electronics Engineers (IEEE) and the Electronic Industries Association (EIA).

Because the OSI Reference Model was created by a standards organization, vendor compliance was optional. However, soon after the introduction of the OSI Reference Model in the 1980s, large corporations began to mandate the use or commitment for future use of the OSI standards. This pressure for compliance was further enforced by the Government OSI Procurement (GOSIP) programs put in place by the governments of the United States and United Kingdom. This led most of the major manufacturers of computer hardware and software to make a commitment to build and deliver OSI-compliant products.

In brief, the OSI Reference Model defines seven layers of interaction between platforms. From bottom to top, those layers are:

1. **Physical.** The physical and electrical characteristics of transmission media
2. **Data link.** How data is packaged and transmitted over the physical media
3. **Network.** How routes between systems are discovered and followed
4. **Transport.** The delivery and tracking method for moving data between systems
5. **Session.** The establishment and maintenance of end-to-end links to enable the movement of data
6. **Presentation.** The structure and format of the data transmitted between the systems
7. **Application.** The services responsible for interfacing the data with the user or user application programs

However, the important aspect of the OSI Reference Model is not the definition of the seven layers. Instead, the real value lies in the standards that have been created as a result of the model. Some of the standards that have come to life in vendor products as a result of the OSI Reference Model include:

- The 8802 series of LAN standards, which define the operation of Carrier Sense Multiple Access with Collision Detect (CSMA/CD), token-passing bus, and token-passing ring networks. These standards were adapted from the IEEE 802 series of standards.
- The File Transfer Access and Management (FTAM) standard, which defines a common means for the transfer and management of files in a multivendor environment.
- The X.400 standard for electronic mail exchange, which defines a methodology for the exchange of mail between different electronic mail environments. Most major vendors (including IBM and Digital) provide an X.400 interface for their proprietary electronic mail products.
- The X.500 standard for directory services, which provides a common means of defining network objects. This includes, for example, user names, system names, system locations, and other related attributes. One of the key uses for X.500 is to establish a global user directory in conjunction with the X.400 standard for electronic mail exchange.
- The Central Management Information Service and Central Management Information Protocol (CMIS and CMIP), which work together to provide network management information. They are organized as an agent/collection pair, with CMIP as the agent and CMIS as the collector.

Although products are certainly available that adhere to these standards, one of the more interesting (and frustrating) details is that different vendors may implement these products for different transports. For example, IBM originally offered FTAM over X.25 while Digital offered it over Ethernet—in this case both vendors offered an FTAM solution, but provided no clear means of connecting the two together.

Other standards of importance that have come (or are coming) from the OSI Reference Model but have not yet been incorporated into any vendor products include:

- The Virtual Terminal Services (VTS) specification for terminal access
- The Distributed Transaction Processing (DTP) standard for transaction handling
- The Remote Database Access (RDA) standard for distributed database access
- The Job Transfer and Manipulation (JTP) specification for network jobs
- The Office Document Architecture (ODA) standard for compound documents (text, data, graphics, voice, and video); this standard is also an important part of the OSI Electronic Document Interchange (EDI) strategy

The overall scope of the OSI Reference Model is necessarily huge. Because of its size, standards take a long time to be developed and agreed upon. Although this may lead to the perception that the acceptance of OSI standards is slowing down, the simple fact is that the availability of the standards themselves is quite slow.

TCP/IP Protocols and Services

The TCP/IP were by-products of the U.S. Department of Defense's (DoD) ARPANET project in the early 1970s. The purpose of ARPANET was to allow consulting agencies and related government activities to share and exchange information concerning various DoD projects. Accomplishing this task required the creation of a set of protocols and services to span the wide variety of computer systems used by the government and all of the interrelated agencies (Figure 4.3).

The TCP/IP provide the basic delivery mechanisms for traffic within and between networks. The TCP is responsible for the end-to-end delivery of messages while the IP handles the routing of messages in a network. A third protocol, the User Datagram Protocol (UDP), normally accompanies TCP/IP to

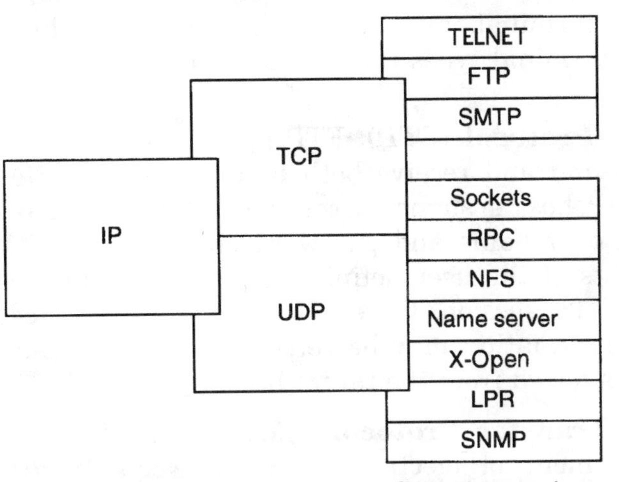

Figure 4.3 TCP/IP strategy.

provide a means of implementing program-to-program communications. UDP is similar to TCP except that it provides a faster delivery mechanism because it does not include the error checking and message recovery features of TCP; message delivery and recovery is the responsibility of the programs using the UDP transport.

In an interoperability environment, the underlying operation of TCP/IP contributes virtually nothing. Instead, it is the ancillary protocols and services layered on top of the TCP/IP protocols that contribute significant value to the connectivity cause. Specifically, the "big three" application-oriented protocols commonly associated with TCP/IP are:

1. **TELNET.** The TELNET protocol facilitates interactive terminal access to TCP/IP host systems. Although TELNET was originally designed as a simple, character-oriented interface for TTY-style devices, the protocol provides a means of "negotiating" custom options for more sophisticated terminal control. Negotiation occurs at connection time and allows the host to define the minimum operating requirements for the session. More importantly, this mechanism allows terminal emulation to be layered on top of the TEL-

NET protocol. Thus, a TELNET session may emulate a Digital VT100 terminal, an IBM 3270 terminal, or hundreds of other terminal types through the use of negotiated options.

2. **File Transfer Protocol (FTP).** FTP is an interactive facility used to send and receive both binary and text files between TCP/IP host systems. Accessing a target host requires a valid user name and password on the host, with the access rights of the user defining the read/write capabilities of the FTP session. Once a session is established, file directory information may be retrieved, and files may be sent to or retrieved from the target host.

3. **Simple Mail Transfer Protocol (SMTP).** SMTP facilitates the movement of electronic mail between TCP/IP hosts. SMTP is an underlying service that provides mail delivery services in the network, but does not communicate directly with the end user. End-user services (creating mail, reading mail) are handled by any of a large number of software programs that operate between the user and SMTP (such as MAIL, MAIL-X, or MUSH). Like X.400, SMTP is frequently implemented as a gateway protocol to interconnect dissimilar electronic mail or office automation products.

TCP/IP has been around a long time and it has picked up its fair share of add-ons and enhancements. But the most significant enhancements to TCP/IP have come out of its relationship with the UNIX operating system; TCP/IP has been the de facto network protocol for UNIX systems for many years. Items that are of special interest to the field of interoperability include:

- **Sockets.** Programs in the UNIX environment use a mechanism called *sockets* to perform program-to-program communications. A socket is an interface to the underlying TCP/IP services. Each socket has a series of services (program calls) available to initiate links, send and/or receive information, and terminate links. Most socket implementations allow the program to use either TCP or UDP as the underlying transport.

- **Remote Procedure Calls (RPC).** Like sockets, RPC is a program-level service for program-to-program communications in TCP/IP networks. The RPC interface is a higher-level service than sockets and isolates the program from most of the gritty details of the underlying transport services. In the world of UNIX systems, two popular RPC approaches exist. The best known and most licensed methodology was developed by Apollo (before its acquisition by Hewlett-Packard) as part of its Network Computing System (NCS) line of products; the second RPC approach was developed by Sun Microsystems as part of its Open Network Computing (ONC) family of licensed products.
- **Network File Services (NFS).** Sun Microsystems developed a methodology for sharing file volumes and directories among several systems. Sun's approach, NFS, is layered on top of TCP/IP and allows a host system to "mount" file sets of other hosts. Because Sun licenses NFS at no charge, hundreds of companies have included support for the NFS-style of file access in their products.
- **Name servers.** A name server is a designated system that contains the definitions for users and systems in the TCP/IP network. Multiple name servers may be employed in one network. Among other things, name servers allow traffic to be addressed to systems by their name or alias. The name server translates the name into an Internet address, which is then translated into the actual hardware address by the Address Resolution Protocol (ARP).
- **X-Open.** The X-Open family of protocols and services is frequently implemented in conjunction with TCP/IP (although it technically may be implemented in virtually any type of network). The X-Open family provides graphics-oriented services to support client/server environments. The most recognized member of the X-Open family is the X-Windows standard for multitasking, graphics-oriented application services.
- **Line Print Remote (LPR).** LPR was developed by a TCP/IP steering committee to facilitate printer sharing among systems. Under LPR, print output, and control infor-

mation associated with that output, may be passed from one system to another until it reaches the system responsible for the destination printer.

- **Simple Network Management Protocol (SNMP).** SNMP was developed by a TCP/IP steering committee to enhance network management in a TCP/IP environment. Under SNMP, network agents collect data on network usage and failures, and then report these findings to a main management program. SNMP has become so popular that is now used in a variety of non-TCP/IP networks, including HP, Digital, and IBM networks.

The OSF Distributed Computing Environment

Finding a common methodology for program-to-program communications across many (but not all) platforms has been a focal point for IBM, Digital Equipment, and Hewlett-Packard, jointly operating under the veil of the Open Systems Foundation (OSF). The OSF solution lies within their definition of the Distributed Computer Environment (DCE); the foundation for the DCE program-to-program communication methodology is based on the HP/Apollo's NCS technology (Figure 4.4).

The OSF is a consortium of computer manufacturers and related vendors committed to developing products—that is, products, not standards—that facilitate distributed, multivendor computing environments. Some of the key members of the OSF include IBM, DEC, and the founding member, Hewlett-Packard.

Hewlett-Packard described the focus and purpose of the OSF in a document entitled "OSF and the Open Systems Market: An HP Perspective," published in May 1989:

> On May 17, 1988, eight internationally prominent computer companies joined together to form an independent foundation to develop and provide an industry standard software platform. These founding companies were motivated to form this alliance by the rate of technical innovation and the demand for worldwide cooperative computing within the software industry. They recognized that only through open process cooperation, not single vendor solutions, could open software come of age. The Open Software Foundation emerged from the contributions of resources by the original eight sponsors.

OSF was not formed to develop another set of standards. Rather, OSF is acting as an integrator of technology by starting with the base of Berkeley 4.2 and System V.2 operating systems and building an industry standard operating environment through an open process. The open, cooperative process for evolving standard systems will unite the software industry and provide the best available technologies for all users. By building and supplying a complete operating environment rather than just specifying components, OSF complements the open software industry like no other organization.

Two items are particularly noteworthy in this Hewlett-Packard statement:

1. The document clearly states that the purpose of OSF is to develop products. Elsewhere in the same document Hewlett-Packard goes on to state that OSF products may or may not conform with other international or de facto standards. Instead of blindly yielding to standards, OSF is committed to a review process that solicits technology and

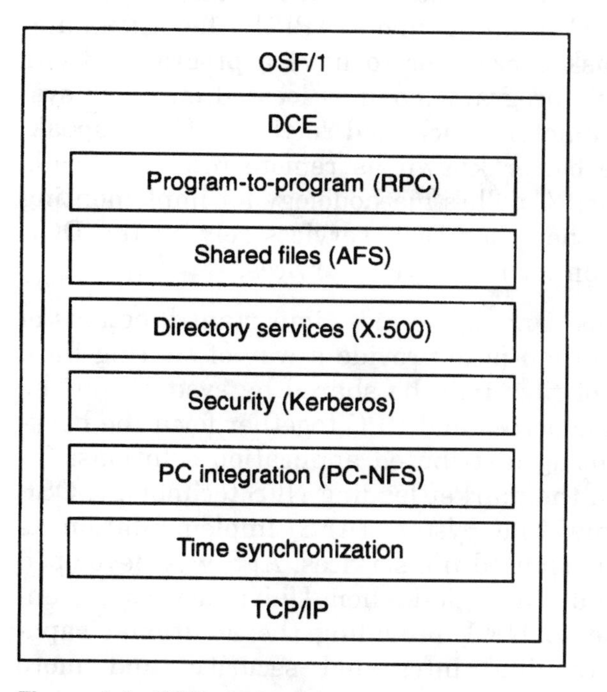

Figure 4.4 DCE strategy.

reviews based on its own merits. If some of this technology turns out to be OSI-compliant, all the better.

2. The document identifies the birthplace of OSF products as the world of UNIX. The references to Berkeley 4.2 and System V.2 indicate that OSF will use these two implementations of UNIX as the starting point for developing its own operating system (OSF/1). Additional technology will be layered on top of the operating system to provide network, distribution, and cooperative services.

In short, the initial focus for OSF was to develop a UNIX-compatible operating system and then surround it with tools to facilitate cooperative processing.

The DCE is the first pass at a set of tools to surround the OSF/1 operating system. The functionality provided by DCE includes:

- **Program-to-program communications.** At the center of DCE is the ability for programs on different systems to communicate with one another, such as IBM's Advanced Program-to-Program Communication (APPC) facilities and Digital's task-to-task service, or to have a program on one system actually call program modules located on other systems, passing parameters back and forth. In UNIX-speak, these services are better known as remote procedure calls (RPC). OSF chose HP/Apollo's methodology for implementing RPC, and most of the other DCE services rely on the DCE RPC implementation for underlying services.
- **Shared file access.** One of the most important functions of any distributed solution is to provide a way of sharing files. Under DCE, sets of files may be shared by systems on the network. Shared file access and RPC together form the backbone for implementing distributed application solutions. Instead of going with the market-leading NFS technology, OSF selected the Andrew File System (AFS) implementation as the basis for its distributed file services. AFS was developed jointly by IBM and Carnegie-Mellon University as an enhanced alternative to NFS, providing the additional capabilities of local caching, integrated security, and more

sophisticated file directory structures. AFS also provides backward compatibility to existing NFS file servers.

- **Directory services.** The OSF directory methodology was proposed by Siemens and works in conjunction with the X.500 standard. In the simplest context, the DCE directory services provide a means of globally identifying users and systems participating in the network.
- **Security.** Because user and application activities will often span multiple systems, sensitive information may frequently be carried on the network. DCE security provides a means for encrypting and securing such information so that it cannot be intercepted and scrutinized by unauthorized eyes. This authorization process also includes user identification validation. The basis for the DCE security implementation is Kerberos, a security service jointly developed by Hewlett-Packard and the Massachusetts Institute of Technology.
- **PC integration.** DCE recognized up front the need to provide PC integration. DCE PC integration services permit participation in the shared file structures and the ability to share printers. To handle this aspect of DCE, OSF chose Sun's PC-NFS implementation as the core technology. Under the PC-NFS approach, PCs can "mount" NFS file sets and treat them like virtual disk drivers. For example, the "/usr/users/sales" directory on a file server could be mounted as drive "S:" on a PC.
- **Time synchronization.** The purpose of time synchronization is to ensure that all participating systems share a common basis for real-time clocking. This is a particularly important service in light of transaction processing and distributed database services where the time of day is a key element to transaction logging and/or database recovery.

In all the previous cases, the OSF chose an existing methodology for providing a particular service. But this does not mean the specific methodology is incorporated into DCE intact. In most cases, OSF modifies the methodology or technology so it is custom fitted to the OSF environment. This means that all of the products chosen by OSF will continue to have a life of their own outside the domain of DCE, and that compatibility between the DCE implementation of a service and an outside implementation of a service is guaranteed. For example, a commercial implementation of AFS may not be 100 percent compatible with the DCE implementation.

While this collection of services may seem rather unique, this is not really the case. Sun Microsystems, the leading manufacturer of engineering workstations and one of the dominant vendors in the general UNIX market, has a similar collection of services that it markets under an umbrella called the Open Network Computing (ONC) architecture. ONC technology is available on a for-sale basis as a set of run-time modules, or it may be licensed for incorporation into other (non-Sun) operating environments. Most of the major computer manufacturers have at least licensed Sun's NFS technology, which is undoubtedly the best-known aspect of ONC.

In point of fact, DCE resembles Sun ONC to such an extent that many analysts have come to wonder if OSF really stood for "ostracize Sun forever." After all, DCE closely parallels ONC, but little Sun technology is part of the DCE architecture. And the fact that OSF membership includes the number 2, 3, and 4 engineering workstation manufacturers (behind Sun) has not helped create a "Sun-friendly" impression. All things considered, the absence of fundamental Sun technology in DCE has set up a confrontation in the open market between the Sun camp (which includes AT&T) and the OSF camp.

Sun's response to the OSF DCE environment was the development of Solaris, an operating system designed to operate on multiple platforms (RISC- and Intel-based, in particular). Sun's ONC services are integrated into Solaris, and so, like the OSF DCE environment, create a distributed, multiple-platform environment.

In terms of the IBM environment, DCE does *not* resemble any of the established architectures in the IBM midrange or mainframe markets (the PC market is arguable both ways). Clearly DCE is not the same as IBM's SNA because SNA is a much broader architecture oriented to the networking aspects of distributed processing. Furthermore, DCE is not equal to IBM's SAA, because SAA is focused on distributed applications. To be sure, IBM has services within the scope of both SNA and SAA that can provide the same functionality as DCE—they are just not packaged in one eclectic set.

In contrast, Digital's DECnet product does offer many of the services and functions provided by DCE. The most important difference between DECnet and DCE is that DECnet is a proprietary architecture designed to operate with Digital systems. Support for DECnet services is integrated into the standard Digital operating systems like VMS. This makes porting DECnet out of the Digital environment very difficult.

DCE is unique in that it is not a closed, proprietary architecture, nor is it a totally open architecture driven by standards organizations. Instead, DCE fits somewhere in the middle, neither fish nor fowl, neither open nor closed. This leads to a number of interesting questions, which follow.

Will DCE race through the market like a raging hurricane, pounding OSI, DECnet, and SNA services into the jagged rocks of yesterday's technology?

The chances of DCE replacing SNA, DECnet, and OSI are pretty slim. IBM and Digital have invested over 10 years of research and development into SNA and DECnet, respectively, and it is difficult to imagine that either company would throw away that kind of investment in favor of an upstart architecture bred from the UNIX environment. Similarly, the commitment to the international set of OSI standards is firmly rooted in the market. For example, the U.S. government has mandated OSI compliance in its GOSIP regulations. The probability that the international community would change its mind at this stage is also pretty unlikely.

More likely is the scenario where DCE services will co-exist with other distribution services, such as those provided by SNA, DECnet, OSI-compliant products, and any other future distributed architectures that come along. This means that systems must begin to make the transition from monolithic, single-network systems to multistate machines capable of conversing with a number of different logical or physical networks using a variety of protocols and services.

Will DCE crash into TCP/IP like the iceberg that struck the *Titanic*?

Probably not. In the initial release of DCE, TCP/IP is used as the underlying transport mechanism for DCE services. The

DCE architecture does, however, make every possible effort to isolate users and application programs from TCP/IP; in effect, TCP/IP can neither be seen nor heard in the DCE scheme of things.

This approach is remarkably analogous to the Sun ONC architecture, which also uses TCP/IP as the underlying network service. The simple truth is TCP/IP has long been the de facto network for UNIX systems and most implementations of UNIX come bundled with TCP/IP. Given this broad base of acceptance, TCP/IP was not only the logical choice, in many ways it is the only choice acceptable to the market. This approach allows the market to use DCE concurrently with a vast array of UNIX utilities and services that rely on TCP/IP.

The relationship between DCE and TCP/IP is not cast in stone. In fact, the DCE architecture is designed to allow other operating systems and network services to participate in a DCE network. Therefore, DCE may be implemented in a number of non-UNIX environments (such as IBM and Digital environments), with or without TCP/IP. But for now, DCE and TCP/IP are friends and not foes (at least in the UNIX environment).

Will DCE become the modern de facto standard for multivendor computing?

This answer is entirely up to the market. DCE is not a standard, it is a product. If enough people buy DCE, it will become a standard the same way that TCP/IP became a de facto standard—people bought it, used it, and demanded it everywhere. On the other hand, if only a small segment of the market buys into DCE technology, then it will not become a significant player.

The bottom line is that although IBM, Digital, Hewlett-Packard, and a horde of others endorse DCE, they cannot guarantee its success in the open market; that is up to the marketplace.

Conclusion

Unquestionably, the key element of an interoperability strategy for a multivendor OLTP environment is the intersystem communication interface. In most cases this choice then drives the interoperability strategy. For example, if IBM's APPC interface is selected as the interface of choice, then it follows that the interoperability strategy will be gateway oriented.

Selecting the intersystem interface in the first place is, of course, no simple task. The selection process must take into consideration a number of technical issues, including:

- Operating systems in use
- Native program-to-program communication interfaces
- Existing application programs and programming languages
- Data structures and storage formats
- Logging and recovery requirements
- Response time requirements
- Physical attachment options
- Availability of gateways or standards-based products

Influencing all of these considerations are the needs of the OLTP applications. If, for example, the primary purpose of the OLTP environment is to implement a distributed database, then those strategies that provide benefits such as guaranteed message delivery and/or message logging have a significant advantage over other solutions. Alternatively, if the purpose of the OLTP environment is to perform statistical analysis of real-time process control data generated from a variety of control units, then speed and data structures have more weight.

In the end, it is the functionality of the application that makes or breaks a multivendor OLTP implementation. If the processing threads are not properly selected or not well routed, the resulting application tapestry will be rough and ragged. But if proper analysis is performed, and the best-possible threads are employed, the resulting tapestry will not only be a thing of beauty, it will also be an extraordinary business asset.

About the Author

John Enck is a data communications and networking specialist with over 12 years of hands-on experience. Presently a network analyst with Forest Computer Incorporated, Mr. Enck has also worked for Burroughs Corporation, Electronic Data System Corporation, the Illinois Law Enforcement Commission, and the U.S. Department of Defense. He is the author of A Manager's Guide to Multivendor Networks, published by Cardinal Business Media; of "Signals," a monthly column appearing in *NEWS 3X/400*; and of articles featured in *DEC Professional*, *HP Professional*, *NEWS 3X/400*, *MIDRANGE Systems*, *UniReview*, and *Network World*.

Acknowledgments

Portions of this chapter have been adapted from:

"Cross-Training Your Systems," *NEWS 3X/400*, December 1991. Copyright 1991 by Duke Communications International. Used with permission.

"Signals: A DCE Primer," *NEWS 3X/400, April 1992. Copyright 1992 by Duke Communications International. used with permission.*

Chapter

5

OLTP and System Reliability

Jeffrey Gui
Sequoia Systems, Inc.

Introduction

System fault tolerance and improved system reliability have become increasingly important considerations for IS managers evaluating the benefits of on-line transaction processing (OLTP) systems. There is today a growing awareness of the advantages of improving the availability of the systems and the integrity of the data that a company relies on to do its processing.

There are many reasons for this increased interest in fault-tolerant, high-availability, and high-reliability systems. The main reason is that IS managers responsible for OLTP systems have measured the costs of system downtime and concluded that it is cheaper to pay for an increased reliability system than it is to pay for the costs of additional downtime experienced with a traditional system.

By definition, an OLTP system is only doing useful work when it is on-line. Any system failure that takes an OLTP system off-line will leave the users of that system unable to work. The costs of downtime vary depending on the OLTP application, but range from customer dissatisfaction to lost revenue, lost productivity, and corrupted data.

A survey of MIS executives[1] across a representative sample of large, U.S.–based companies with on-line computer systems concluded that their OLTP systems had a mean failure rate of 8.9 times a year, a mean downtime of 4 hours per failure, and a cost of $329,321 per outage for those sites reporting a revenue loss.

Another reason for the increased interest in higher-reliability systems is that the success of OLTP systems has led to their being given an increasingly important role in the operation of their businesses. As businesses have become more reliant on their OLTP systems, the costs of downtime have increased. IS managers expect this trend of increased reliance on OLTP systems to continue.

Finally, the introduction and widespread adoption of RAID (redundant array of inexpensive disks) in recent years has introduced a much wider audience to the concept of paying more to obtain higher system reliability. IS managers who are familiar with RAID will reasonably ask what steps they can take to further increase the reliability of their systems. There are many system architectures available that offer incremental steps toward to improved system reliability, culminating finally in a robust, fault-tolerant system.

The purpose of this chapter is to discuss the incremental steps toward higher reliability that are available in today's marketplace. The costs and benefits of each of these steps will be discussed to help clarify the decision of how much increased reliability should be included when selecting an OLTP system today.

System Reliability

A "fault-tolerant" module is by definition one that is tolerant of faults; i.e., one that will keep functioning even if any hardware component within the module fails. The term module is used here to refer to a portion of a larger computer system. Modules would include power supplies, disk drives and other input/output (I/O) devices, main memory images, buses, CPUs (central processing units), etc.

The basic building blocks needed to build a fault-tolerant or high-reliability module are redundancy, monitoring, verification, and isolation.

Redundancy is needed to provide two or more copies of the module, so that if one fails there is a usable backup. This backup can be either a "cold" or "hot" standby, meaning it is doing no useful work until called upon to take over, or it can be an active module, able to perform its own work plus take over for the failed unit when necessary.

Monitoring, verification, and redundancy are all needed to detect when a fault has occurred. For example, running two or more CPUs with the same inputs and outputs and the same clock is referred to as running the redundant CPUs in lockstep. The lockstep CPUs should always be doing exactly the same thing at the same time, which is checked by monitoring and comparing all the inputs and outputs to the CPUs. If one of the CPUs has a fault, it will show in the verification circuitry as a miscompare between the CPUs. All the CPUs running in lockstep are together doing the work of a single CPU and by doing so are able to detect any fault in any of the CPUs.

Detecting faults by verification requires either this sort of lockstep comparison within a module or redundant information added to data and protocol handshakes. This latter type of redundant information is used to check that all intermodule transfers proceed as expected, and that the redundant data, such as parity, error-correction code (ECC), or cyclic redundancy check (CRC), is valid after the transfer, proving that the transfer or the storage medium did not corrupt the data.

After the verification circuitry detects a fault, the monitoring circuitry is responsible for taking corrective action and for reporting the fault to the system and/or user. The monitoring circuitry will disable the faulty hardware, switching to use solely the functioning backup hardware. The failure will be reported, so that the faulty hardware can be replaced, returning the module to a redundant, fault tolerant state.

Isolation is needed so that the redundant modules are completely separate and unable to affect each other, and so that the faulty module can be identified and replaced. If redundant components were not fully isolated, then the failure of one component could cause its partners to fail, affecting the system as a whole.

Whenever a module is insufficiently duplicated, monitored, verified, or isolated, then there are single hardware components in that module that can fail and crash the whole system, referred to as single points of failure.

Definitions

High-Reliability Systems A highly reliable system can be built by using hardware components that are less likely to fail: i.e., that have a larger mean time between failure (MTBF). However, in a large computer system, the number of hardware components is large enough that the probability of failure of one of these many components is still high. In addition, certain hardware, such as disk drives, are inherently more likely to fail due to the inclusion of mechanical rather than electrical components.

To improve reliability further requires using fault-tolerant modules, implemented using redundancy, monitoring, verification, and isolation. High-reliability systems usually refer to systems that have been engineered to include at least some fault-tolerant modules.

A common example of high reliability is an implementation of disk storage using RAID disks. RAID disk arrays are designed to provide redundant data, which can be used in case of a media failure in one of the drives. If two disks keep the same data and if one fails, then the other can supply the data, requiring a pause only to allow the hardware or software to detect that the first drive has failed and to switch to the backup drive.

A high-reliability system is protected from some hardware failures (e.g., disk drive failures) but the system is not protected from all hardware failures: a CPU, memory, or even a disk controller failure can cause the system to crash. In other words, in a highly reliable system with a RAID disk array, the disk module has been made highly reliable, but there are still many single points of failure in the system.

Although disks are the most common modules to be made highly reliable, various high-reliability vendors have selected other modules that they have made highly reliable through monitoring, redundancy, verification, and isolation (see the section on hardware reliability for a more thorough discussion).

High-Availability Systems High-availability systems introduce a redundant, "hot-standby" system, which is able to take over in case of the failure of the primary system. In many respects, a high-availability system is a high-reliability system, where the system itself is the module that is being duplicated. This is discussed in more detail in the section on hot-standby systems.

The main difference between high-availability and fault-tolerant systems is in the level of fault monitoring they provide. There is no self-checking within the modules in a high-availability system, i.e., the modules are not run in lockstep. The only faults that are detected are hard faults that cause the primary system to become completely inactive. Faults that allow the primary system to continue running, but running incorrectly, are single points of failure that will not be detected or recovered from.

A typical high-availability implementation will provide two systems, primary and standby, that are complete except for sharing I/O devices, such as RAID disk arrays. These systems include some external monitoring and verification hardware to control whether the primary or backup system is active. This architecture can be rapidly constructed, reducing complexity and time to market.

Fault-Tolerant Systems A fault-tolerant system is one that provides sufficient redundancy, monitoring, verification, and isolation so that a single point hardware failure anywhere in the system will be detected and prevented from propagating to the rest of the system. A single-point hardware failure that occurs in a robust, fault-tolerant system is always recoverable, and the system will not crash.

Every hardware module in a robust, fault-tolerant system has been engineered to be fault tolerant, and all inter-module data paths have been duplicated and made fault tolerant as well. Uptime and MTBF are maximized in a robust, fault-tolerant system, since all single points of failure are detected and recovered from.

In addition to higher uptime and greater MTBF, a widely overlooked advantage of robust fault tolerance is lack of data corruption. In nonfault-tolerant systems, whether standard or with high-reliability subsystems, there are hardware faults that can crash the system. However, there are other hardware faults that can corrupt data, and this corruption can go undetected.

For example, consider a value stored in a CPU's data or address register. If a single bit in this register is changed due to a transient hardware failure, then this value can be propagated through the system, undetected by any hardware or software.

In fault-tolerant systems that can detect any single point of failure, data corruption due to hardware failure is not possible, since this fault would be detected and recovered from. This protection from any single point of failure both protects the database from corruption (a $1.00 transaction does not become $1,000,000) and also prevents corruption that can lead to an apparent software crash (e.g., dereferencing a corrupted address pointer). With a robust, fault-tolerant system, hardware and software faults can be distinguished, so that a user is not faced with hardware crashes that seem to be caused by an unknown software bug.

A related advantage to robust, fault-tolerant systems is that hardware faults are isolated to the component that failed. Because of this, any faulty module can be removed as soon as it fails the first time and will not be left to reoccur, potentially causing repeated crashes or corruption until the source of the fault is isolated.

Terminology Inconsistency The difference between fault-tolerant and high-reliability / high-availability systems is one of fault coverage. High-reliability and high-availability systems are tolerant to some hardware faults, namely those faults that occur in fault-tolerant modules that have been adequately protected via redundancy, monitoring, verification, and isolation. Faults in nonprotected modules, or faults that are not detected, will cause high-reliability and high-availability systems to crash or corrupt data. In contrast, fault-tolerant systems are engineered to be tolerant to all hardware faults.

A high-reliability system, for example, one with RAID disks, is sometimes loosely referred to as being fault tolerant, but incorrectly so. It would be correct to say that a system with RAID provides a fault-tolerant disk module, but the system as a whole is clearly not fault tolerant. This inconsistent terminology is unfortunate, because it makes it difficult to evaluate the actual degree of reliability offered by different vendors. Because the term *fault tolerant* is sometimes used when *high reliability* is really meant, I will use the term *robust, fault-tolerant* to refer to a system that is protected from any single point hardware failure.

High reliability should be seen as a spectrum and not an absolute. The more high-reliability modules in a computer system, the greater that system's MTBF and the less downtime it will experience, on average. In contrast, robust, fault tolerance is an absolute: There is sufficient redundancy engineered into the system so that the system will detect, correct, and continue running after any single point hardware failure.

Importance of Increased Reliability

The effects of OLTP system faults can be far-reaching, extending from the system database all the way out to a company's customers.

When an OLTP system crashes, a company's customers can become dissatisfied with the service the company is offering, potentially causing lost business. Internal employees relying on the affected system, and the IS department maintaining the system, can lose productivity, require overtime work, and can also become dissatisfied. The company using the OLTP system can lose revenue, lose customers, and sometimes even be liable for penalties or fines. The system database can lose transactions or otherwise become corrupted, requiring complex manual steps to restore database integrity—if the corruption is even detected in the first place.

Some of these effects have a measurable monetary impact on the company using the OLTP system. It is easy to compute the cost of penalties or fines or the cost of employee lost productivity or overtime. When downtime causes lost revenue, it is also sometimes possible to measure the monetary cost of this effect, too. An IS department can use its own history of crash frequency and duration to compute the costs of downtime and access its needs for greater system reliability.

After computing the easily measured costs of system downtime, the other more intangible effects should be considered, such as the effects of downtime on lost customers, customer dissatisfaction, and data corruption. Although harder to measure, these effects can be just as important in assessing the need for increased reliability.

If increased reliability were free, the choice would be easy, there is no question that increased reliability is beneficial for every OLTP application. But increased reliability is not free, and, in general, the higher the degree of reliability a system provides, the more redundant hardware it uses and the higher the hardware component cost. The other consideration, then, becomes not just how much fault tolerance / high availability any given application requires, but how much this level of protection will cost.

Costs of Increased Reliability

As defined above, fault tolerance, high reliability, and high availability are all provided by redundant hardware. This redundancy increases the amount and complexity of hardware needed to do a given job, and this will clearly increase the cost of these systems. The fact that increased reliability always requires increased redundancy is important, because it implies that there will always be some additional cost to increased reliability.

When comparing systems from different vendors, it should be remembered that the more protected modules in a system, the higher the redundancy and the higher the hardware component cost. At the low end of component cost will be high-reliability systems that protect a single module, such as high-reliability systems that provide RAID disks. At the high end of component cost will be fault-tolerant systems that protect a system from all single points of hardware failure.

When comparing systems from the different robust, fault-tolerant vendors, it is important to keep in mind that each vendor has chosen a different architecture to achieve redundancy, verification, and isolation, and these approaches imply different component costs. For example, robust, fault-tolerant vendors use either two, three, or four CPUs, running in lockstep, to achieve a single virtual-CPU module. Each robust, fault-tolerant architecture provides the same degree of protection, although at a different component cost.

A robust, fault-tolerant architecture that uses two-way lockstep CPUs can have approximately the same hardware component cost as a high-availability or network fault-tolerant architecture. All of these architectures require approximately twice the hardware of a traditional nonhigh–reliability system.

Of course, system cost is not always directly proportional to component costs, due to differences in overhead and markup. Therefore, the important distinctions when choosing between increased reliability vendors are the same distinctions that are important for comparing any system: software application, open systems support, and price/performance, and expandability, with the added consideration of the degree of increased reliability achieved.

Increased Reliability Implementations

Some of the modules that have been made highly reliable by different vendors will be examined in this section. System software is a very important component of a reliable system, which is often overlooked in discussions of fault tolerance and high reliability.

Software Reliability*

Faulty software is responsible for a substantial portion of OLTP system failures. Some studies estimate that approximately 25 percent of OLTP system failures can be attributed to operating system (OS), layered product, or applications soft-

* Software fault tolerance is sometimes used to refer to an approach where whole computer systems are duplicated across a high-speed network. I have referred to this approach as *network fault tolerance*, described in a following section.

ware.[1,2] All OLTP systems, whether built using standard or enhanced reliability hardware, benefit from enhancing the reliability of their system software.

The most critical effort required to increase software reliability is often referred to as *code hardening*. Code hardening consists of removing existing software faults and possibly redesigning and recoding to decrease the possibility of other unobserved but latent software faults. Hardening should also include insertion of numerous kernel validity checks, so that faulty code can be quickly identified during the testing cycle.

Hardening code requires careful software design and coding, as well as extensive testing and debugging. The testing and debugging cycle is of critical importance, especially testing seldom-used error paths to increase code coverage.

To harden code in an open systems environment requires a commitment to improving the quality of the source code, rather than simply allowing bugs to persist because they are present in the "standard" code. Of course, care must be taken while hardening code that the changes to be made do not break compatibility with the open system standard code being modified.

Because of the difficulty of modifying standard code without breaking its compatibility, it is sometimes preferable to reimplement code, so that higher code quality standards can be imposed from the design stage forward. The open systems interface can then be provided from the kernel out, through libraries and standard utilities.

There are additional techniques that can be used to improve software reliability. These techniques include panic avoidance through process restart, panic recovery by software state modifications, and hardware write protection of selected kernel text and data. A system that periodically saves consistent memory image checkpoints[3] can attempt process restart or termination when a panic occurs, backing a process up to a previous consistent checkpoint, in an attempt to avoid timing-related or process-related software faults. Another approach to handling software panics is to actively recover from panics by making state modifications at the time of the panic. Hardware write protection can prevent errant pointers or errant kernel streams from corrupting critical code or data.

Any evaluation of the reliability of an OLTP system should include an analysis of the system software, checking whether the system software is running unmodified code, or if steps have been taken to improve code reliability, by using techniques such as those cited above.

Hardware Reliability

Systems can be classified by analyzing which hardware modules in the system are fault tolerant (i.e., duplicated , monitored, verified, and isolated) and which are not. Table 5.1 lists some of the more common fault-tolerant modules and systems that are available and shows which faults these types of systems are protected from.

An attempt was made to organize this section by presenting modules in order of increasing reliability; i.e., the most likely to fail be listed first. This ordering is not absolute, however, since implementations from different vendors inherently vary in their reliability. Nevertheless, this order can be used as a

Table 5.1 Fault Protection Coverage

System Type	Power Fault	Disk Fault	Disk Controller & I/O Bus	RAM Memory Fault	Arbitrary Memory Fault	CPU Failure	Arbitrary Single Point Failure	Data Corruption
Standard Reliability								
UPS/BBU	X							
RAID 1–5		X						
Duplex RAID 1 [Mirror]		X	X					
ECC Memory				X				
Shadowed Memory				X	X			
Hot-Standby CPU						X		
Robust Fault Tolerance	X	X	X	X	X	X	X	X

guide for choosing which modules should be made highly reliable for a given OLTP system. The reliability of a system is no greater than the reliability of its least reliable module, so when increasing a system's reliability, the least reliable modules should be protected first. For example, when buying a system with a hot-standby CPU you should also specify an uninterruptible power supply with battery backup, since a power system has a much lower MTBF and is more likely to fail than the CPU.

Power System An uninterruptible power supply (UPS) with battery backup (BBU) is a cost-effective, first step towards increasing OLTP system reliability. A UPS conditions the power supplied to the computer, preventing power spikes that can damage components and cause a system crash.

In addition, a UPS with BBU can keep a system running through a short-term power loss. Most power failures are short term, lasting less than the several minutes needed to discharge most BBUs. A UPS with BBU automatically switches to the battery when power fails and switches back after power is restored, so that the system remains functioning without any downtime or data loss. Longer term power failures can be protected against by using a motor-generator UPS, which adds a generator to the power system to keep a system functioning indefinitely from its own power source.

A UPS can be integrated into a computer system, with the system monitoring the power status. If power loss is long term, then the system can shut itself down gracefully, eliminating the risk of losing critical data. When power is restored, processing can continue from where it left off, without data loss.

To further improve power system reliability requires redundant power supply modules. This additional reliability can be worthwhile because of the higher failure rate of power system components compared to digital components (due to the high-current analog circuitry). A fault-tolerant power system can be achieved either by providing a separate and isolated power supply for each system module or by duplicating and load sharing across two power modules, and providing isolation, detection, and auto-switching between the two in the event of failure.

RAID and Mirror Disks Disks have traditionally been the least reliable computer system hardware module. Although disk reliability is steadily improving, a recent study[1] still attributes approximately one half of all on-line system hardware failures to disk subsystems. Because this is statistically where the most hardware crashes occur, improving the reliability of disks is therefore a necessary step to improving system reliability.

A paper was published in 1987 that described several architectures for implementing high-performance, fault-tolerant disk modules.[4] These are collectively referred to in the article as *RAID*, an acronym for redundant array of inexpensive disks. The RAID disks are connected in different configurations, named RAID 0 to RAID 5, which correspond to different levels of price and performance. These numerical designations are not ordered; i.e., RAID 5 is not necessarily better than RAID 1, or vice versa.

The RAID configurations RAID 1 through RAID 5 provide a fault-tolerant disk module, which can tolerate the failure of a single drive in the disk array without data loss. The more popular of the RAID configurations, RAID 1, Duplex-RAID 1, RAID 3, and RAID 5, are shown in Figure 5.1.

The simplest of these implementations, RAID 1 and Duplex-RAID 1, have been in use by fault-tolerant vendors for many years and are equivalently known as mirror disks. RAID 1 connects two equal-sized disks as partners, each of which is an exact copy (mirror) of the other. All data is simultaneously copied to both drives in the pair, which appear to the system to be a single disk drive.

If the RAID controller or other monitor detects that one of the disks is either not responding or returning error status, that drive is disabled, and the other drive becomes the sole active member. Most RAID implementations allow the disabled drive to be replaced without halting the system; this is called *hot swapping*.

Because both drives are active in parallel, there is no performance disadvantage to RAID 1 and Duplex-RAID 1, each of which can perform as well as a standard non-RAID implementation. In fact, these RAID implementations may perform better, because the disk chosen for disk reads can be selected from the mirror pair to minimize head seeking. Furthermore,

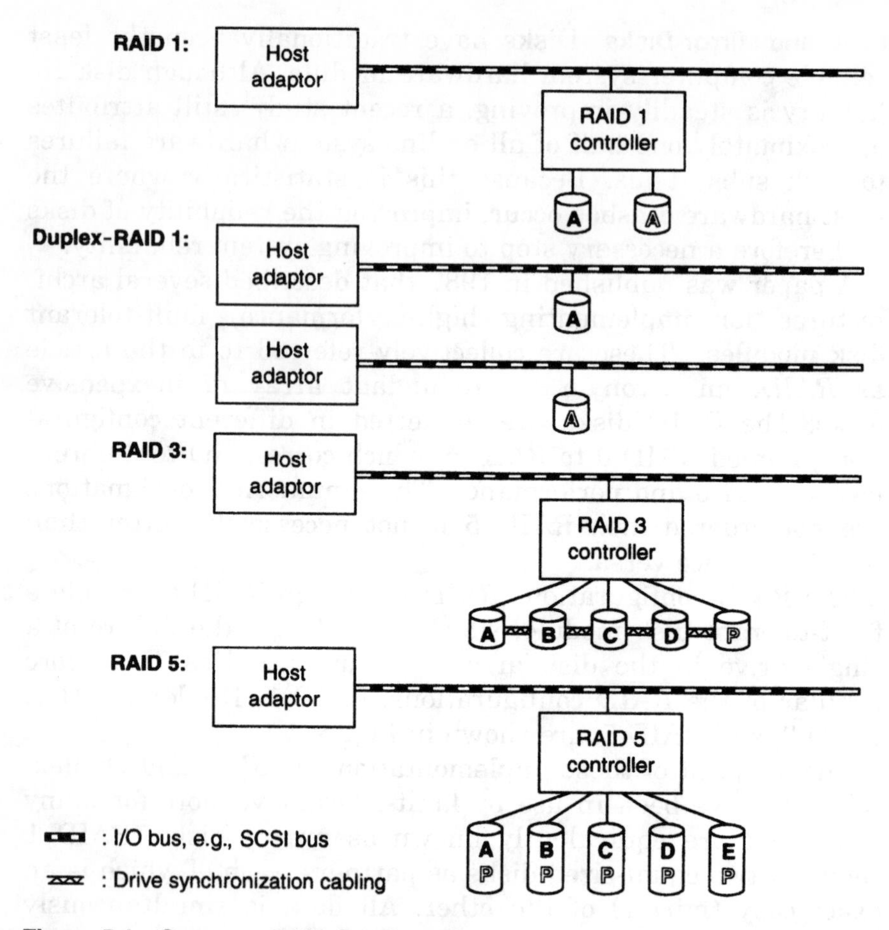

Figure 5.1 Common RAID Configurations

sector striping (RAID 0) can be combined with RAID 1 and Duplex-RAID 1 to further increase performance; this is occasionally referred to as RAID 10.

There is no performance degradation in a RAID 1 or Duplex-RAID 1 system if a drive fails. There is, however, a potential performance loss when the failed drive is first replaced, since the new drive must be re-mirrored with the surviving drive. This can be done while the drives are otherwise idle, however, to minimize the performance impact. Once the mirroring is complete, performance returns to the pre-failure level.

Duplex-RAID 1 is a software implementation of RAID 1 that uses increased isolation to increase the fault-tolerance coverage of the disk module. As can be seen in Figure 5.1, Duplex-RAID 1 requires no RAID controller, instead using software to maintain duplication across the two disks. In RAID 1 through 5, the single host adaptor, I/O bus, RAID controller, and power supply are all single points of failure. Duplex-RAID 1 removes all of these single points of failure, increasing fault coverage.

Although Duplex-RAID 1 is a software implementation, it can perform as well as a RAID 1 hardware implementation. Performance is not affected, since the software needs only to start I/Os on the mirrored host adaptors, which is done in parallel.

RAID levels 2 through 5 seek to provide fault-tolerant disk modules at a lower cost than that of RAID 1, by reducing the redundancy required. RAID level 2 provides the same level of fault protection as RAID 1 by using ECC, but the cost savings from RAID 1 have been insufficient to warrant much vendor interest. RAID levels 3 through 5 provide a similar degree of fault protection as RAID 1, but at different levels of performance and cost.

RAID 3 uses parity to reduce the redundancy required. Instead of copying all the data, as RAID 1 does, a RAID 3 controller breaks every word of every sector into N bits (in Figure 5.1, N is 4). The controller computes parity on those N bits. Each of the N bits—plus the parity bit—for each word are sent to a different drive. If any of the N drives fail, the parity drive is used to reconstruct the data in the failed drive.

RAID 3 is usually implemented with synchronized drives so that all drives in the array are at exactly the same disk location at the same time. They seek and rotate together and in fact appear to the system as a single spindle. The data throughput of this virtual single-spindle drive is very good, potentially much better than RAID 1, depending on the I/O bus speed.

For this reason, RAID 3 is very appealing for systems that are used to transfer very large blocks of sequential data, such as graphics or video data.But for OLTP applications, with many small, random I/Os, RAID 3 does not provide the advantage of multiple spindles, with overlapped seek and rotational latency times, which is important for improving OLTP performance. For OLTP, four sets of two-disk RAID 1 or Duplex-

RAID 1 arrays will dramatically outperform a five-disk RAID 3 array.

Of course, RAID 3 is potentially cheaper than RAID 1, since it requires less duplication than RAID 1, which potentially lowers the cost: For example, the same capacity is provided in the above example with eight RAID 1 disks and five RAID 3 disks. But RAID 3 is usually implemented using drive synchronization, which can raise the per-disk cost, and requires a shared RAID controller, which can be expensive, and it has multiple single points of failure where as Duplex-RAID 1 does not.

RAID 3 is best suited to applications that require massive amounts of sequential data access and that can accept limited fault tolerance. However, this is not a good match with most OLTP applications.

RAID 5 also uses parity to reduce the amount of duplication required, but calculates parity at a sector level instead of a bit level. Any time a sector in a RAID 5 array is written, the data and parity drive must first be read at that sector location, the parity recomputed, and the parity drive written with new data, before the sector itself can finally be written. In RAID 4 the parity drive is always the same drive, making that drive a severe performance bottleneck; in RAID 5 the parity drive rotates between all the drives in the array.

The extra I/Os to the parity drive are required on all writes, which makes RAID 5 write performance significantly slower than that of RAID 1 implementations. RAID 5 reads perform the same as RAID 1 reads, since the parity drive is not used. A five-disk RAID 5 array has the same capacity and the same disk read performance as four two-disk RAID 1 arrays, as long as all drives are functioning, since the parity drive is not used. Unlike RAID 1 or RAID 3, however, the failure of a disk in a RAID 5 array significantly slows down both read and write performance, since the data for the missing drive must be computed from the parity drive.

RAID 5 is sometimes implemented in software, which saves the cost of the RAID 5 controller, but a software implementation does not improve the fault tolerance of the array, and it makes write performance even worse, since the parity is computed at a main CPU, introducing additional overhead to the extra reads and writes that are required.

RAID 5 is best suited to applications that read their database often, but write it infrequently. This is not suitable for most OLTP applications, which need to update their database often. However, for a read-intensive application that does not require the extremely high level of reliability provided by Duplex-RAID 1, a RAID 5 hardware or software implementation could be a cost-effective way of getting RAID disk protection.

ECC-Protected Memory A parity bit encoded with a data word provides detection of any single-bit failure in the data word. Parity is a very cost-effective means of detecting single-bit data failures, costing, for example, only one extra bit per thirty-two bit word. However, parity is limited to single-bit fault detection and cannot be used to correct errors where the failed component is unknown.

ECC memory, by adding more encoding bits, adds the ability to not only detect failures, but also to correct them. ECC works by computing parity on subsets of the data and using the information from overlapping subsets to locate the position of the error. Because ECC computes codes, duplication of every data bit is not required; the amount of extra hardware required to store the ECC bits is much less than double. For example, a seven-bit ECC code for each thirty-two-bit word is sufficient to correct any single-bit error in the data word and to detect any double-bit errors. Using more ECC bits allows correction of greater than one-bit errors.

At seven bits per thirty-two, ECC memory requires less than 25 percent more RAM than standard memory. This is well worth the cost for any but the least crash-sensitive OLTP application.

ECC protects against some data failures in memory; it is usually used to protect against single-bit RAM failures. However, ECC does not protect against arbitrary multibit RAM failures, nor does it protect against failures in the hardware circuitry surrounding the RAM chips. Protection against these failures requires *shadowed memory*.

Shadowed Memory Memory reliability can be improved over that supplied by ECC memory codes by protecting all of the memory circuitry via shadowed memory. Shadowed memory provides complete duplication, similar to mirror (RAID 1) disks. Any detected failure in the memory circuitry, including non-RAM failure and multibit, uncorrectable ECC RAM failures, are recoverable with shadow memory.

As with mirror disks, all writes to memory must be made to both the primary and shadow memory. If the primary memory fails, or if it gets an uncorrectable ECC error, the primary memory is marked as failed and the shadow memory reconfigured as the primary.

Shadow memory requires complete duplication of the memory hardware, and so it is more expensive than ECC memory, doubling the cost of the memory system. Shadow memory is usually only provided by robust, fault-tolerant systems, although it could be supported by other high-reliability systems.

Parity-Protected CPU Some recent microprocessors have been designed to include various degrees of fault-detection circuitry, usually parity checking. Examples include parity checking of on-chip caches, micro-code ROM, and address and data buses.

As discussed above, parity is useful for detecting some faults, but parity alone cannot correct detected faults. A non-fault-tolerant, nonhigh-availability system with a parity-protected CPU that fails a parity check will typically crash, so this protection is not sufficient to prevent downtime. The main advantage of using a parity-protected CPU, therefore, is that it is less likely to silently corrupt data, although data corruption is still possible.

Because a parity-protected CPU costs approximately the same as an unprotected CPU to manufacture, it is likely that more CPUs will be designed with this checking feature in the future. For those systems that do not require robust fault tolerance, a parity-protected CPU is a valuable tool which can be used to inexpensively detect a small portion of the possible data corruption in a system.

Hot-Standby System A system consisting of two fully functional subsystems, one primary and the other hot standby or backup, is often referred to as a high-availability system. The backup system waits to take over for the primary in the event the primary system suffers a fault that causes it to be unable to continue to operate. Typically, the only hardware that is shared between the primary and backup subsystems are the I/O devices, such as disks, and the switch over circuitry that determines which subsystem has the right to access those I/O drives.

There is sufficient redundancy in the backup subsystem of a high-availability system to replace the primary subsystem when it fails. There is not sufficient monitoring or verification to detect all faults, however. Hot-standby systems do not run CPUs or other system hardware in lockstep and lack intra-subsystem protocol monitors. The only detected failures are ones that cause an outright reset or failure to respond of the primary subsystem. This makes a high-availability systems susceptible to many single points of failure and to all hardware faults that cause undetected data corruption.

The better the fault detection in a high-availability system, the more its reliability increases. Therefore, there is a distinct advantage to using hardware, such as a parity-protected CPU, that is self fault detecting. Using a parity-protected CPU increases the fault coverage of a high-availability system, although there are still many single points of failure and data corruption.

The other main shortcoming of hot-standby systems has been that transactions that have not been committed at the time of the fault are lost and must be repeated. Some vendors have attempted to reduce the time and cost of this occurrence by introducing disk I/O logs to record mid-transaction I/Os so that incomplete transactions can be completed. This approach is not always effective, however, and adds a performance penalty, due to the need to flush these logs to disk.

A high-availability implementation requires less redundancy than most robust, fault-tolerant implementations and so can have a lower hardware component cost. The hardware component cost of a fully-configured high-availability system is approximately twice that of a nonhigh–reliability system if the backup subsystem is to deliver the same performance as the primary system in the event of a recoverable system fault.

Hot-standby high-availability systems increase uptime and MTBF beyond that of high-reliability systems. And, because the two subsystems that are used to construct a high-availability system are essentially standard systems with all fault-detection hardware external to the subsystems, high-availability systems can be designed and built comparatively easily. High-availability systems have therefore been successful at capturing a large share of the market that wants increased reliability, but does not require the ultra-high reliability of robust, fault-tolerant systems.

Robust Fault Tolerance Robust fault tolerance includes protection of all of the modules discussed in the previous sections, plus it adds either lockstep operation or protocol protection for all remaining hardware in the system.

For example, all CPUs, whether main system CPUs or I/O processor CPUs, are duplicated and run in lockstep, as described in the section on system reliability. This duplication provides detection of any fault in a CPU or surrounding circuitry, even a transient fault that corrupts data but does not crash the system. With lockstep operation, what would have been an undetected transient fault becomes a miscompare between the hardware circuitry running in lockstep, which is detected and recovered from, as are all other hardware faults. Because lockstep operation is done at standard CPU clock rates, there is no performance loss from running hardware circuitry in lockstep.

Lockstep operation is not limited to CPUs, but is performed on all other hardware circuitry that is not otherwise protected. This includes all of the fault-detection circuitry, which must be duplicated and verified to prevent a failure from letting a fault go undetected.

Parity and ECC are used to protect circuitry whenever possible, since it requires less duplication and therefore lower hardware cost than lockstep operation. Shadow memory protects against multibit RAM failure or other memory hardware failures. Disks are protected with Duplex-RAID 1 (mirroring), with the disks duplexed on different I/O processors so that there is no single point of failure.

Some hardware is more efficiently checked with protocol monitors. For example, system buses are protected with parity to detect any single-bit failure and with protocol monitors to verify that transactions across the bus complete successfully and that the data transferred is valid.

The combination of all of the above produces a robust, fault-tolerant system, which detects and recovers from any single-point hardware failure. Different fault-tolerant vendors have chosen different architectures to achieve robust fault tolerance.

The main difference between fault-tolerant architectures is the amount of redundancy provided, e.g., whether two, three, or four-way lockstep redundancy is used. This difference can have important effects on system pricing (proportional to the amount of redundant hardware used), recovery times (the time required to re-configure and continue operating after a fault is detected), expandability (minimum and maximum system CPU, memory, I/O processor, and device configurations supported), and performance.

One architecture that provides robust fault tolerance is shown in Figure 5.2. This architecture uses two-way lockstep redundancy with all spare modules active unless faulty. For example, both buses are active, doubling bus throughput, and

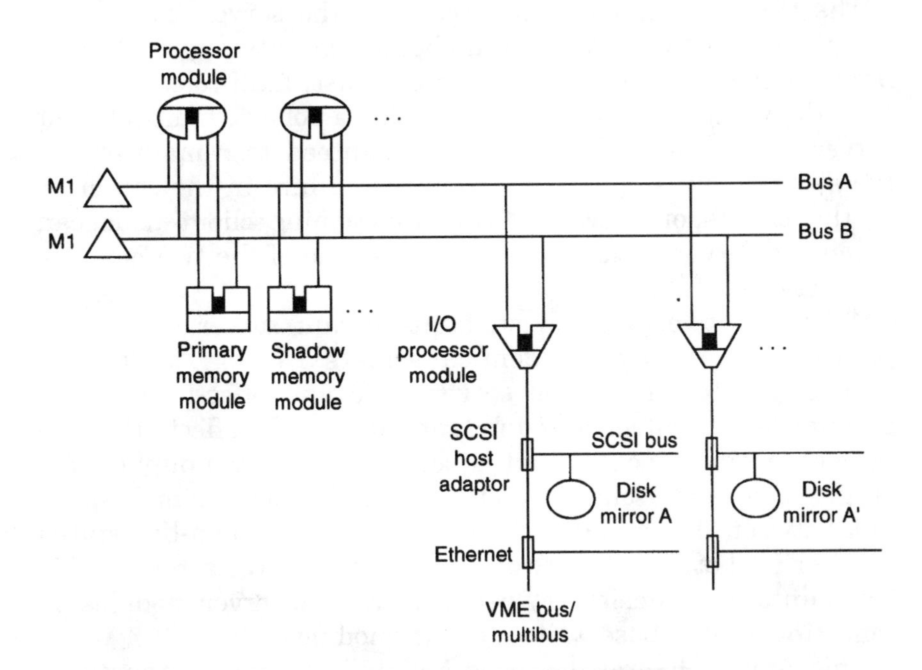

Figure 5.2 Example of a robust fault-tolerant hardware architecture.

all CPUs are active with no hot standby. The hardware component cost of this architecture is approximately twice that of a nonhigh–reliability system.

Network Fault Tolerance In a client/server network, the fault tolerance requirements are different than those of a standalone system. The client, and processes running on the client, are considered expendable; it is the server database that must be protected from downtime and corruption.

Protecting a client/server network requires: (1) two-phase commit, in case the client fails in mid-transaction to prevent corruption of the server database; (2) redundancy in the network, with each client/server connected to more than one network, so that if a network goes down, the server is reachable over another path; and (3) protection of the server database, either with a single high-reliability server or by using a network fault-tolerant architecture with two identical servers.

The first two requirements are necessary regardless of the architecture chosen for the server.

The third requirement, protection of the server, can be accomplished in two ways. The highest-reliability approach is to implement the server with a single robust, fault-tolerant server with two network connections. With a robust, fault-tolerant server, the server's database is guaranteed to remain operational after any single-point hardware failure in the server or in the clients or networks. Any functioning client node can reach the server database over at least one of the two network connections.

An alternative to a robust, fault-tolerant server is network fault tolerance using two identical servers. Network fault tolerance duplicates the whole server node and effectively treats each node as half of a redundant module. In effect, the two servers form the module that is being protected via duplication, verification, and isolation. Software and a special high-speed link between the servers enforces duplication and on-line status monitoring between the two modules. Software is responsible for maintaining consistency between the two server modules by reflecting all database writes to both modules.

This approach provides good reliability when compared to most high-reliability and high-availability systems, but it does not provide the same level of protection as a single robust, fault-tolerant server node.

The redundancy is complete in a network fault-tolerant system, because the whole server node, including disks, buses, memory, and CPU is duplicated. Fault monitoring, isolation, and verification are not complete, however. There are single points of failure in the high-speed link hardware that can crash both servers, an example of insufficient isolation. More important, the data that is part of each transaction is not being verified for correctness, leaving the possibility that undetected data corruption can occur.

Because the only verification that is done is for one module to check that the other module is alive, only hard faults that cause a server to crash will be detected and recovered from; transient faults that leave a server running will not be detected.

Aside from incomplete fault tolerance, there is another disadvantage to network fault tolerance: There is a performance penalty from the I/O duplication that is done over the high-speed link. There is, however, also a notable benefit to network fault tolerance: The servers are physically separated, aiding in disaster recovery.

The cost of a network fault-tolerant architecture is easy to compute: twice the cost of a fully configured single server, plus the cost of the high-speed link adaptors and cabling, plus the cost of software to maintain the mirroring. The hardware component cost is slightly more than twice the cost of an unprotected server or approximately the same as a high-availability or two-way lockstep redundant fault-tolerant architecture.

Depending on the server chosen, this can deliver attractive price/performance, so in cases where robust fault tolerance is not required, network fault tolerance is an effective way to increase reliability across a client/server network.

Conclusion

An IS department considering the purchase of an OLTP system should evaluate its needs first from the standpoint of application requirements, such as open systems platform, database systems, network requirements, etc. System price-performance and expandability are also important considerations at this stage.

Another important consideration is the criticality of system uptime. This can be evaluated by attempting to quantify the internal and external costs of system faults and downtime. If it is found that the OLTP availability is critical enough to justify additional expenditure, then systems from different vendors meeting that level of availability should be considered.

Unfortunately, evaluating the degree of high reliability that systems from different vendors provide is often not easy. Vendors have failed to come up with a rating system to compare their systems for either the percentage of hardware protected from single point hardware failures or the historical results of their tendency to crash. This is unfortunate, because a useful quantitative value, similar to performance benchmarks, would help enormously in comparing systems.

The only available alternative is to examine a system's software and hardware architecture, looking for all modules that have been properly protected with redundancy, monitoring, verification, and isolation. Un-hardened software and unprotected hardware are susceptible to system faults and can cause system crashes or data corruption.

Disk fault tolerance via RAID or mirrored disks, power system fault tolerance via UPS/BBS, and memory system fault tolerance via ECC, are now widely available and substantially improve MTBF. Most attempts to improve OLTP system reliability should include at least these fault-tolerant modules.

Increasing system availability beyond this level costs more money. However, especially for OLTP systems, crashes can cost much more money. Recognition of the enormous costs of system downtime is leading many IS departments with critical OLTP applications to move to ever more high-reliability and robust, fault-tolerant systems.

About the Author

Jeffrey Gui is Senior Consulting Engineer at Sequoia Systems, Inc. in Marlborough, MA. He holds a Master's degree in Computer Science from Harvard University.

References

1. "The Impact of Online Computer Systems Downtime on American Businesses," FIND/SVP Strategic Research Division for Stratus Computer, 1992.
2. "Fault Tolerant Computers for the AIN Environment," Gartner Group for Tandem Computer, 1992.
3. "Sequoia: A Fault-Tolerant Tightly Coupled Multiprocessor for Transaction Processing," *Computer*, February 1988.
4. "A Case for Redundant Arrays of Inexpensive Disks (RAID)," University of California, Berkeley, Report No. UCB/CSD/87/391, December 1987.

Part 3

OLTP and UNIX

Chapter

6

A Professional's Guide to UNIX

Alan Paller
Computer Associates

For two decades UNIX was easy to ignore. Used primarily in scientific and engineering applications, or for university research, it offered little that was of interest to International Standards (IS) managers. It is becoming tougher to ignore.

As the open systems movement gained momentum during the past few years, UNIX has been portrayed as the solution to open systems challenges of software portability, vendor independence, and interoperability. A large marketplace has developed for commercial applications of UNIX in government, retail, insurance, and many other industries. In fact, the commercial UNIX market (which excludes engineering, scientific, publishing, and CASE workstations) exceeded $2.5 billion in 1991 and is growing at least 20 percent per year.

This chapter offers a candid assessment of the strengths and weaknesses of UNIX, the problems commercial UNIX users face, and the prospects for resolving those problems. It answers the questions most commonly asked by IS directors who are evaluating UNIX and shatters some of the myths that make UNIX appear either better or worse than it actually is.

The Value of Moving to UNIX

The rise in popularity of UNIX is driven by two forces. First, UNIX offers a powerful price-performance advantage for certain applications, solving a trio of problems that software developers (and their clients) need to solve:

- It allows extremely large programs to run without extensive time-consuming overlaying (switching portions of software back and forth between disk and memory because memory is constrained).
- It provides multiuser access to a single machine.
- It provides access to new higher-powered, lower-cost RISC-based computers. Because RISC computer manufacturers are engaged in intense competition, they are increasing performance and reducing prices on a continuous basis.

Many commercial applications demand large programs, fast, low-cost machines, and multiuser access on low-cost computers. Retail store operations, manufacturing automation, and branch automation are only three examples in which UNIX will impact millions of users during the 1990s.

Multiuser access allows clerks, machine operators, or tellers to work simultaneoulsy. These applications demand large programs because graphical user interfaces (GUIs) and innate intelligence needed to serve lower-paid workers utilize huge amounts of computer memory. Yet, high-speed computing is required to provide responsive customer service. Also, low prices are mandatory because enterprises are buying numerous machines.

All these needs combine to make UNIX the operating system of choice in all three categories (retail, manufacturing, and bank branch automation) because UNIX is the primary operating system used on RISC computers and RISC provides the features these applications require.

UNIX is not always chosen for these and similar applications. When IS executives become involved, proprietary solutions from IBM (AS/400 computers), DEC (VAX), and Hewlett-Packard (HP 3000 computers) are more often selected. They are chosen primarily for security and reliability, the two areas in which proprietary solutions have traditionally held a wide lead over UNIX.

The second force driving the growth of UNIX as a cornerstone of enterprise computing is less tangible and yet equally as powerful. UNIX is perceived by some buyers to be the only *open* operating system.

Government agencies on both sides of the Atlantic have moved aggressively to UNIX in an attempt to free themselves from dependence on proprietary platforms from which they cannot economically escape. Their motto is "Fool me once, shame on you. Fool me twice, shame on me." They do not want to be fooled twice. Right or wrong, they are moving to UNIX as an initial step toward the key open systems goal of software portability.

UNIX for Large-Scale, Mission-Critical Production Applications

The suitability of UNIX for large-scale, mission-critical production applications depends on which UNIX is chosen and what supporting tools are available. Several systems vendors (HP, DEC, NCR, and IBM are leading examples) have stabilized their versions of UNIX and have had several years to ensure their versions respond to the needs of clients using them in commercial applications. However, none of those vendors has satisfied growing user demands for what they consider minimum glasshouse capabilities needed to support high-volume, mission-critical applications. Those capabilities include security control and management, backup, archiving, tape management, problem monitoring and help desk management, automated operations, performance monitoring, accounting and chargeback, print spooling, and report distribution.

All these capabilities can combine to ensure that computer systems are operational, responsive, and accountable. The lack of these tools in the past led to untimely halts in operations, lost or incorrect information, angry users, and forced turnover in IS management positions. Today, no one attempts to run IS without these basic management capabilities. However, UNIX systems have been notoriously weak in precisely these management disciplines.

Companies that have chosen UNIX have generally avoided using it in applications in which mainframes have traditionally been used: mission-critical transaction processing and large database support. Instead, commercial UNIX systems have found their homes in business data processing in small- and medium-sized organizations, as processors for stores and divisions of large organizations, and as LAN servers in all sizes of corporations. In such relatively small-scale operations, a failure would be unpleasant but not catastrophic.

UNIX could not be ready for large-scale, production applications until third-party utility suppliers brought proven systems management solutions to UNIX. In addition, even the smaller commercial buyers of UNIX and those who depend on it for local area networks (LANs) have long felt the need for mature systems management tools (see Figure 6.1).

Impact of Different Versions on Software Portability

The number of versions of UNIX is a significant problem for independent software vendors (ISVs) but should not be an impediment for effective use of UNIX for commercial buyers. ISVs must support many different machines, but buyers need only choose one at a time.

Each hardware vendor offering UNIX provides a version that differs substantially from others. It may be different in input/output routines, in utilities, or even in advanced user functions. An ISV writing software must build, document, and maintain versions of its software for each UNIX on which programs are to run.

However, translating a program from one UNIX to another (porting) is usually quite simple. Weekend ports are not at all uncommon. Users can choose UNIX with confidence that any software they write will be portable. ISVs, on the other hand, must package and document versions for each UNIX variant and must maintain and handle user questions on all versions. They must hire specialists on all versions—it only costs money. Consequently, ISVs are outspoken proponents of a single version of UNIX. Users, for the most part, do not care (except when it affects the cost and support of the software they need).

When commercial applications move to UNIX, systems managers discover that most management problems eradicated on their IBM mainframes have reappeared in UNIX. The list below describes some of the more common frustrations UNIX systems managers face in commercial applications.

Managing Data on Disks and Tapes

- When disk space is exhausted, work stops
- When a job needs a file that has been archived, work stops
- Backup consumes so much time that some operators do not do it
- Remote backup is too slow and clogs the network
- Backup tapes are not protected and may be overwritten, plus key backups may be lost

Security of data

- No way to know when information was accessed
- Password protection and permission scheme are vulnerable
- No controls on file use by time of day and calendar
- Super user can access any resource and change any management controls
- No management systems that allow policy-based security administration
- Managing security in growing networks demands excessive effort and cost

Managing the Workload

- The UNIX "scheduler" (cron) is time-of-day and date-based; it does not know what predecessor jobs may not have run and does not use triggers
- Submitted work is not tracked; therefore, it is difficult to know what is happening.

Managing Printing

- The UNIX spooler (lp) is cryptic with numerous hard-to-remember commands.

Report Distribution

- Entire reports must be printed even if only a small part is needed
- No systematic, manageable on-line report delivery
- No tracking of manual report delivery
- No report retention (archiving) controls

Accounting for Use of the System

- UNIX system accounting information is difficult to manage

Figure 6.1 Thirty deficiencies in standard UNIX systems management.

- UNIX system accounting does not reflect reality of organization structure: too many bills, no integration, and difficult to analyze
- Difficult to find data on resources and users, unless you are a UNIX wizard
- No easy way to do overhead allocations, split charges, discounting, and credits

Managing Problems and Helping Users

- No help desk tools
- No facilities to detect problems when running unattended
- No way to automatically escalate unresolved problems

Console Management

- Because it is difficult to handle messages automatically, many do not get handled at all
- Difficult to trace activity by source
- No way to automate operations remotely; systems administrators are needed everywhere

Performance Monitoring

- Difficult to view CPU utilization, device access times, terminal response times, and other factors affecting user satisfaction

Overall Management

- No common database of systems-management information, no integration among systems-management features, and no GUI to ease the tasks of systems management

Conclusion

As users demanded solutions, the UNIX community responded. In the first quarter of 1992, Hewlett-Packard (HP) of Cupertino, CA began bundling a solution called Unicenter for UNIX with all HP midrange and high-end UNIX servers. In a rare show of UNIX industry unity, Sequent Computer Systems (Beaverton, OR), Pyramid Technology (Mountain View, CA), and Sun Microsystems (Mountain View, CA) have all agreed to join in offering Unicenter to their UNIX server clients. In September 1992, David Tory, president of the Open Sofware Foundation, announced that Unicenter would become Distributed Management Environment (DME) compliant as soon as DME becomes available. As Unicenter matures, UNIX systems managers will have the same level of security, manageability, and reliability that had traditionally been available only on mainframes.

Figure 6.1 ***(Continued)***

It is unlikely there will ever be a single UNIX. Such a development would make UNIX a commodity and undermine the differentiation hardware vendors need to survive. Each vendor will continue to add a few highly visible and useful features to its UNIX offering that make it a little better than another company's UNIX. Those features, commonly called proprietary extensions, make the jobs of software developers easier and attract those developers to the vendor's hardware.

Although UNIX offers easy portability among machines, it is not the kind of transparent portability PC users are accustomed to with MS-DOS machines. Still, it would be enough were it not for the siren song of the proprietary extensions that each vendor offers with its UNIX. Software developers are lured into using the extensions because they save development time or make an application a little easier to use. Once developers use one of those extensions, they are locked into that vendor's version of UNIX. Many of the complaints about porting difficulties have been caused by users lured into using proprietary extensions.

Despite these caveats about portability, for users simply wanting to implement distributed, multiuser computing with large programs on cost-effective RISC machines, any of the stable UNIX versions is adequate. The hardware cost saving that comes from downsizing to RISC machines can be so great many users simply choose a version of UNIX and carry on with the job of distributing computer power. They will worry about portability once the current job is completed.

Security in UNIX

UNIX security has been weak. Thousands of UNIX systems have been installed with feeble password managment and with one or more well-known holes through which smart programmers can enter and cause havoc with Trojan horses and other malicious logic. Most managers have heard at least one horror story about hackers breaking into UNIX computers and doing damage or committing crimes.

Much of the weakness in UNIX security lies in the simplicity of its password system and the availability of "super user" status, which allows all system safeguards to be circumvented. Both of those deficiencies are expected to be corrected during 1992 (see Figure 6.1).

Transaction Processing Power

Only a few companies presently are running on-line transaction processing (OLTP) applications on UNIX, and then only in medium-sized operations. However, the role UNIX plays is growing as the power of the machines on which it runs increases. Already, the HP 9000/800 family of computers provides some of the lowest cost per transaction per second of any OLTP offerings. By 1995, UNIX will be considered a mainstream solution for OLTP, with transaction rates well in excess of 500 transactions per second.

Acceptance of UNIX for OLTP will be significantly enhanced as missing systems utilities become available for UNIX and as security improves.

Distributed Computing

Systems administration costs are a large and growing part of the budget for UNIX operations. Too much of the savings offered from moving to lower-cost RISC-based computers has been squandered in increased administrative staff needed to manage the widely distributed computers.

Costs are not the only problem. System administrators in UNIX have been required to write their own system administration software or, at a minimum, to modify and adapt unsupported systems administration sofware they downloaded for other sites. Expertise, needed to build and modify such software, is in short supply and comes at a high price.

The problems systems administrators face are multiplying. Where once they managed two to five computers, their networks have grown to dozens of machines. Where once all their computers came from a single hardware vendor, they now face a heterogeneous assortment of machines. The hodgepodge of machines was purchased by autonomous offices that once thought they would be independent but now want to share access to common resources and communicate with one another via their computers.

Heterogeneity is reaching a new high in the early 1990s. Companies include moves to integrate their proprietary mainframes and minicomputers into networks that include UNIX systems and even DOS- and Macintosh-based personal computers (PCs).

If old habits are not broken, the position of systems administrator will become one of the fastest growing professions in the world. The costs of administration will eradicate the promised savings of downsizing to smaller, less expensive hardware.

Companies that own IBM mainframes and are acquiring UNIX systems for commercial applications already face the problems of multiplatform distributed systems management. When IS executives focus on the problem, they immediately recognize that this problem could actually offer a solution to another difficult problem. Their mainframe activities are declining, and they need to find jobs for the trained staff who know the disciplines required to maintain high service levels of availability, responsiveness, and security. They would like to find a way to use the existing staff to manage the heterogeneous systems. A name for their quest is "single-point control" or "single-point administration." In the words of one CIO, "We want to have 20 people managing 200 machines instead of needing 200 people to manage them."

Among the vital needs for single-point administration are security, tape management, scheduling, problem management, and help desk and report distribution. Single-point security administration will allow assigning security access once for each user in the organization rather than once for each user for every computer. Combined scheduling keeps jobs that depend on information produced on a remote machine from being started until the remote machine has completed the necessary work. Combined tape management allows moving tapes from machine to machine without fear a wrong tape will be mounted or vital information will be on a scratch tape.

On mainframes, mature systems management tools are already in place. The only hope for single-point administration is to have active links between existing mainframe tools and new management tools created for systems administration of distributed computers. The commercial UNIX industry, led by HP, has recognized that such integrated systems management will be a critical factor in the acceptance of UNIX to provide viable solutions.

Conclusion

UNIX is here to stay. Already, 20 percent of new IS spending is for UNIX-based systems. It is the fastest-growing component of the computer systems market. Its acceptance will grow only as shrink-wrapped software comes to UNIX, as well-crafted user interfaces replace cryptic commands of the UNIX of the past, and as senior management begins to trust UNIX computers through the advent of integrated systems management software that protects UNIX computers and keeps them running smoothly and efficiently.

About the Author

Alan Paller is the UNIX product champion at Computer Associates International, Inc., focusing on UNIX and open systems, Executive IS (EIS), and downsizing. He is the author of *The EIS Book: Information Systems for Top Managers*, several articles, and is a frequent lecturer on EIS and open systems.

Chapter

7

OSF/DCE-Based Distributed Transaction Processing

An Implementation Approach

Scott Dietzen
Transarc Corporation

Introduction to OLTP

On-line transaction processing (OLTP), or simple transaction processing (TP), is the foundation of commercial data processing throughout the world. TP systems, or monitors, offer the computing enterprises a secure, reliable means for recording sales, orders, transfers, reservations, or any other updates to data that is shared—potentially among several thousands of users. TP monitors must preserve those updates, even in the face of system or application failures. For example, the record of a credit card sale should not be lost when a machine crashes. TP systems also ensure the consistency of data, even when it is geographically distributed. This is achieved by protecting multistep operations from partial failures, so that no funds will be lost in a funds transfer, even if the associated debit initially succeeds but the corresponding credit fails. Finally, TP monitors protect business applications and data from conflicts that may result when they are broadly shared.

OLTP is now entering its fourth decade and has a rich history in systems like IBM's Customer Information Control System (CICS) and IMS database management system (IMS). These and other TP monitors evolved as system designers recognized common requirements in the on-line systems they were building:

- The assurance of reliable, real-time access to large databases
- The preservation of data integrity in the face of concurrent updates and system failures
- The scalability to admit large numbers of simultaneous users without sacrificing performance
- The security of limiting data access to authorized users only through prespecified channels (i.e., only through audited applications)

By meeting these requirements, OLTP systems guarantee access to and the integrity of mission-critical data that is used to run an enterprise—account balances, inventories, customer records, portfolio contents, flight bookings, and so on. Through these guarantees, TP monitors simplify the programming, operation, and maintenance of mission-critical applications.

Today, the majority of OLTP applications and systems run on mainframes that serve large data processing centers; two traditional examples are airline reservations and international banking. However, TP monitors are increasingly used for many other computing needs, for example, retail point of sale, manufacturing control, telecommunications, government, health care, insurance, legal services, and image processing. In fact, Gartner Group has predicted that by 1995 more than half of the new applications using relational database management systems (RDBMSs) will employ a TP monitor. While RDBMSs supply basic transactional properties, TP monitors are better positioned for interoperability between databases, interoperability with other TP monitors, choice of a range of integrated screen managers, highly optimized performance, ironclad security, and the scalability to deliver application services to widely separated users.

Introduction to Encina

Presumably, an enterprise seeks to make its applications portable and interoperable across a wide range of platforms. The solution is to adopt a standard distributed computing infrastructure that may be layered upon a variety of different networking and operating systems, shielding applications and their administration from the underlying complexities of heterogeneity. Figure 7.1 shows such a general architecture for distributed transaction processing.

Transarc's Encina is a comprehensive client/server OLTP solution that fits centrally within this framework. Encina is integrated with both screen managers on the client side, and RDBMSs and other resource managers on the server side. It also offers connectivity to other OLTP monitors such as CICS via Logical Unit 6.2 (LU 6.2)/Systems Network Architecture (SNA). Encina uses and exposes the base-distributed services of the Open Software Foundation's (OSF's) Distributed Computing Environment (DCE). By building upon this DCE foundation, Encina inherits the benefits of this foundation: transparent access to remote services, enterprisewide scalability, automatic protection of services from unauthorized access, privacy for applications distributed over unsecure networks, isolation of damage caused by incorrect or unauthorized applications, POSIX-standard high-performance concurrency technology, and secure global file sharing.

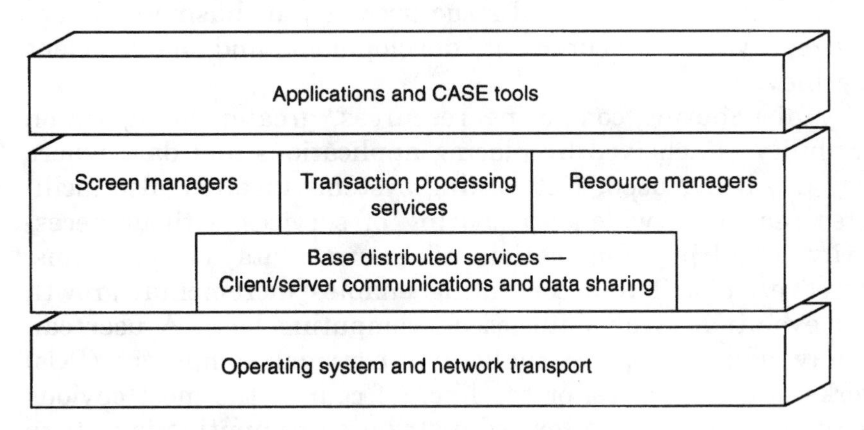

Figure 7.1 Open, distributed TP system architecture.

Encina also has state-of-the-art features, such as full recoverability, high performance, security, comprehensive management services, and an open, modular construction. Encina tracks and complies with relevant industry standards, including those of the American National Standards Institute (ANSI), the Institute of Electrical and Electronics Engineers (IEEE), the International Standards Organization (ISO), OSF, and X/Open Ltd.

Encina will be available on a range of vendors' platforms, including those from IBM, Hewlett-Packard, Hitachi, NEC, Stratus, and Sun.

Evolution in Computing

The migration toward open, distributed transaction processing is the culmination of four technology evolutions in computing.

Distributed Computing

Today, a business is likely becoming less centralized. At the same time, smaller, more affordable networked systems are offering services previously performed solely by large, centralized ones. Through distributed computing systems, autonomy is gained for the federated subsystems that make up an enterprisewide computing base. By matching computing services to the evolving organizational structures of your business, decentralized system procurement, development, and management is achieved.

By distributing computing resources, greater configuration flexibility is acheived by placing applications and data where they are being used. Networking systems together also facilitates real-time, wide-area sharing of services without necessarily requiring duplication of secure data or programs. Moreover, distributed computing enables incremental growth and evolution of an enterprise's computing base: A user can simply add or replace individual personal computers (PCs) workstations, servers, or the like. Of course, the most obvious motivation to migrate toward distributed computing is to take advantage of the improved price/performance of microcomputers. However, distributed systems also can provide greater reliability and availability, which is achieved through redundancy in hardware and software. Finally, end users can be more productive when using the advanced graphical user interfaces (GUIs) associated with inexpensive but powerful desktop computers.

Open Systems

Although distributed computing addresses many business challenges, it also may introduce further complexity into the computing environment. The primary obstacle is linking heterogeneous computing platforms in a manner that applications can communicate with one another, can be run on different machines, and can be effectively administered. Open systems address these issues by enabling the following:

- **Portability.** By emphisizing common application programming interfaces (APIs), open systems permit applications developed on one platform to run on others.
- **Interoperability.** With common communication protocols, open systems permit distributed applicatons to work together by sharing data and/or computing resources.
- **Evolution.** Modularity and published internal interfaces ease adoption of new technologies as well as new standard protocols and interfaces.

The result is that open systems provide the flexibility to meet changing computing requirements with little sacrifice of investment.

Client/Server and Object Orientation

True client/server technologies like DCE permit applications to be separated into presentation logic (implemented in front-end clients) and business logic (implemented in application servers). This allows the developers of application services to focus on defining and implementing abstract business services (or objects) that offer a coherent set of business procedures (or object methods). A banking service, for example, might offer deposit, withdrawal, inquiry, and transfer operations. Business functions could then be published in a corporate manual, to be used and reused by the developers of front-end clients or by the developers of other application services. Under this paradigm, specifics of the data model are hidden behind an abstract interface and, hence, are free to evolve over time (e.g., moving from a relational to an object-oriented model) without necessarily impacting the other components of a system. Well-defined application server interfaces also permit business services and databases to be shared among a diverse set of clients: from a bank teller user interface to an automated teller machine (ATM) to an on-line decision-support application.

This paradigm is truly client/server because, unlike many approaches, it allows the application designer to chose the interface between the client and server. For reasons discussed below, this offers greater program modularity, increased ease of evolution, better performance, and stronger security.

Transaction Processing

Transaction processing technologies have had to undergo much change to meet the needs of open, client/server, distributed computing. Traditionally, a transaction was thought of as the mainframe-based application procedure a terminal invoked to process a particular screen: Busines logic and presentation logic were packaged together as a single *host* transaction. To meet the distributed, client/server model, it is necessary to expand the notion of what a transaction is.

Consider the transaction illustrated in Figure 7.2, which could just as easily be part of client or a server application. In this example, `debit`, `credit`, and `enterAuditData` represent abstract business procedures that have been composed together within a funds transfer "transaction." Each operation might be a local procedure call to services within the same programs or a *remote procedure call* (RPC) to services running on remote nodes. In this way, a single transaction can encom-

```
transaction { . . .
   debit (salaryExpense,amount);
   credit(accountsPayable,amount);
   enterAuditData(employeeIdentifier,amount,date);
   . . . }
```

Figure 7.2 Example transaction in the C programming language.

pass applications and data distributed over local or wide area networks. The above transaction could also have included database commands (e.g., embedded SQL or ISAM), queuing commands, or communications with other TP monitors. The programmer, however, need not worry about managing conversations, packing messages, routing requests, data conversion, or how `debit`, `credit`, and `enterAuditData` are bound together as part of the same distributed unit of work; all this and more is managed by the underlying system.

Also crucial to this more general transaction model is nesting—the ability to define transactions within other transactions. For example, the implementer of an `enterAuditData` service should be free to start another transaction, so that if the auditing database were temporarily unavailable, an alternative action could be taken (i.e., reliably queuing the audit for later entry) rather than aborting the entire funds transfer. In general, nested transactions allow you to simplify the structuring of larger transactions. They are fundamental to modular and object-oriented programming methodologies in which basic services (i.e., base transactions) are combined to form higher-level services (i.e., more complex transactions) without regard to the details of their implementation. With systems that only support flat transactions, transactional functions or objects can only use and be used by nontransactional functions or objects. Otherwise, run-time errors result. Such restrictions are in direct opposition to modular programming practices.

DCE and Encina combine the above technology advances in a comprehensive, commercial OLTP solution, and, among commercial systems, Encina is unique in its support for nested transactions. Another view of Encina, however, is that it permits applications of transaction processing concepts to a broader class of applications; that is, open, distributed TP is relevant to more than the migration of traditional OLTP applications. First, as applications are distributed, there is a general need to ensure that computations on different machines can be synchronized, so that one does not get ahead of another. There is also the need for the components of the applications to achieve consensus, so that mutually dependent operations succeed together. Finally, distributed applications face a greater range of failures—network, software component, system, machine, and media—from which they are expected to recover and continue forward processing. Transactions offer an easy-to-use mechanism for programming robust applications that must face precisely these complexities.

Evolution in Application Architectures

During the 1990s, progress on molular programming techniques, as epitomized in client/server and object-oriented methodologies, will have a substantial impact on MIS operations. Figure 7.3 shows a typical application architecture for a distributed transaction processing environment. Shown on the left are several front-end client applications, which could be running on PCs, workstations, or the concentrators for terminals or other devices. A client's presentation logic could be developed by directly using lower-level GUI toolkits such as Motif, or through higher-level fourth-generation languages (4GLs) or forms managers. Front-end clients also include DCE and Encina libraries for issuing requests to the business or application servers running in the second tier.

The application servers implement business logic by accessing resource managers (i.e., databases), other application

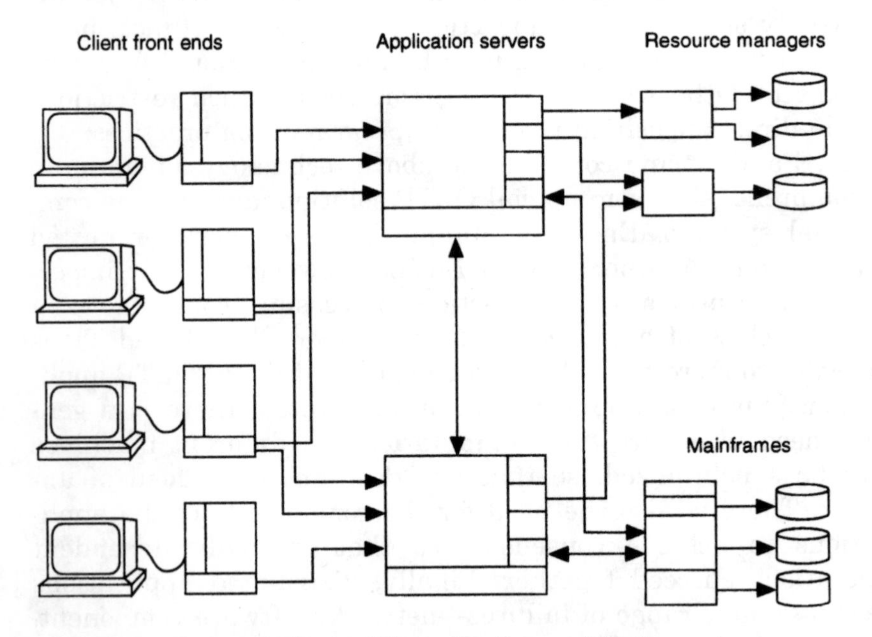

Figure 7.3 Open, distributed TP application architecture.

servers, and/or host services. Client/server programming methodology dictates that the data modeling commitments—to structured query language (SQL), indexed sequential access method (ISAM), text files, or structured objects—be hidden behind an abstract interface. Requests to host-based services are also hidden behind the application server interface. This way, the implementation of such a service could later be seamlessly moved to an open platform. For example, host-based Customer Information Control System (CICS) applications and data could be migrated to Encina (even in an on-line fashion) without affecting the remainder of the distributed application.

The architecture in Figure 7.3 offers substantial advantages over one in which client applications can access databases directly. Although appropriately authorized users should be able to browse and update a database, it is dangerous to give arbitrary clients unrestricted access to corporate data. Instead, one typically seeks to channel general access to mission-critical data through only trusted, audited applications. These *application servers* usually reside on the same machine as the database itself, and are hence more secure than desktop clients. (Server machines are most often under lock and key.) Application servers are further protected by access control lists to restrict business services to only appropriately authorized clients. In this way, malicious or errant clients cannot compromise secure data.

Placing an application server between a front-end client and resource managaer also provides greater performance. Application servers permit business logic to reside on the same machine as the database. The alternative—for example, shipping representations of SQL tables to a client for processing—entails additional network and computing overhead. New application servers can also be added to address your processing needs or upgraded to new versions without affecting the database or front-end clients. As will be discussed in the administration section below, application servers provide the natural focus of control for distributed TP monitors.

Migration Strategies

The majority of the OLTP market today resides on mainframes, primarily IBM hosts. To enable migration to open TP monitors, systems like Encina most provide access to existing OLTP applications and data. Only in this way can an MIS organization gradually evolve its computing base by focusing increasingly more development on open systems.

Encina enables this migration by providing interoperability through an IBM standard distributed processing protocol, LU 6.2. This permits Encina applications to access CICS applications and data without running any new special-purpose software on the host. Indeed, from the perspective of CICS on the host, Encina appears to be just an external CICS region. CICS applications that support distributed processing today can interoperate with Encina without modification; others require small enhancements. This strategy also permits connectivity in the opposite direction: By supporting dispatch from the host to Encina, you may offload processing from an overburdened mainframe onto open systems without affecting the mainframe's terminal network. In addition to CICS on the host, Encina offers this bidirectional interoperability with other TP systems that speak LU 6.2 or for which there exist LU 6.2 gateways (such as IMS or DB2).

Figure 7.4 illustrates this approach. An Encina application anywhere on a DCE network can communicate with the host

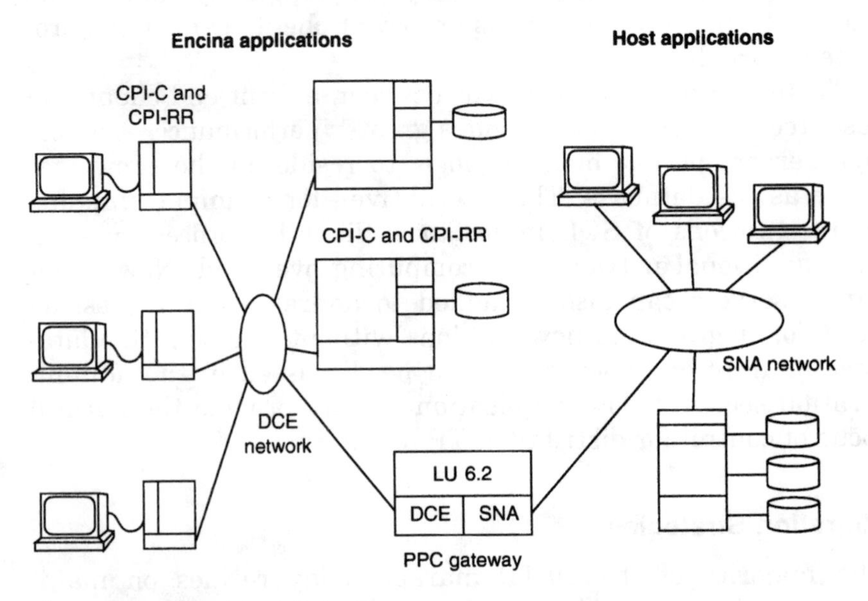

Figure 7.4 Migration strategies.

through the Encina Peer-to-Peer Communications Services (PPC). The API for this communication is the X/Open and Systems Application Architecture (SAA) standard Common Programming Interface for Communications (CPI-C). With Encina, CPI-C applications need not reside on an SNA-networked machine. Instead, any Encina node can carry on a conversation with the host, provided that the DCE network contains at least one SNA gateway machine. The same is true in the opposite direction: A host can dispatch requests to any of the DCE-networked Encina application servers. System administrators can thereby configure applications without worrying about the underlying network topology. By permitting redundant gateway machines, this architecture also removes a potential single point of failure.

Perhaps most importantly, Encina's host connectivity is designed to support LU 6.2 *sync-level two*, whereby consistency between a host and open system can be guaranteed transparently to the applications. Within a single tranaction, Encina can update an RDBMS on a reduced instruction set computer (RISC) server and a CICS resource on the host. Such transactional guarantees, uniquely demonstrated among open systems by Encina and Encina-based CICS/6000, are essential for robust communications. Without them, there is no way to protect the operations between the host and open system from failures. (Encina's sync-level two support is dependent on capabilities within the underlying platform's SNA services. An Encina vendor can provide information on availability for specific platforms.)

While Encina includes an LU 6.2 gateway today, Encina will support other TP protocols so that Encina applications may interoperate with a range of other TP monitors. Predominant is the Open Systems Interconnect (OSI) TP protocol (as defined by ISO), which Transarc has committed to integrating with Encina. Encina is well positioned for this and other such integrations because of its open, modular architecture. The relevant internal interfaces of Encina are published, allowing Encina to more straightforwardly interoperate with arbitrary TP technologies. Standards like OSI-TP and those coming out of X/Open, as well as nonstandard legacy TP systems, may be integrated by layering veneer on top of Encina published interfaces.

For porting host batch programs, Encina provides a COBOL interface to its record-oriented file system, the Structure File Server (SFS). SFS is a transactional file system designed to scale to large numbers of concurrent users and large (multigigabyte) data files without sacrificing performance. The SFS supports full recoverability and provides fast (log-based) restart after failures. Through the use of the SFS, batch applications may seamlessly share data with an on-line system.

Administration

In general, administrative interfaces are at least as important as application programming interfaces, given that the cost of managing the applications over time can outgrow the cost of their development. However, coherent management of *distributed OLTP* applications is even more crucial, because of the need to support high availability (or even continuous operation) and the need to shield the system administrator from the complexity of a network computing environment.

An administrator needs a simple, systemwide view of the operation and configuration of the various application and system components, a single logical operator's console for the entire system. From any node in the network, an authenticated administrator should have access to this console to monitor services, errors, and performance, and to (remotely) take actions to address recognized needs. It is not acceptable for routine operations to require administrators to directly access individual machines. Distributed administration services should use the secure client/server communications of DCE. In this way, traditional interactive (command-line) administration as well as programmatic management interfaces for the construction of GUI administrative utilities or administrative applications are offered (Figure 7.5)

A DCE-based OLTP environment offers the concept of a cell for structuring a distributed system. A cell is simply a collection of systems, applications, and users that have been placed under a common security and administrative authority. Each of the service providers in a cell, from low-level systems services to high-level business applications, registers their current physical location (and perhaps other information) in a secure directory service provided by DCE. This protected name space

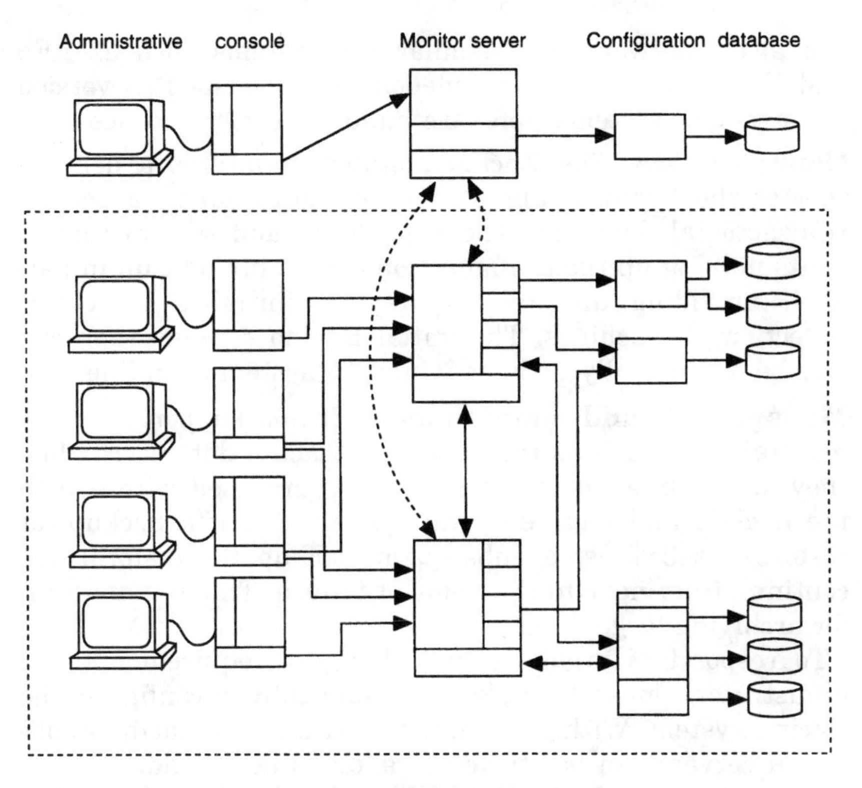

Figure 7.5 Distributed system administration.

may then be queried by authorized applications and administrators to determine the availability and location of services they require. As distributed systems and applications make reference only to these logical names, clients and servers can be freely relocated without modification. System administrators choose the degree to which enterprise services are exposed within cells or exported to other cells.

Encina and DCE provide a range of administrative features for both the applications and underlying system components.

- **Software installation and distribution.** The distribution of systems and applications software is aided by the Distributed File System (DFS) of DCE. DFS permits programs to be transparently executed on any machine in the network, without an administrator having to manually distribute copies of the software to individual machines. DFS manages the transfer and local caching of a program while it is in use. Encina can also interwork with similar file systems such as AFS and NFS, as well as with independent tools such as version management systems, software build, and test facilities.

- **Configuration.** The Encina Monitor maintains a description of the business application configuration in a secure, transactional database. The application and system components making up the configuration can be brought up in parallel, providing an efficient way to initialize an entire collection of machines. The initial Encina configuration can also be dynamically updated while the system is on-line.

- **Management and maintenance.** Encina supports routine maintenance, such as the backup of Encina databases while they are on-line. In fact, transactions are used within both the backup and restore operations, so that if a backup (or restore) itself fails, a subsequent backup (or restore) can continue from near to the point of failure. This is important for archiving large databases.

  To respond to problems and changing requirements, administrators must be able to dynamically reconfigure the Encina system. With Encina, new instances of Encina application servers can be started to address peak loads. Out-of-date or malfunctioning ones can also be gracefully shut down by having them refuse new requests while completing those pending.

- **Monitoring, instrumentation, and diagnostics.** Encina assembles information about the behavior of a system for presentation to the system operator. These facilities enable the administrator to determine when something has gone wrong, to help to isolate the problem, and then often to correct it. For example, an operator should be able to easily enumerate transactions that have blocked (perhaps due to a machine failure) and to invoke a heuristic decision to free up essential data. System- and application-defined diagnostic conditions are prioritized, and collection can be disabled below a configurable threshold. In this way, more detailed information can easily be collected during debugging without affecting production operation.

  Encina also optionally maintains performance profiles of various application services. Encina keeps track of the number and type of the requests that each of the service providers is delivering and each of the clients is consuming, as well as maintaining the amount of computing time devoted to processing those different requests. Transparently to the administrator, Encina also monitors the health of the application servers and other processes under its control and automatically attempts to restart failed instances.

- **Application and system upgrade.** To achieve continuous availability, Encina must permit application software to be upgraded without interrupting service. Encina provides facilities for bringing up new versions of application servers while the old continue to operate. After testing has been completed, the production load can be gradually shifted to the new applications servers. Clients could be upgraded as users reinitialize their environments. DCE also includes support for upgrading client/server interfaces, so what would be incompatible versions of client and server software can co-exist without interfering with one another. In fact, Encina permits you to have separate development and production cells sharing the same machines. This means that a development environment can be brought up, thoroughly tested, and then gradually integrated with production services.

Open, distributed TP monitors must work with a range of resource managers, networks, and operating systems that make up the computing base. Administration of a system is simplified by the availability of uniform tools for managing all of these components. Administrative services and their incorporation within vendors' administrative tools partially address this issue. Flexible administrative interfaces are also needed to facilitate integration with a variety of administrative frameworks. The Distributed Management Environment (DMD) presently being developed by the OSF is one such comprehensive framework. The DME builds upon DCE to offer a standards-based, object-oriented GUI environment for the administration of an entire computing environment: networks, systems, and applications.

Security

For an enterprise to take advantage of global public networks such as the Internet, it must protect the privacy and integrity of its applications and data. Technologies like DCE are designed to facilitate secure distributed processing, even over public networks.

A DCE-based distributed computing environment assures you that only audited applications are available to your clients. DCE provides authentication services to ensure that clients know the identity of the servers with which they are communicating and vice versa. Clients are thereby protected from malicious servers masquerading as standard application or system services. Service providers, in turn, use authentication in conjunction with DCE access control lists (ACLs) to restrict access to only appropriately authorized clients. ACLs contain the users and groups permitted to use the individual business services. ACL protection is generally provided for both administrative as well as processing interfaces. With Encina, an access control list is associated with each of the application servers. These ACLs are maintained in the Encina configuration database and thus are protected from loss or corruption. The authorized system administrator can then dynamically update these ACLs with no change to the application code and with no interruption in service (except for clients subsequently denied access).

The level of security an enterprise requires will differ between services and networks. For secure networks in which all participants are trusted, DCE security may be disabled. For less secure networks, the authentication of distributed participants can be required. DCE provides authentication at varying levels of granularity, from an entire conversation down to the individual network packets. A system administrator can also choose to protect the contents of network communications from malicious or inadvertent tampering. (This is accomplished by including encrypted checksums in the messages.) The highest level of DCE security is to combine authentication and content protection with full data encryption. Client/server conversation is thereby assured protection and privacy even over a public network. The end result is that data and services are protected from inadvertent or malicious access and corruption in a manner that is transparent to the application devlopers.

Encina also provides facilities for environment retrieval, such as for the construction of audit trail records that establish the user and application services responsible for specific operations. Of course, these facilities use the underlying DCE security services to guarantee the record's authenticity.

Performance

In terms of raw MIPS, RISC processsors today offer higher levels of performance than mainframes. Of course, mainframes remain the best single architecture for very large, monolithic databases, because of their input/output capabilities. However, even large databases may be economically migrated to smaller platforms, provided they admit natural partitions. Of course, as discussed in migration strategies, Encina permits you to use the host in conjunction with PCs, workstations, and servers, thereby achieving greater performance at less cost by making more optimal use of the computing base.

Encina employs a modern architecture geared towards high performance in a distributed environment.

- **Process model.** Encina uses a library-based approach that allows transaction definition, coordination, and recovery to be done from any Encina program. This eliminates the need for additional processes to perform these tasks, the extra communication for participants to interact with these processes, and the additional points of failure these processes represent.
- **Scheduling.** TP monitors are frequently used in the benchmarking of database systems because of the scheduling optimizations they provide. Instead of a corresponding server process for each active client, Encina more optimally schedules client requests over a smaller set of service providers. This provides better performance without sacrificing client isolation.
- **Load balancing.** As illustrated in Figure 7.6, Encina supports the replication of application services to remove single points of failure and to permit the load to be spread over multiple business servers, whether on the same machine or on different machines. This load balancing is tunable, so that a greater share of the load may be given to higher bandwidth

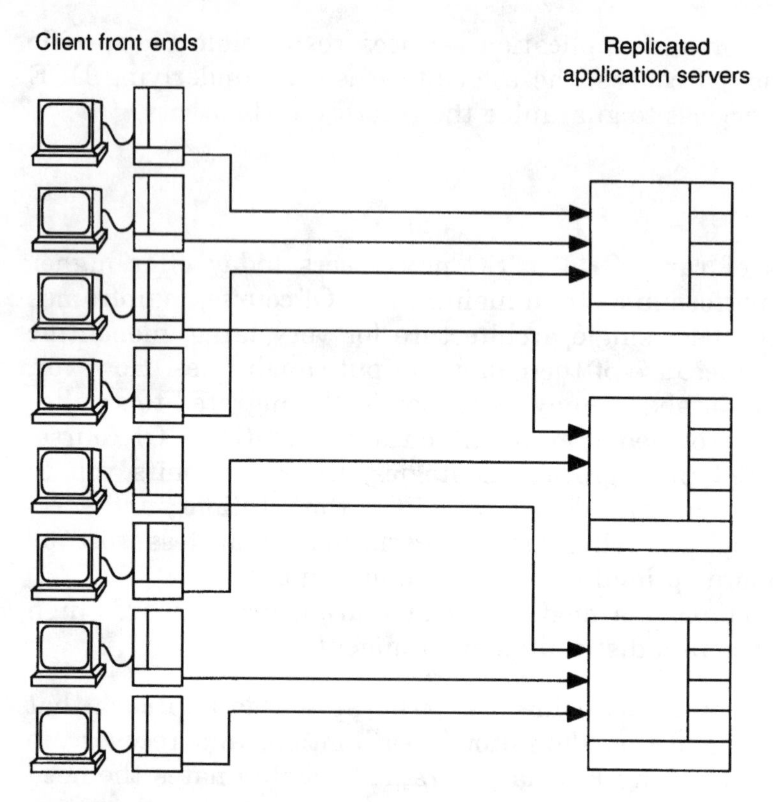

Figure 7.6 Load balancing.

processors. It also will dynamically adjust to changes in the number of application servers available.

- **Concurrency.** Another advantage of client/server computing is its natural parallelism: A client can issue requests to several application servers in parallel, and concurrent servers may respond to many client requests simultaneously. Encina and DCE simplify the management of such concurrency by providing a structured paradigm, POSIX standard threads, and supporting APIs. Threads are superior to implementing concurrency than using separate processes.*

Consider the revised funds transfer transaction illustrated in Figure 7.7; concurrent is an Encina programming con-

* Threads share the same address space in memory so that the physical processor can change its focus much more quickly than with conventional processes. Because they share an address space, different threads can communicate far more efficiently than separate processes.

```
transaction {...
   concurrent {...
      debit(salaryExpense,amount);
      credit(accountsPayable,amount);
      enterAuditData(employeeIdentifier,amount,date);
      ...}
   ...}
onCommit
   printf("Transaction succeeded.");
onAbort
   printf("Transaction failed.");
```

Figure 7.7 Example of Encina concurrent transaction

struct that uses DCE threads to execute its branches in parallel. Concurrency reduces the latency of the above transaction, since each of the remote services will execute simultaneously.*

Threads make high-performance programs easier to write, debug, and maintain. POSIX threads can be and are being implemented on a range of multiprocessor systems. Systems and applications that use POSIX threads, unlike those using other threading models, are designed to be run on these machines without revision.

For the transaction of Figure 7.7, implicit nested transactions ensure the safety of concurrently executing the `debit`, `credit`, and `enterAuditData` operations. These operations could otherwise conflict in the same way two *top-level* transactions can. Application development is thereby simplified because Encina transparently manages intratransaction concurrency in the same manner as intertransaction concurrency.

Reliability and Availability

Another attraction to distributed computing is that applications, systems, and hardware can be configured with redundancy, so that failures do not interrupt service. DCE, for

* This concurrency is achievable even on a uniprocessor. With POSIX threads, first the `debit` branch is run until its message is sent. That thread then blocks and the `credit` thread is executed, and so on. The three threads are joined at the end of the `concurrent` statement. The application programmer need not explicitly synchronize different threads unless they are updating shared data in some fashion.

example, provides for the replication of its primary services, so that the loss of a machine or network connection cannot bring the whole system to a standstill. The Encina architecture is similarly designed to offer such redundancy. Furthermore, transactions provide a simple, well-understood paradigm for managing failover, so that applications can be shielded from failures. Nested transactions are fundamental for achieving this, since they provide a straightforward means to protect a higher-level transaction from failures in underlying system or application services. With nested transactions, a more complicated transaction, such as one that accesses a number of servers as well as a host, can be successfully completed even through some portion of it initially failed. Without nested transactions, the application programmer has no means to limit the scope of failure inside of a transaction.

There are several other ways in which Encina gives reliability beyond its support for fully recoverable data storage, replication of services, and failure isolation and recovery:

- **Protection of administrative data.** Encina uses a secure, transactional database to maintain system configuration and monitoring information. Administrative data is thereby protected from failures as well as unauthorized access and can be updated dynamically to reconfigure or upgrade an on-line system with no interruption in service.
- **Limited consuption of resources.** Along with application configuration, the system administrator provides intervals for transaction time-out, so that service providers cannot be blocked for a prolonged period waiting for a failed client.
- **Limited scope of failure.** Encina applications are isolated within separate processes that only communicate through secure DCE communications. This means that application components are free to migrate between machines without changes to their application and without affecting the remainder of the system. More importantly, this model protects other application and system components from failures: Errant or malicious applications are precluded from compromising system services (for example, damaging configuration and routing information) or from interfering with independent applications. This is accomplished in a way that

preserves high performance, using DCE's and Encina's modern process architecture and their support for the local caching of information (e.g., security, routing tables) other TP systems place in shared memory. Caching combines the performance of shared memory without the accompanying loss of security and failure isolation.

- **Failover via reliable queuing.** As discussed in the queuing section below, Encina offers a robust means for interapplication communication. Suppose an essential server is currently inaccessible to a client. With the Encina queuing technology, that client could enqueue the task for later processing, instead of aborting the pending transaction.

Enterprisewide and Global Scalability

Both DCE and Encina were designed to offer global, enterprisewide computing services. Much of the relevant discussions have been made elsewhere: transaction nesting for failure isolation (transaction processing section); the lack of points of failure in the architecture (reliability and availability section); support for reliable queuing (queuing section); and distributed administrative services (administration section). The important and, as of yet, undiscussed scalability benefits of Encina and DCE include:

- **Global services and information directory.** With DCE and Encina technologies, you can define a single integrated name space for the registration of service providers throughout your enterprise: whether that be text or binary files, system services, or application services. This global directory—supported by DCE standard services including X.5000 standard naming—allows you to transparently share data and services throughout your organization. At the same time, security protects restricted data and services even over public networks (see under security).
- **Cells.** DCE and Encina cells provide the primary structuring paradigm for the administration of sets of users, machines, and services. Cells may be thought of as "islands" of processing, since the majority of service requests are usually intracell. However, the same technologies are used to tran-

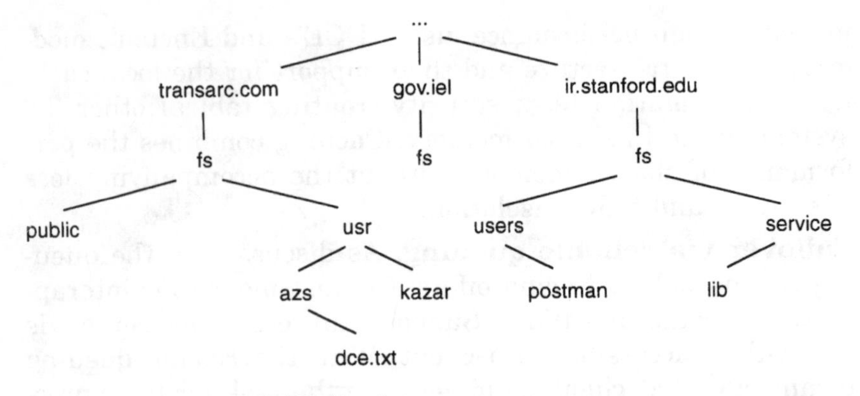

Figure 7.8 Example DFS directory.

sparently access resources outside a current cell. Perhaps the best example of this is the DCE Distributed File System (DFS), through which users and applications may transparently share files located around the world. DFS offers a uniform global directory (illustrated in Figure 7.8) to enable enterprisewide or even worldwide distributed file sharing. Security for DFS is enforced through the authentication, authorization, and encryption features discussed earlier. Advanced caching schemes ensure that performance is not sacrificed, and even that local POSIX sharing semantics are applicable to the distributed file system. The latter means that users on separate continents simultaneously editing a file see the same behavior as if it were all taking place on a single machine.*

- **Internationalization.** Both DCE and Encina were designed to support the representation of multibyte characters and strings; the definition of message catalogs, so that system output can be in the appropriate language and collation sequences, so that data may be sorted in other languages.

---

* The DFS component of DCE evolved from AFS 3 and was developed by Transarc. While central to the Encina/DCE environment, the Distributed File System is not strictly required by Encina and is also not part of the initial DCE product shipments of some vendors. On many platforms, including AIX, Transarc's AFS offers an interim solution and migration path to DFS.

Record-Oriented Data

While the SQL data model of RDBMSs is rich, it is not the best choice for every application. For example, programmers may have artificially contrived table representations for nonrelational portions of data simply so that it can be transactionally stored in an SQL database. RDBMSs typically hide from an application developer more of the detail of how data is organized on disk, but real-time applications or those that require the storage of very large amounts of data may depend upon greater flexibility. A further reason to augment SQL with other data models is that an organization may have existing investments in alternative APIs such as X/Open ISAM and VSAM.

The Encina SFS fills the need to manage alternative record-oriented data with full transactional integrity, recovery, and security. It supports ISAM-compliant and VSAM-style APIs. SFS scales to meet needs by supporting many concurrent users sharing very large files spanning multiple disks. SFS employs the underlying DCE and Encina technologies to offer application developers modern paradigms such as multithread access and nested transactions.

Queuing

Typical business transactions are structured so that each step of the transaction must complete successfully before the entire transaction is finished. For many applications, particularly those with which users directly interact (e.g., funds transfer, data entry, point-of-sale), response timne is crucial. In such cases, it is required that the outcome of transactions be guaranteed without waiting for all steps associated with the transaction to commit.

The Encina Recoverable Queuing Service (RQS) allows complex business functions to be segmented into individual transactions without sacrificing transactional guarantees. Critical data can thereby be enqueued in real time, then dequeued independently for further (a.k.a. "batch") processing. RQS is accessed transactionally—the failure of either the enqueuing or dequeuing transaction would cause any queue modifications to be rolled back. The enqueuing client is thereby assured that subsequent failures cannot result in lost requests. For example, you could use RQS to transfer data over a wide area network (WAN), since an entry is deleted on the originating side only after it has been reliably enqueued on the receiving side. Moreover, RQS serves as a reliable buffer for on-line applications on either side of a WAN by shielding them from latency and failures.

RQS, then, provides an "out-of-band" alternative for robust communications between transactional applications. RQS offers priority ordering of queue contents so that you may best schedule your dequeuing services. It further permits many simultaneous queuers and dequeuers and, like the SFS, scales to hold many gigabytes of data. So that an enterprise can reduce its capacity-processing requirements, queues can be allowed to grow over the course of a business day with the backlog handled during off-peak hours.

RQS further addresses performance needs by permitting the "pipelining" of requests through a series of service providers. For example, an order-processing system might update a number of resources on each request: inventory, customer account, shipping schedule, and billing. With RQS, a single request could easily be routed between these services without requiring any data copying. Following failures anywhere in this process, operations resume where they left off.

DCE Component Listing

The Open Sofware Foundation's DCE provides the facilities for defining distributed client/server applicatons that are interoperable and portable across a range of hardware platforms, operating systems, and network transports. DCE includes a number of components, illustrated in Figure 7.9, leveraged by Encina: remote procedure call (RPC) for client/server communications, multithreading for concurrency, a name service for locating servers in the distributed environment, and security service ensuring the authenticity of distributed participants as well as for protecting resources and communications. Built upon these underlying technologies is the data sharing serv-

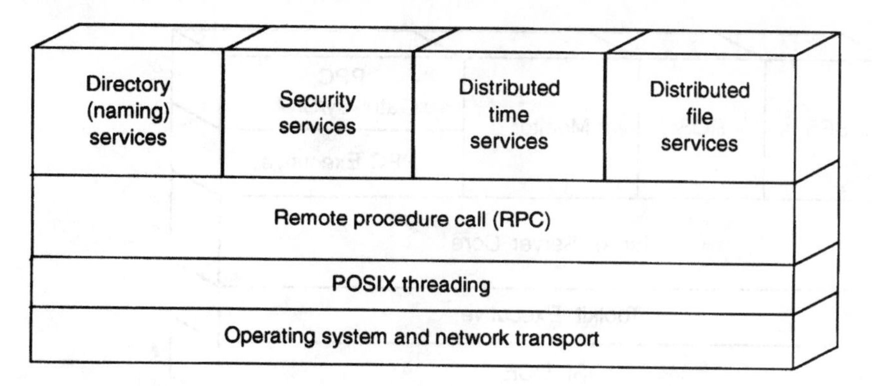

Figure 7.9 DCE components.

ices of DCE, the DFS. The DFS, which is based on Transarc's Andrew File System (AFS), permits the seamless sharing of files (from ASCII to binary) over the network in a manner that ensures ease of access, security, and performance (see enterprisewide and global scalability).

Encina Component Listing

The Encina product suite, illustrated in Figure 7.10, is composed of

- **Toolkit Executive**, which extends the services of DCE with core technologies that enable client/server transaction processing. The Executive runs on each node that is a transactional participant, from a front-end PC to a workstation to a back-end server. The Executive includes the high-level application programming interface (API) of Transactional-C, which provides support for transaction demarcation and concurrency control. The Executive also includes extensions to the DCE remote procedure call communication mechanism, which transparentaly provides transactional integrity to distributed computations.
- **Tookit Server Core**, which extends the services of the Executive to provide for managing recoverable data. On the one hand, the Server Core provides the tools necessary for constructing DCE-based, transactional resource managers. On the other, the Server Core provides the necessary librar-

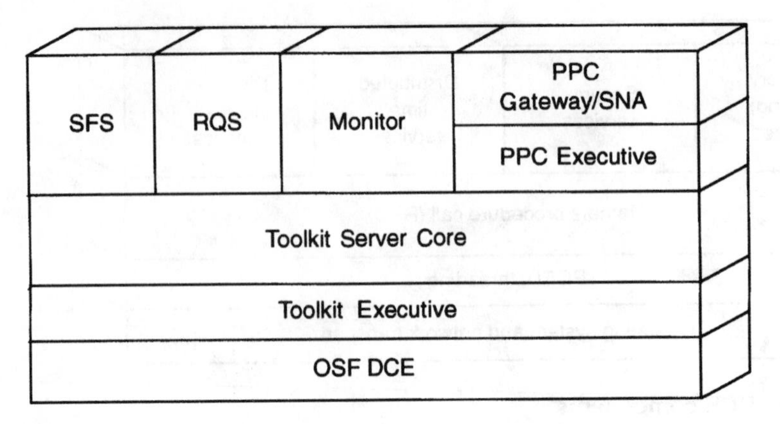

Figure 7.10 Encina components.

ies for transactionally accessing X/Open-compliant resource managers (e.g., supporting RDBMSs) via the XA standard interface.

- **Monitor**, which extends the functionality of the Encina Toolkit and DCE to provide a comprehensive environment for deploying, monitoring, and managing distributed TP applications.
- **Structured file server (SFS)**, which is a record-oriented file system, offering transactional integrity and supporting ISAM-compliant and VSAM-style APIs. To organize record-oriented data, the SFS offers multiple file layouts: entry-sequenced, relative, and B-tree clustering. The SFS also supports multiple secondary indexes, as well as both transactional and nontransactional access. A range of locking strategies is available to enable trade-offs between full transactional serializability and higher degrees of concurrency.
- **Recoverable queuing service (RQS)**, which is a recoverable resource manager like the SFS, but which instead offers a queuing interface. Key features include flexibility in system configuration and usage, high reliability, large capacity, and support for high levels of concurrent access.
- **Peer-to-peer communication (PPC) services**, which support transactional, bidirectional peer-to-peer communica-

tions with host-based and other TP systems. PPC employs LU 6.2/SNA for linking to host and provides an emulation of LU 6.2 over DCE. The PPC is composed of the Executive and SNA Gateway. The Executive permits any application in the DCE network to use PPC to communicate with the SNA Gateway or with another such application. The Gateway provides the translation between the DCE-based peer-to-peer conversation supported by the PPC Executive and the LU 6.2/SNA protocol understood by the host.

Together these components deliver a complete, integrated environment for open, distributed transaction processing.

About the Author

Scott R. Dietzen, Ph.D., joined Transarc at the beginning of 1991 working in the area of technical marketing for the company's Encina transaction processing products. He is currently Principal Technologist, Transarc Sales Group.

Dr. Dietzen received his Ph.D. in computer science from Carnegie Mellon University. His dissertation is concerned with the development of programming languages and environments that support generalization. In addition, he has broad technical interests in programming languages and systems, software engineering, theoretical computer science, and artificial intelligence. Dr. Dietzen also holds a B.S. degree in applied mathematics and an M.S. degree in computer science from Carnegie Mellon University.

Transarc Corporation

Transarc Corporation is a leading developer of systems software products for open, distributed computing environments. With headquarters in Pittsburgh, the company's products focus on key areas of distributed computing, including file systems and transaction processing. Transarc is also the developer of the OSF DCE Distributed File Service (DFS). Transarc's Encina family of products for open on-line transaction processing is licensed openly to many system vendors, including Hewlett-Packard, IBM, Hitachi, NEC, and Stratus.

Acknowledgments

A number of my colleagues at Transarc made contributions to this article. In particular, thanks go to Erik Brown, Satish Dharmaraj, Sandy Esaias, Peter Oleinick, Mark Power, Mark Sherman, and Alfred Spector.

Chapter

8

Improving UNIX for OLTP

Roland N. Luk
Hewlett-Packard Corporation
General Systems Division

Introduction

The success of UNIX in the engineering application environment is well established. Running mission-critical, on-line transaction processing (OLTP) applications on UNIX has become more attractive because of the promise of standards-based solutions and price/ performance benefits. As a result of the tremendous demand and appeal to run business applications on UNIX, system vendors are involved in making UNIX more robust for OLTP by tuning the operating system and integrating key technologies and solutions which have only existed in proprietary systems in the past.

Running OLTP applications successfully on UNIX requires a hard look at how the system vendor can address basic issues such as performance, high availability, data integrity, and security. In addition to these requirements, additional technologies and tools are needed to support application development and system management. Increasingly, there is a need to execute transactions in a client/server distributed computing model.

This chapter examines how Hewlett-Packard is addressing the needs of this growing market, and how the market is rapidly evolving towards new and exciting technologies.

OLTP Market Evolution

The nature of business computing has drastically changed since the days of batch processing, when data requests were collected together, converted into a machine-readable format, and then brought to a central computer for collected processing. Reports resulting from batch processing reflect the most current information up to the last batch job that was performed. On-line transaction processing brings the end user closer to the computing environment, allowing data to be entered via terminals and processed immediately.

Large mainframe proprietary environments were the primary and only means of batch and on-line business computing during the 1960s and 1970s. In the late 1980s, a complement of variables such as acceptance of Reduced Instruction Set Computing (RISC), attractive price/performance of UNIX-based solutions, maturity of UNIX and relational database management system (RDBMS) technologies to meet OLTP challenges, as well as the momentum towards open systems have all contributed to the rapidly growing UNIX OLTP market. During the 1990s, new technologies in the areas of distributed OLTP, client/server, graphical user interface–based tools, and interoperability at the software transaction level will emerge and mature. Figure 8.1 depicts some of the key OLTP industry trends.

UNIX OLTP Market Size

One of the biggest growth opportunities for UNIX applications is in OLTP. Figure 8.2 shows the overall UNIX OLTP market size from 1990 to 1994. The rapid growth rate has influenced a lot of hardware and software vendors to jump on the bandwagon to deliver OLTP solutions on UNIX.

OLTP Requirements

Individual customers have varying OLTP needs, depending on the size and nature of the business operations. Some of the

Early 1980s	Late 1980s	1991	1992 and 1993
• Centralized mainframe TP systems • Terminal-based CICS applications • IBM OLTP dominance	• Increased use of mission-critical OLTP • Increasing number of users and database size • RISC/SQL acceptance • Commercial UNIX acceptance • Distributed databases • High availability fault tolerance • OLTP performance price/performance improvement	• Transaction management for DOLTP TP monitor 2-phase commitment • MP scalability • X/Open Distributed TP Standard XA • CASE solutions for distributed OLTP *Development of distributed OLTP solutions starts*	• Distributed management environment for distributed OLTP • GUI-based DOLTP applications • Distributed OLTP TP applications • Interoperability with heterogeneous TP systems *First distributed OLTP solutions available*

Figure 8.1 OLTP trends.

most important criteria that OLTP vendors are measured against are shown in Figure 8.3. These criteria are discussed below.

1. **Performance and price/performance.** Both hardware (H/W) and RDBMS vendors are increasingly being asked to show OLTP system throughput based on "standard" benchmarks. In addition, the total cost of the system, which includes a 5-year cost of ownership, is being analyzed closely

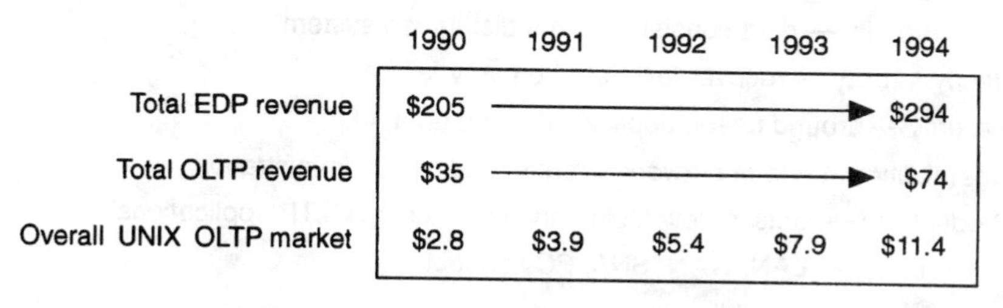

1990
1991
1992
1993
1994
Total EDP revenue
$205
$294
Total OLTP revenue
$35
$74
Overall UNIX OLTP market
$2.8
$3.9
$5.4
$7.9
$11.4
(Figures are in billions)

Figure 8.2 UNIX OLTP market share.

by MIS decision makers. The latest industry standard benchmarks for OLTP are the Transaction Processing Council (TPC) benchmarks, which include the TPC-A and TPC-B benchmarks. TPC-A exercises the system components necessary to support OLTP invironments characterized by multiple on-line terminal sessions and significant disk input/output (I/O). TPC-B exercises the database components in OLTP environments characterized by significant disk I/O, and it is a batch versus an OLTP benchmark in that no terminals, networking, or think-time are included. The metrics reported by TPC-A and TPC-B include throughput expressed in transactions per second as well as the associated prices ($)/TPS.

2. **High availability.** Mission-critical applications require absolute data integrity and no downtime (both planned and unplanned). In general, customers are concerned with limiting the maximum length of time that a system is down.
3. **Scalability.** Customers want their investment protected and would like to see a highly flexible set of upgrades at minimum cost through board upgrades or added expansion.
4. **Distributability.** As RDBMS technology evolves and customer environments become more complex and distributed, there is a need to manage transactions across multiple distributed sites.

- Performance — TPS and S/TPS
- High availability — uptime
- Scalability — broad product line, board upgrades, MP
- Distributability — manage distributed OLTP across multiple heterogeneous systems and databases
- Data integrity — data consistency in a distributed system
- Recoverability — recover lost data from any failure
- Security — around users, applications, and data
- Operability — ease of network, system, and user administration
- Productivity — tools in developing and maintaining OLTP applications
- Connectivity — LAN, WAN, SNA, PC connectivity

Figure 8.3 OLTP market requirements.

5. **Integrity.** Distributed systems over multiple sites and departments need facilities to ensure that no lost transactions occur which may cause inconsistencies in the various databases.
6. **Recoverability.** As failures occur, either hardware or software, the system, including the databases, must be rapidly restored to the most stable point before the failure.
7. **Security.** Data is a valuable asset. It must be secure in today's increasingly networked system environments.
8. **Productivity.** OLTP systems will require sophisticated application development tools such as fourth-generation languages (4GLs) and computer-aided software engineering (CASE) to support new application devlopment as well as helping existing applications evolve towards new technologies or models (e.g., client/server, object-oriented solutions).
9. **Operability.** Client/server networked environments will require networked-based system management tools for OLTP environments.
10. **Connectivity.** Corporate mainframe and workstation personal computer (PC) connectivity will be stressed such that LANs, OSI, and IBM connectivity solutions will require increased integration.

A Strategy for Success

The weaknesses of UNIX for OLTP are being addressed by various OLTP vendors. Criticisms in the past have focused on realiability, the UNIX file system, data integrity, as well as process and memory management.

Performance and Price/Performance

Performance and price/performance are two fundamental metrics used to measure system vendors. The trend in OLTP is to move the system closer to the actual users, which means a greater demand for fast on-line data access. Because the volume of these transactions usually is large, response times between transactions are also important. Buyers are also concerned about the cost of these systems. Hence, vendors

- Maturing SQL technology
- SQL adaptations for UNIX
  - — Raw I/O
  - — Minimized context switching
  - — Shared memory
- OLTP performance on HP-UX
  - — Fast IPC mechanism
  - — Asynchronous I/O
- Close ties with RDBMS vendors

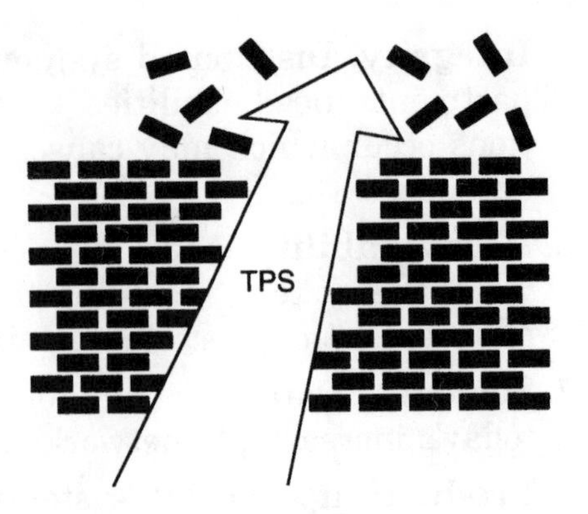

Figure 8.4 Breaking transaction performance barriers.

(PCs to mainframe) will usually quote a $/TPS number (the lower, the better) along with a TPS figure (the higher, the better).

Figure 8.4 shows that traditional barriers for UNIX in OLTP are increasingly being addressed.

One of the characteristics of OLTP is the heavy use of interprocess communication (IPC), which, to the operating system, means a lot of process context switching. Some of the database vendors use a two–process/user architecture, and IPC calls are being made constantly between the two processes. A faster IPC mechanism that optimizes the number of context switches available is needed for third-party software vendors, who can benefit from this feature.

Another needed feature of the operating system (OS) is asynchronous or nonblocking I/O to the disk. This basically allows a process to continue executing while the I/O is being processed. The asynchronous I/O feature includes the ability to get notification after the I/O is completed. This feature is important for DBMS, for example, which uses a single back-end process for multiple front-end processes. The asynchronous I/O feature prevents the single back-end process from blocking the other front-end processes that are trying to gain access to it.

A criticism of UNIX is the limitation of the file system for OLTP. OLTP applications need fast access to large files randomly, and the UNIX file system is designed to access mostly small files. The important point here is that most of the major database vendors have by-passed the UNIX file system and have essentially created their own file system through the UNIX raw I/O disk feature. This allows the flexibility for database vendors to take full control of buffer allocation schemes and disc I/O algorithms.

Database vendors are also tuning and enhancing their structured query language (SQL) products to include features such as multithreaded server, disk I/O optimizations, and precompiled procedures to enhance CPU utilization. RDBMS vendors are doing these optimizations because they feel that it is not the relational model, but the implementation of it, that prevents them from delivering high-volume transaction performance. Multithreaded database servers such as the one provided by Ingres allows each back-end server to process multiple front-end client processes, thereby reducing the number of processes created. This is quite different from previous vendors' architectures, which imposed a two-process model for each user.

Disk I/O optimizations used by major RDBMS vendors include things like multivolume tables, group commit, and deferred writes. Multivolume tables allow a relational table to be transparently partitioned or "striped" across multiple disk volumes, resulting in the increased utilization of the available disk I/O bandwidth. Group commit eliminates log file bottlenecks. A log file is used to ensure transaction data integrity. Every transaction commit will normally generate one I/O to the log file. With group commit, the log information from different transactions is grouped together and flushed in a single I/O.

Deferred writes allow a database server to commit transactions without writing the changed data to the disk immediately. The frequently changed data can remain in memory and be flushed at a later time. Data integrity is maintained with deferred writes because the transaction log is flushed during commit time.

Compiled database procedures are used by almost all database vendors. Database procedures are SQL commands that are grouped together, precompiled, and stored in the database, thereby reducing context switching and IPC time. These optimizations are only a small sample of how database vendors are reducing operating system overhead.

As a result of the tuning and enhancements, it is becoming apparent that UNIX can match the performance of higher-priced proprietary systems.

High Availability

There is an increasing demand in the OLTP market for highly available systems to run mission-critical applications. This demand is particularly strong in the manufacturing and telecommunications industries. The key features under high availability, which customers need, include data integrity, no planned downtime, and minimal unplanned downtime.

Data integrity is defined as the need to maintain consistent and durable data even after failure occurs. Planned downtime is the time the computer is unavailable for doing scheduled operations such as preventive maintenance, disk backups, and hardware and software updates. Unplanned downtime is the time a system is unavailable because of a system failure.

The system availability needs will vary depending on the cost associated with lost time to perform the business transactions due to the system being down. Service-oriented firms such as airline or hotel reservation systems and telephone services will require 24 hours by 7 days availability. Other companies have less stringent requirements.

New hardware features such as processor failover and hardened file system are being added. Processor failover allows a standby processor to back up one or more primary processors in a loosely coupled network. The hardened file system allows a file system to maintain higher reliability such that the reboot time involved in file system checking is greatly reduced.

Scalability

OLTP customers want the flexibility of expandable systems with wide performance ranges, including the scalability provided by high-end multiprocessor systems. Customers want their hardware and software investments protected, which translates to providing a scalable growth path with portability in mind.

Distributability, Data Integrity, and Recoverability

In the 1990s, we will see networked heterogeneous systems become a reality. Users will want to perform and manage distributed transactions across these systems transparently. Data integrity and recoverability issues become more complicated in a distributed environment.

Networked systems include client/server configurations with intelligent workstations such as MS-DOS, OS/2 PCs, and UNIX workstations. Distributed transaction processing is the future trend in OLTP and key technologies for distributed computing are appearing on UNIX.

Transaction Processing Monitor One of the key technologies needed to support distributed OLTP on UNIX is a transaction processing (TP) monitor. A TP monitor handles many of the same tasks that an operating system does, such as scheduling of resources and managing user requests. In networked environments, the TP monitor can also direct database transaction requests to an idle processor, which enhances the capacity of an OLTP application.

TP monitors are more cost effective in high-volume transaction environments with more than 100 users, and most UNIX OLTP systems are currently limited to about 100–200 users on the high end. Although UNIX OLTP systems can handle 100–200 users without difficulty, putting more users beyond 200 requires additional software features and tuning. An OLTP monitor, through its ability to efficiently schedule and manage transaction requests and services, promises to deliver more users for the same hardware configuration. TP monitors that extend the client/server model across the network and offload screen or forms processing to local workstations are expected to deliver on that promise.

Another key benefit of a TP monitor is the ability to coordinate transactions in a distributed OLTP computing environment. The two key features that enable this are transaction logging and a protocol called two-phase commit. A transaction log is used to store the status of a transaction's progress and the state of systems involved.

Two-phase commit allows a TP monitor to tell all involved systems to prepare to commit their transaction parts. If all of the systems respond affirmatively by saying that they are ready to commit, only then will the TP monitor send the global commit instruction. Otherwise, an abort message is sent to all participating sites, thereby ensuring data integrity in a distributed manner.

To help enable recovery after failures, most TP monitors include a log that stores the history of a system's operation which can, in turn, be used to reconstruct a system after a failure. Another point about recovery is when a transaction fails, a TP monitor can detect the system failure and notify the application of origin. It is then up to the application to abort or retry the transaction. Besides these OLTP run-time execution features, a TP monitor usually includes software development tools to help develop these applications, as well as an administrative support environment to help users install, configure, monitor, and manage these systems.

Figure 8.5 illustrates an example of a global transaction, which consists of subtransactions executed in a distributed, heterogeneous environment.

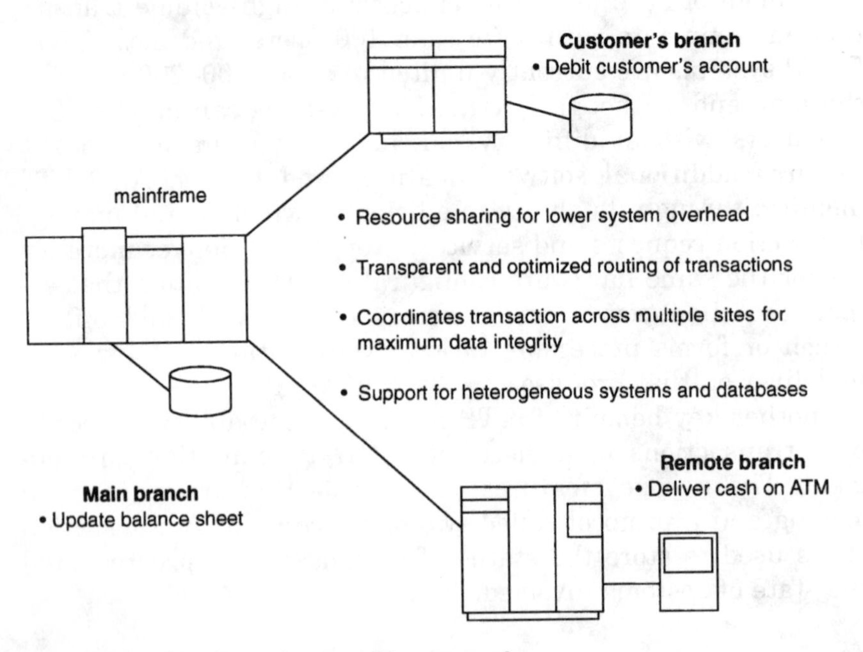

Figure 8.5 Distributed transaction example.

Emerging OLTP Standards Distributing the execution of transactions across a heterogeneous set of platforms is a difficult task since the environment needs standardization and cooperation. Open OLTP will require that a set of common application programing interfaces (APIs) be defined and implemented by all. X/Open has defined an OLTP model consisting of basically three functional components: application, transaction manager, and resource manager. Resource manager includes RDBMS, file systems, and print services. Applications and transaction managers work together to request resource managers for a certain task. A transaction manager includes most of the TP monitor features discussed earlier plus some communication services for an application to access. However, the approach X/Open might take on communication services is to break up the communication services to another module such that an application can deal directly with the communication services without going through the transaction manager. One of the first interfaces under definition is the XA interface, which is the interface between the transaction manager and resource manager. A formal XA proposal was distributed to various X/Open companies and users for review and it was finalized in the fall of 1991. Figure 8.6 shows the X/Open OLTP model.

Some of the key interfaces being defined are the XA interface described earlier, the ISO remote database access (RDA),

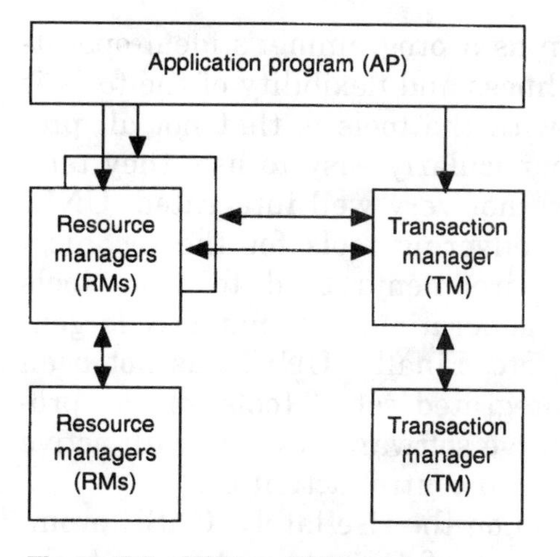

Figure 8.6 X/Open DTP model.

and the ISO distributed transaction processing (DTP) protocol, which defines the interface between two TP monitors cooperating in a single transaction. In addition, X/Open expects to tackle the AP/TM interface in the near future. All these various efforts are being undertaken to deliver users of DTP systems with the following ultimate benefits:

1. **Interoperability.** The ability to have transaction programs that operate on several different RDBMSs, which may be on different sites
2. **Application portability.** The ability to move applications to different systems easily
3. **Interchangeability.** The ability to substitute databases without major rewrite efforts for OLTP programs

Productivity

OLTP systems will get more complicated as new technologies emerge and begin to be integrated with existing or new applications. One of the biggest considerations when purchasing an OLTP system is the availability of software development tools. Customers today are faced with issues such as application backlogs, poor-quality software, large maintenance efforts, and migration problems as they move code from one system to another. Customers will also start facing new challenges such as development of client/server and distributed OLTP applications.

UNIX has been well known as a programmer's ideal operating system because of the richness and flexibility of the tools it provides. The only problem with the tools is that not all programmers find UNIX tools particularly easy to use; they tend to be point tools and they are not very well integrated. UNIX has also been criticized for delivering tools for the technical environment. Commercial environments tend to have tools such as database design and generation, automated code generation, 4GLs, report writer, etc. Finally, UNIX has not been well known for having an integrated set of tools for the production and maintenance of large software systems with active software project management and control activities.

The CASE business has been on the rise lately. CASE promises to deliver an integrated set of tools to automate tasks

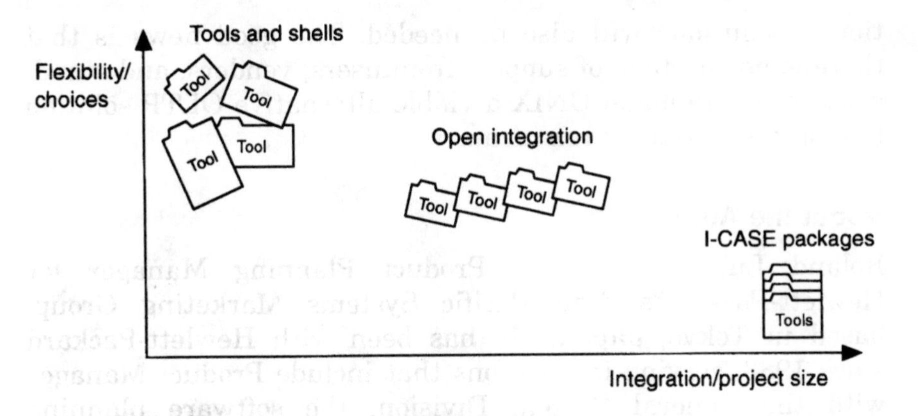

Figure 8.7 Commercial CASE solutions.

across the entire software development life cycle and to increase development productivity, quality of software, and reduce maintenance costs.

Customers will choose their tool set depending on two major variables. The first consideration is the flexibility or choices of combining tools from different sources; the other is the degree of integration needed as well as the project size. An implied factor here is that the less integrated tool set will demand a lower price in the market. Figure 8.7 shows this varying set of commercial CASE solutions.

There are trade-offs to consider when choosing the tools and shells solution versus the integrated CASE (I-CASE) solution. Tools and shells are less costly but deliver less productivity because of the low degree of integration and usability. I-CASE solutions from third parties offer higher productivity at a higher cost, and they usually involve investing in a vendor's proprietary solution.

Conclusion

UNIX OLTP will be maturing as new technologies mature and are integrated. Even though vendors and users are still struggling with the problems of how to build bigger, more powerful, distributed OLTP systems, the key ingredients for success are appearing quickly.

Clearly, standards in OLTP will need final definition, acceptance, and implementation. Further optimization and integration of solutions will also be needed. The good news is that there is no shortage of support from users, vendors, and standards groups to make UNIX a viable alternative OLTP solution to costly, proprietary mainframes.

About the Author

Roland Luk is currently Product Planning Manager for Hewlett-Packard's Asia Pacific Systems Marketing Group, based in Tokyo, Japan. He has been with Hewlett-Packard since 1983, serving in positions that include Product Manager with the General System Division, the software planning group responsible for OLTP-related information management products.

Mr. Luk is a graduate of the University of California at Berkeley with a degree in computer science.

Part

4

OLTP and CICS

Michael Snyder's contributions to this work have the obvious common theme of CICS, IBM's flagship on-line transaction monitor. Underlying this is a set of challenges that are generic to OLTP in general: communication between programs in like or unlike computer systems; data integrity; and serving customers when they need it rather than at the convenience of the data processing people.

Movement toward client/server processing often requires that there be a robust and well-defined pipeline between the desktop client workstation and the CICS-based behemoth which manages the corporate "data of record." Chapter 10, on SNA Logical Unit 6.2, defines the CICS end of this pipe from the application programmer's perspective, based on the experience of writing and debugging a prototype application, which performs database updates in both session partners.

Chapter 10 places heavy emphasis on the data integrity issues raised when both the client and the server are causing database updates which must either be committed or rolled back in perfect synchronism. It also discusses the exact sequence of actions that a CICS program must render as a participant in LU 6.2.

Data integrity is much more precarious in the OLTP world than in the batch processing world, with which we all felt so safe and comfortable. An unsatisfactory batch update can be backed out and redone later; with OLTP there is no such option. Chapter 11, a data integrity tutorial essay, discloses, again from the CICS practitioner's viewpoint but with industrywide applicability, all the stitches which must never be dropped in on-line database updating. It applies both to batch and on-line programming.

Round-the-clock OLTP becomes important to customer service and market share when competitors begin using it in their business strategy. Chapter 9, on the CICS 24×365 goal, illustrates that constant database update access to all applications requires an artful and disciplined approach to system design, investment in leading-edge systems software, and cubic money.

Chapter 9 confronts data integrity and its impingement on the 24-hour goal. It also addresses the measures that must be taken to preserve database response time goals, which directly conspire against those of high availability. As with his other writings, Mr. Snyder brings a current practitioner's experience to the table.

Chapter

9

CICS for 24 Hours a Day?

Michael Snyder
Kaiser Foundation Health Plan, Inc.

The Problem

Many data processing shops hear from their users (loud and often) that taking down the Customer Information Control Systems (CICSs) for batch processing is putting a crimp in the corporation's need for high-availability on-line applications.

The users cannot believe it is such a giant challenge; the technical staff often has only a vague collection of unresearched objections. This makes the reply unconvincing. What to do? Data processing is supposed to help the company compete for customers, not hinder it. The programmers have some explaining to do. If the customers start walking, guess who will be next!

For instance, a company's market may become spread across several time zones. In the wee hours, when the headquarters CICS systems have to be shut down for batch processing, it is the time when offices far to the east are opening for business.

There are many roadblocks to high CICS availability. This chapter is the result of one organization's identification of the problems and remedies in an environment of Virtual Storage Access Method (VSAM), Information Management

System/Database (IMS/DB), and IBM Database 2 (DB2). It is quite a bitter pill to swallow when there are lots of on-line applications designed for only 9-to-5 availability. This is because there were thousands of sins of omission committed in the past. These must be undone today—at tremendous expense.

The organization never considered running CICS 24 hours a day, all year long. This shop's goal was 24 hours a day for a week or two at a time.

Finger pointing becomes circular. System software used to be the major inhibitor; applications were designed within those constraints. System software now leads the evolution to high availability; the applications must catch up.

It takes real work to differentiate between sins affecting response time and those that impair availability. Even if a system delivers 1-minute response, it is still available to those with enough stress-tolerance to use it. This chapter looks at phenomena which truly take the application out of service, in whole or in part.

To gain some sense of scale in the following discussion, note that the author's installation runs 50,000 production batch jobs a month. Its network of over 10,000 terminals generates in excess of 4 million CICS transactions per day. There are 18 production regions with up to 21 hours scheduled daily availability. Around 100 CICS applications exist, 10 percent of which could use high uptime. Most of the latter are used in hospitals, which are 24-hour institutions.

Application Design

Do not assume that every functional part of a CICS application must be available 24 hours a day and that every batch job must be capable of data sharing. Batch that shares no data with CICS can go its merry way. The application must be divided into the components that fall into the high-availability regime and those that do not. This requires good documentation.

Database management systems offer availability features. IMS/DB has Database Recovery Control, IMS Resource Lock Manager, and block-level data sharing where a mixture of batch and CICS applications may concurrently update a database. Data integrity locks are placed on control intervals of the database. DB2 is endowed with a similar set of properties.

Omission of checkpoint/restart logic in batch IMS or DB2 update programs tends to make data sharing unrealistic. If data sharing batch programs do not commit their work as they go along, they accumulate data integrity locks on all the control intervals they update. A long batch run can gradually deny the database to CICS and other batch jobs. This affects all updaters, IMS readers with integrity, and DB2 readers. And it greatly escalates the odds of deadlock. If the program blows up, it takes roughly as long to back out its uncommitted updates as it did to make them in the first place. Then the work remains undone, which is entirely rude.

IMS offers a facility for batch programs to issue checkpoints during processing. These irrevocably commit the database updates done to that point. If the program abends, it can be restarted from the last checkpoint with repositioning of sequential input and output files and restoration of selected areas of working storage (control totals, for instance). Database browse repositioning is the application's responsibility (DB2 Version 2.3 can retain browse position). Sequential input and output files must be managed as Generalized Sequential Access Method (GSAM) databases in order to be repositioned automatically. SYSOUT files, which are used throughout the job (rather than only at startup or end), must be managed by GSAM and printed with IEBGENER or equivalent utility.

Restarting an abended program from the last commit point is important because it is often unacceptable to restart it from the beginning, reapplying the updates it had already committed. Adding to inventory on hand, for instance, would not be prudent to do twice. Any update that uses the preexisting data value must not be repeated; plus it is rather a waste of computer time.

Because DB2 offers commit but no restart facility, its batch updates must run under IMS control to properly share data unless home-grown restart methods for DB2 are developed and generalized.

Application programs must be modified for checkpoint/restart and it is not easy. It requires finding the place in the code to insert the checkpoint, identifying the variables to be preserved across a restart, and placing the restart logic. Try doing this on some crusty old program (converted from Autocoder).

Some programs that read IMS databases with integrity or DB2 tables can cause throughput problems due to their read integrity locking. Rather than browsing along, constantly changing its database position, such a program reads just one or a few records, then does a lot of other work. Its read integrity lock persists, preventing updaters from accessing the last-read control interval.

There are two ways to deal with this problem. If the program can afford to lose browse position, it can issue a commit after it has read the data it needs, which will release the read integrity lock. The program can ignore restart provisions, since it is read-only and relatively unlikely to abend.

The other way, if up-to-the-minute data is not required, is to make a copy of the database for read-only jobs.

CICS applications should contain several transaction identifiers (IDs) for differentiation of read-only and update functions. For granularity, functions that use different sets of databases should be defined as separate sets of transaction IDs. This allows those that do database updates to be selectively disabled when their particular databases are not available for that. Meanwhile, the read-only programs can keep at it. Whether the users will get any benefit from this depends on business requirements.

Let us consider application robustness in the face of database outage, scheduled or unscheduled. This leads to steeply diminishing returns due to the complexity of dual-mode processing. Such designs also tend to be difficult to test. One of the less expensive tricks is for the application to write update transactions to a holding file when the target database is unavailable. This file would be edited and processed later when the database becomes available again. It is not trivial.

Be universally and doggedly suspicious of purchased applications. They consistently tend not to be designed for high-availability operations.

The problems can be cured only with huge amounts of programming labor. Faster iron will have minimal effect, if any.

VSAM

Native VSAM files used both by CICS and batch, which are updated by either, can ruin the program. They are almost never readable with integrity when any address space is updating them.

Certainly, SHAREOPTIONS(2) specifies that one address space may update the dataset while many others read it. However, the catalog is not updated when the file takes a secondary extent. During a control interval or control area split, some inserts and deletes, and secondary index updates, the index is not consistent with the data. Also, it may be of dire consequence for a program to read uncommitted data in; for instance, a debit/credit type of file which is out of balance between the posting of the offsetting entries. Finally, update sharing between mainframes is totally uncontrolled; it is almost too scary to contemplate.

There are only two safe uses of native VSAM. They equate to SHAREOPTIONS(1):

- Read-only by multiple address spaces during CICS uptime and updating in batch during a scheduled CICS outage
- Updating by CICS and denied to batch programs during this time; batch access is allowed only during a scheduled outage

There are at least two products on the market that provide VSAM sharing with integrity. Investigation shows that they meet the requirements of a subset of applications.

IMS offers the Simple Hierarchic Indexed Sequential Access Method (SHISAM) where a VSAM key-sequenced dataset is managed by IMS as a database rather than by the application as a file. This enables block-level data sharing and checkpoint/restart. It is the ultimate means of sharing a native VSAM key-sequenced dataset (KSDS) in a mixed CICS and batch environment. It requires modification of all programs that share the file; the input/output (I/O) statements must be converted to IMS calls.

After due consideration of data processing's future, one is tempted to rule that an alternative far more useful than SHISAM is to convert VSAM files that need sharing into DB2 tables; but it will be expensive, no matter what is done.

High-Availability CICS: Finishing the Job

In this last part of the chapter, the following topics will be discussed:

- Database design
- Database backup
- Database reorganization
- Change management
- Unavoidable scheduled outage
- Standards

Ideas are presented *without* universally advocating any of them. The merit of one must be gauged in the context of the pertinent applications. Remember that some of them can slightly increase response time of on-line transactions, but this can be addressed with the addition of more computing power.

Database Design

Even with properly designed data sharing, it is not a good idea to let heavy batch work run into the time when CICS is really busy. The following ideas are for keeping it within bounds.

Partitioning of DB2 table spaces allows multiple copies of the same batch job to run in parallel, each handling one partition. To limit its activities to one partition, the program must read a control card telling it which key range to process.

Likewise, IMS databases can be procedurally partitioned. This feature is not offered by IMS; it must be accomplished by defining the partitions as a series of databases. An IMS batch program would be pointed to a program specification block (PSB), which contains just one of the partitions.

Programs that view the partitioned IMS database as a single entity will be sensitive to the partitioning. The whole database would be included in the PSB with each partition being a program communication block (PCB). The program must specify the PCB of the target partition for every I/O request.

Database Control (DBCTL) is a feature of IMS Version 3, where data management is removed from CICS Version 3 and batch regions and centralized in one set of address spaces as a subsystem. Architecturally it looks a lot like DB2: a server for CICS and batch regions using its databases, creating one set of logs instead of many. It provides automatic backout of abended batch work, which should be more reliable than separate backout steps in job control language (JCL).

IMS Version 3 Data Entry Databases (DEDBs) have high-availability features. These include transparent disk I/O error recovery and sequential processing enhancements. They do not directly support secondary indexes.

Database Backup

DB2 table spaces can be backed up while updating continues. DBCTL provides the same for IMS databases, but there remains a potential problem.

The issue is point of consistency between DB2 and IMS databases and with logs not being integrated between the two subsystems. Databases may be related to each other in a DB2/IMS mix due to application-defined referential integrity constraints or transactions that update databases in both subsystems. Disaster recovery requires that all related databases be restored to congruence with one another. The only way to make a point of consistency backup is for all of the related DB2 and IMS databases to be simultaneously disabled for update while all the copies are made. This *must* be done periodically and will take some time. Design permitting, the application can provide read processing during the backup.

Partitioning of DB2 table spaces and procedural partitioning of IMS databases allows backups to run in parallel.

It is possible to back up an IMS database without taking the time to back up its indexes. Proprietary software exists which will reconstruct them after the database is restored. It does add to recovery time.

If there are VSAM files updated by CICS, IBM's CICS VSAM Recovery product can allow them to be backed up during update. The Storage Management Subsystem and CICS Version 3.2.1 are prerequisite to this. Proprietary products also are available. The point of consistency issue may include these files, of course. VSAM's numerous other problems remain.

Database Reorganization

Indexed *and* hashed databases need reorganization for performance reasons but create availability problems during the process.

Reorganization frequency might be reduced by providing more free space in the definition of a database, but clustering of inserts can ruin free space planning. If, for instance, the current date and time are part of the key, and are not subordinate to other key fields with widely varying values (customer number, for instance), hot spots in the database will tend to use the free space unevenly.

A major problem with reorganization is that it ordinarily takes the entire database out of service during the reload process. Following are some ideas for decreasing the impact.

Partitioning of DB2 table spaces can yield benefits because it offers opportunities to run reorganizations in small pieces (though not in parallel). This can spread the reorganization work over several successive scheduled outages rather than doing the whole job all at once. IMS databases can be procedurally partitioned and reorganized in parallel.

Another way to decrease the scope of IMS reorganization is to use multiple dataset groups. This can segregate volatile segment types (the ones that need reorganizing) from the other ones.

Primary and secondary indexes on HIDAM and secondaries on HDAM can be reorganized without reorganizing the underlying data. The scope can be limited to individual indexes, thus spreading the impact.

An alternative to reorganizing IMS indexes is to rebuild them from the database itself, using an index reconstruction product.

Another way to limit IMS reorganization impact is to use IBM's Surveyor to find those key ranges that actually need it. With this information, a partial reorganization of the database can be accomplished. This appears to depend on free space, and the result might not yield as good a result as one might hope.

IMS DEDBs can be reorganized while updates carry on. If reorganization during scheduled CICS uptime is unavoidable and the application design permits, IMS non-DEDB databases might be used read-only during reorganization. Readers use the disorganized database. After reorganizing, the database is quiesced and the disorganized copy taken off-line. The reorganized copy is renamed as the active copy, and updating resumes. DB2 offers a similar facility but requires that Plans be rebound as part of the switchover.

Change Management

Resource Definition On-line (RDO) allows applications to be changed without recycling CICS. This will reduce the length of outage.

Changes to the CICS Database Definition Directory (DDIR) and Program Specification Block Directory (PDIR) require a recycle unless DBCTL is implemented. Then it would require only a brief outage of the affected applications.

Auto-install allows terminals to be added to the CICS network as they log on. It does *good* things to startup elapsed times.

Unavoidable Scheduled Outage

After all the arguments are done, the inevitable conclusion is that applications (if not CICS itself) will remain subject to periodic outage. The minimum may be 26 or 52 per year and it will be very costly to achieve.

It will be tempting to squeeze an unrealistic amount of batch processing into the scheduled outage rather than modify all those programs for checkpoint/restart. This is retrograde thinking and must be stamped out, as it will quickly lead to failure of the high-availability effort by compromising it to death.

Storage fragmentation can require that a CICS region be periodically recycled for stall prevention. Extended Recovery Facility is not the universal answer today because of nontransferability of common work area and main memory temporary storage.

Standards

To prevent more of the same old sins from sneaking into application designs, new standards are in order. These need not be imposed on all designs, just the ones that need high availability. New applications always should be assumed subject to the regime and negotiated out of it (if appropriate), *not* the other way around.

There must be no native VSAM files used concurrently by CICS and batch which are updated either by CICS or batch.

Other native VSAM files must use SHAREOPTIONS(1) to prevent data integrity surprises.

Batch programs that update databases must implement checkpoint and restart. Checkpoint frequency (number of updates or elapsed time in seconds) must be a run-time variable so it can be tuned.

VS COBOL II should be the standard compiler for COBOL shops, if for no other reason than it makes CICS storage fragmentation and program compression less of a hazard.

Applications should have separate CICS transaction IDs for read-only and update, limiting the impact of database outage. This also makes security, performance analysis, tuning, and problem diagnosis much easier.

Get the standards committee signed up for the high-availability movement. If that group can get the management to approve and enforce law, then it will be done. Put action deadlines in the standards. Make those who move software into production responsible for enforcement. Give them tools for scanning source code for musts and must-nots. Make the waiver process humiliating.

The whole deal will trash the development work schedule. People will howl and threaten to gnaw your skull. Does the board of directors want it? Go for it.

About the Author

Michael Snyder has worked in all aspects of application software development since 1968. His major areas of emphasis since 1984 have been application performance analysis and technical education for his constituency of 200 application programmers.

Working for a giant health care provider has made him particularly sensitive to data integrity in the belief that harming a patient is the province of the physician, not the computer programmer.

His employer is Kaiser Foundation Health Plan, Inc., Walnut Creek, California. His shop runs a network of 15,000 CICS terminals, which originate over 7 million transactions on the average Monday. A capacity-planning committee of a dozen highly talented colleagues helps keep this train on the tracks.

Chapter

10

Logical Unit Type 6.2 Applications in CICS

Michael Snyder
Kaiser Foundation Health Plan, Inc.

Distributed transaction processing (DTP) is the Customer Information Control System (CICS) implementation of Systems Network Architecture (SNA) Logical Unit (LU) Types 6.2 and 6.1, enabling direct synchronous communication between application programs. Pairs of transaction programs send application-defined messages back and forth in a "conversation" using a set of old and new Terminal Control commands. When implemented via LU Type 6.2, it is also called Advanced Program-to-Program Communication (APPC). CICS provides full data integrity for recoverable resources updated by either or both of the DTP partner transactions.

This chapter, while purporting to be mainstream, does not address the whole spectrum of DTP function. Its emphasis is on the processing of commits and backouts of updates to recoverable resources in mapped LU 6.2 conversations. In that area the subjects of CONFIRM, ISSUE ERROR, and ISSUE ABEND are omitted as not being essential to successful applications.

Perils of Database Updating

To contemplate the issue of data integrity and recoverable resources, consider a bookkeeping application where entries are made into a ledger. The ledger consists of debits and credits, which are balancing pluses and minuses. When a program updates the ledger, it posts a debit, then a credit in two database update actions. After both entries are posted successfully, the ledger has been transformed from one internally consistent (in-balance) state to another consistent state. At this point the program declares the updates irrevocably "committed" to the database. The system software notes this fact in its recovery log.

When the program makes the first of these two updates (the debit), it transforms the ledger to an inconsistent state because the balancing entry (the credit) has not yet been posted. Furthermore, if it finds a problem in posting the credit, it absolutely *must* reverse the debit rather than leaving the ledger in an inconsistent state. The application requests "backout" and the uncommitted update is rescinded by system software action as if it had never occurred in the first place. The debit–credit set of updates must be committed either as a pair or not at all. This constitutes what IBM calls a *logical unit of work*—an update that durably transforms a resource from one consistent state to another consistent state.

The logical unit of work concept is critical in DTP if both the conversing application programs are updating databases or other recoverable resources. Usually the work they do in concert must be committed or backed out in concert. Were one partner to commit an update and the other abend before accomplishing its update, this could cause a data integrity disaster.

Recoverable resources can include IMS and DB2 databases, VSAM key-sequenced datasets, and intrapartition transient data destinations. Updates to these are noted by system software in a recovery log. Among other things, the log is used to back out uncommitted updates as needed.

DTP Basics

There are some IBM-defined terms that must be absorbed in gaining an appreciation of DTP.

The *front-end transaction* is the one that starts the DTP conversation. It is analogous to one person dialing a telephone to start a conversation with another person. The *back-end transaction* is the target of the front-end's conversation, analogous to a person picking up a ringing telephone. Once the conversation is established by CICS, the front-end transaction sends a message and the back-end transaction receives it. An arbitrary number of messages flow back and forth in an orderly fashion, one message at a time, synchronously. The process must follow the protocol defined by CICS regarding which partner can do what (receive data, send data, commit database updates, terminate the conversation, etc.) at any given *state* in the conversation.

There is no sense of power or privilege implicit in the terms *front end* and *back end.* CICS regards both conversing transactions as equals.

When one of the transactions starts an action to commit or back out updates to recoverable resources, a definite imbalance of power arises between the two. Either the front-end or the back-end transaction can start this action; the one which does this is designated the *syncpoint initiator* by CICS, the other the *syncpoint slave*. Once a commit or backout is started by the syncpoint initiator, the slave has only a few options. This is described later in the chapter.

LU 6.2 can be used between a CICS application and one residing in a non-CICS computer, or between applications residing in separate CICS regions.

In the case of CICS-to-CICS DTP, IBM permits SNA LU 6.2, LU 6.1, or a non-SNA variant called Multi-Region Operation (MRO). In the interest of uniformity and network configurability it is reasonable to use LU 6.2 only. This requires that the connection between the participating CICS regions be implemented via Inter-System Communication (ISC) rather than MRO. These are the two methods by which CICS systems work together in a network.

The DTP protocol under MRO looks a lot like LU 6.1 but the two are not identical. MRO imposes more restrictions than LU 6.1 but a program written for MRO generally will execute under LU 6.1, according to IBM. The confusion factor alone tempts one to dismiss them both.

The ISC requirement can impose limits on the regions in which a DTP transaction can reside. A given CICS region's DTP and function shipping connections to any other single CICS region must be all MRO or all ISC in V2R1. A given CICS region can have MRO connections to one CICS region and ISC connections to another. MRO runs faster than ISC because the latter involves VTAM. But LU 6.2 requires ISC. Many people agree that this is simply the price to be paid; that it is cheaper in the long run than fiddling with anything else. An application can conform either to MRO/LU 6.1 or LU 6.2 with a single stream of code, but not both.

DTP cannot be pseudo-conversational; if one of the partners terminates, the DTP conversation is likewise terminated.

Power to Solve Problems

DTP can be a good alternative to multiple function-shipped I/Os. The front-end transaction in an application-owning CICS region can start a conversation with a back-end transaction in a data-owning region. The front end asks the back end a single question requiring several I/Os. The back end does all the I/O locally and returns to the front end a single message containing the answer. This amounts to a lot less data communication traffic than if the front end had function shipped all those I/O requests and the data records comprising them.

Additionally, DTP enables a spectrum of application power that function shipping was never designed to address. Some examples follow:

- A nondistributed DB2 subsystem can serve only the mainframe on which it resides. A CICS front-end transaction on a different mainframe needing access to that DB2 can use DTP to communicate with a back-end transaction on the DB2 mainframe, which does the work and returns the results.
- LU 6.2 is the industry standard protocol for program-to-program communication between the mainframe and IBM and non-IBM distributed computers and intelligent workstations. When a distributed application on Brand X computer needs access to, say, a VSAM customer file, LU 6.2 will be the communication vehicle.

- If IMS/DB block-level data sharing is not available, DTP is the way to circumvent the problem of a program that has to access with update integrity IMS databases owned by two different CICS regions. Such a program cannot do the job with a single program specification block (PSB), since a given PSB's databases all have to be in the same CICS region. It cannot use two PSBs because the first PSB's work would be committed, as it is closed before opening the second PSB. To solve this problem, the front-end transaction, under its local PSB, can access databases in its CICS region. The back end, under its PSB, can do likewise in its region and communicate the results back to the front end, maintaining cross-region database integrity. (It is true that IMS DBCTL and CICS V3 will help, but the user will not wait; this application is needed *today*.)

Scalpels and Chainsaws

A program can have multiple DTP conversations. For instance, it can comprise the back-end transaction in one conversation and the front-end transaction in another, both going on concurrently. Further, a program can concurrently be the front end in several conversations and/or back end in several. A heroic solution to a simple problem is *not* a good idea! This discussion is addressed to simple one-to-one conversations.

The commands of a DTP conversation are analogous to the human process of using CICS. The front-end transaction's ALLOCATE command, which specifies which CICS region contains the back-end transaction, corresponds to a person logging on to a CICS system at a terminal. The CONNECT PROCESS command, which specifies the transaction identifier (ID) of the back end, matches a person typing a transaction ID at the terminal to invoke an application program. The SEND and RECEIVE commands are like typing in transactions to CICS and staring at its response screen. The FREE command is analogous to typing in the "CSSF LOGOFF" transaction. This bonehead analogy is where the simplicity ends.

The first thing to consider is which CICS region or other network node contains the transaction with which a program wishes to communicate, assuming that the program comprises the front-end transaction. (The back end need not know which node invoked it.) The back-end's network node name must not be hard coded into the front-end program because that negates the systems programmers' ability to reconfigure the network. Instead, consider either a global application-defined "DTP configuration" file or the CICS Common Work Area as a place to store information concerning which network node runs the back-end transaction.

The "mapped LU 6.2" protocol is commonly used in writing application programs. This is elaborated in the chapter "CICS Applications for Logical Unit Type 6.2 Mapped Conversations" in the IBM manual *Intercommunication Guide*, SC33-0519. This manual describes in dizzying detail which execute interface block (EIB) fields must be checked in which sequence and which actions are legal at any given state in the conversation. The rules are complicated and hewn of granite. If a program does anything to violate them, CICS has a superb variety of abend codes with which to reward offenders. All of them result in recoverable resource updates being backed out.

If communicating with a non-CICS system, do not assume that it supports the mapped protocol; it may use only unmapped protocol. This is described in another chapter of the IBM manual.

When a DTP conversation involves the updating of recoverable resources both in the front-end and back-end transactions, LU 6.2 provides tools and rules for coordinated commit and backout. The SYNCLEVEL clause of the CONNECT PROCESS command expresses the level of data integrity requested of CICS in managing the conversation. SYNCLEVEL(2) gives the equivalent of normal CICS syncpointing, which is the safest. If one of the conversation partners is in a non-CICS system, however, never assume that the other operating system supports SYNCLEVEL(2)—many of them do not. This makes data integrity a white-knuckle experience.

SYNCLEVEL(2) invokes a "two-phase commit" protocol where the initiator's DTP commit is actually a "prepare to commit" and the actual commit or backout does not happen until the slave responds or abends. Both partners must issue SYNCPOINT commands in turn in order to commit their updates. Any other sequence of data integrity events will cause the recoverable resource updates of both partners to be backed out.

With SYNCLEVEL(2) the effects of a commit or backout are global to the partner transactions. If an IMS PSB is closed during a DTP conversation or if the conversation causes a commit or backout while an IMS PSB is open, all recoverable resources for both conversation partners are immediately affected. This is a critical consideration for the application designer.

SYNCLEVEL(2) adds overhead to both transactions due to the logging it evokes. Never use it unless it is truly necessary.

SYNCLEVEL(1) offers the CONFIRM data integrity protocol but an abend at the wrong instant will require plenty of manual work to find and resolve. This is not good enough in a large system, with stringent requirements of availability and data integrity.

Coding

This discussion assumes that SYNCLEVEL(2) is in effect and that both partners are updating recoverable resources. It is based on discoveries made in programming a demonstration application wherein a pair of DTP partners update recoverable VSAM files. It has a repertoire of 14 different commit/backout scenarios which can be called up by the experimenter. Either the front-end or the back-end transaction can be the syncpoint initiator. It runs on CICS V2R1.

CICS communicates the progress of commits and backouts in various 1-byte fields of the EIB, which are either "set" (containing HIGH-VALUES, hexadecimal 'FF') or "not set" (LOW-VALUES, X'00').

Also, there is a 4-byte field EIBERRCD, which can contain a variety of binary values. If it is necessary to display EIBERRCD, it must be decoded into 8-byte hexadecimal. Figure 10.1 shows a program fragment that does this.

Commit is implemented by the syncpoint initiator issuing the SYNCPOINT command. Either the front end or the back end can be the syncpoint initiator so long as the state of the conversation permits this. Typically the syncpoint initiator will be in send state. The SYNCPOINT implicitly causes a SEND to the syncpoint slave, which has a RECEIVE command outstanding. The slave's EIBSYNC field is set after its RECEIVE. This tells the slave that the initiator has started a commit and

Following is a VS COBOL II program fragment that converts 4 bytes of binary data in EIBERRCD to 8 bytes of displayable hexadecimal. (Put away that Assembler coding sheet; this COBOL program contains six procedural instructions!)

The modus operandi is to use binary multiplication to simulate a "shift left logical" that chews off 4 bits at a time, then use those 4 bits to subscript into a 16-item array of hexadecimal values.

```
...
WORKING-STORAGE SECTION.
01  HEX-WORK-AREA.
    05  DOUBLEWORD           PIC S9(16)  COMP.
    05  FILLER REDEFINES DOUBLEWORD.
        10  FILLER           PIC X(2).
        10  HALFWORD         PIC S9(4)   COMP.
        10  FULLWORD         PIC X(4).
* FULLWORD holds the original EIBERRCD value.
* When DOUBLEWORD gets multiplied by 16,
* 4 bits get left-shifted into HALFWORD.
    05  LOOPX                PIC S9(4)   COMP.
    05  HEX-SET              PIC X(16)
        VALUE '0123456789ABCDEF'.
    05  FILLER REDEFINES HEX-SET.
        10  HEX-HALFBYTE OCCURS 16 TIMES PIC X.
    05  RESULT-IN-HEX.
*       This receives the 8-byte hexadecimal representation
*       of the 4-byte binary number in FULLWORD.
        10  RESULT-BYTE OCCURS 8 TIMES PIC X.
LINKAGE SECTION
01  DFHEIBLK.
    ...
    02  EIBERRCD             PIC X(4).
    ...
PROCEDURE DIVISION USING DFHEIBLK ...
    ...
    Do something that sets EIBERRCD.
    MOVE EIBERRCD TO FULLWORD.
    PERFORM VARYING LOOPX FROM 1 BY 1 UNTIL LOOPX > 8
*     Grind off 4 bits into low end of HALFWORD.
      MOVE ZERO TO HALFWORD
      COMPUTE DOUBLEWORD = DOUBLEWORD * 16
```

Figure 10.1 Converting binary into displayable hexadecimal.

```
*       HALFWORD now contains a value of 0 to 15 in 4 bits.
*       Add 1 to make it a proper subscript
*       and pick up the hex representation of that data.
        MOVE HEX-HALFBYTE (HALFWORD + 1) TO RESULT-BYTE (LOOPX)
END-PERFORM.
```

This program uses a subscript instead of an index. The computer does binary arithmetic blindingly fast. A subscript is easier to find in a dump. It can be located next to the array it services. A single one can point to multiple arrays. The relative data in a subscript is often more useful than the absolute data in an index for debugging.

Figure 10.1 ***(Continued)***

that the slave must now react. In normal circumstances the slave will issue a SYNCPOINT, implicitly turning the conversation back to the initiator. CICS tells the initiator (via a normal response to its SYNCPOINT command and EIBRLDBK not being set) that the slave committed successfully. The logical unit of work is complete.

The syncpoint slave can respond negatively to the initiator's SYNCPOINT request by issuing a SYNCPOINT ROLLBACK command. This backs out the recoverable resource updates of both partners and tells the initiator (via the EIBRLDBK field being set and the ROLLEDBACK condition being raised) that the slave did this. Since the slave responded with a backout, the initiator has no options and does not take any action to roll back its updates; CICS automatically does this.

The syncpoint slave also can abend in response to a SYNCPOINT, causing the recoverable resource updates of both partners to be backed out. If the abending slave is the back-end transaction, the front end will be abended by CICS with an ASP3 code. If the abending slave is the front-end transaction, the surviving back end typically has nowhere to go, so it can choose either to terminate normally or (preferably) abend.

This ASP3 scenario is the only case where CICS jumps up and murders one of the DTP partners when the rules are indeed faithfully followed. It seems unfair.

The syncpoint initiator can issue a SYNCPOINT ROLLBACK command instead of a SYNCPOINT if it decides that

Table 10.1 LU 6.2 Scenarios and Resource Update Results

Initiator Action	Slave Action	Update Result
SYNCPOINT	SYNCPOINT	Committed
SYNCPOINT	SYNCPOINT ROLLBACK	Backed out
SYNCPOINT	Abend	Backed out*
SYNCPOINT ROLLBACK	SYNCPOINT ROLLBACK	Backed out
SYNCPOINT ROLLBACK	Abend	Backed out
Abend	SYNCPOINT ROLLBACK	Backed out
Abend	Abend	Backed out

*If the abending syncpoint slave is the back-end transaction, CICS abends the front end with code ASP3.

the work must not be committed. In this case the slave sees EIBSYNRB and EIBERR set after doing a RECEIVE and must respond with a SYNCPOINT ROLLBACK or an abend.

Finally, if a program abends at certain states of the conversation, it becomes the initiator of a SYNCPOINT ROLLBACK. The abruptly designated slave will see EIBERR set and must either issue a SYNCPOINT ROLLBACK or abend.

Table 10.1 shows all the legal scenarios and resulting effects on recoverable resources updated by the transactions.

Following is a summary of the EIB fields of interest in LU 6.2. Unless otherwise noted, each is a 1-byte field, which is either set (X'FF') or not set (X'00'):

- EIBCOMPL interacts with the LENGTH or MAXLENGTH and NOTRUNCATE options of the RECEIVE command. If it is set, the entire message has been received. If the program always provides for the maximum size input message, this should not be an issue.
- EIBERR is set if the DTP partner initiates a SYNCPOINT ROLLBACK and sometimes if the partner abends.
- EIBERRCD is a 4-byte binary field containing error information or indication that a SYNCPOINT ROLLBACK has been issued by the DTP partner. It must be checked after every DTP command.
- EIBFREE is set when the DTP conversation no longer is available for use; it has been implicitly or explicitly FREEd.

- EIBNODAT is set if a RECEIVE got no data. This field wants checking after every LU 6.2 RECEIVE. If the partner sent no data (for instance, it did a commit instead of sending data), EIBNODAT may be set and other interesting EIB fields not yet filled in. If EIBNODAT is set after a RECEIVE and neither EIBSYNC, EIBSYNRB, nor EIBERR is set, the program must do one more RECEIVE to get the other fields updated.
- EIBRECV is set if the program is in receive state.
- EIBRLDBK is set if the syncpoint slave responded to a commit with the SYNCPOINT ROLLBACK command.
- EIBRSRCE is an 8-byte field containing the CICS-assigned name of the DTP conversation. The front-end program must save this field in working storage after issuing the ALLOCATE command. The saved value must be used by the front end in the CONVID option of Terminal Control commands which refer to a DTP conversation. If a terminal session locks up during testing, suspect omission of CONVID on a DTP Terminal Control command in the front-end transaction. (The foregoing discussion assumes that the front end is attached to a terminal session.)
- EIBSYNC is set when the DTP partner initiates a SYNCPOINT.
- EIBSYNRB is set when the DTP partner initiates a SYNCPOINT ROLLBACK.

Tables 10.2 and 10.3 show the settings of various EIB fields seen by the front-end transaction for various commit and backout scenarios where the front end does not abend. Table 10.2 covers the case where the front end is the syncpoint initiator, and Table 10.3 shows where it is the slave. The boring appearance of Table 10.2 illustrates the difference between initiator and slave status.

When a program violates a DTP rule and is abended by CICS, some EIB fields important to debugging might not show up in the dump as they were when the program made its misstep. After every RECEIVE, save in working storage the fields just discussed.

Table 10.2 EIB Fields Seen by the Front-End Transaction When It Is the Syncpoint Initiator

Scenario	EIBSYNC	EIBSYNRB	EIBRLDBK	EIBERR	EIBRECV
Front end commits, back end commits, EIB updated	00	00	00	00	00
Front end commits, back end rolls back, EIB updated	00	00	FF	00	00
Front end rolls back, back end rolls back, EIB updated	00	00	00	00	00
Front end rolls back, back end abends, EIB updated	00	00	00	00	00

Table 10.3 EIB Fields Seen by the Front-End Transaction When It Is the Syncpoint Slave

Scenario	EIBSYNC	EIBSYNRB	EIBRLDBK	EIBERR	EIBRECV
Back end commits, EIB updated	FF	00	00	00	FF
Back end rolls back, EIB updated	00	FF	00	FF	00
Back end abends, EIB updated	00	00	00	FF	00

The expected response to a mapped LU 6.2 RECEIVE is EOC (end of chain). The NORMAL condition never occurs.

The most useful form of the SEND command where a response is expected is SEND INVITE WAIT.

The FREE command should be used at the end of conversation unless the transaction terminates shortly thereafter. This makes the LU 6.2 link available to other transactions.

Conclusion

When using the state diagrams in the IBM manual, follow their sequence of EIB field checking fastidiously. This will keep the application innocent of untimely abends and should guarantee its portability between CICS releases.

In designing a conversation, designate one of the partners always to be the syncpoint initiator and the other the slave. Do not program for one of the partners unilaterally to "decide to" assume the initiator duties because the complexities are significant, resulting in excellent opportunities for abend. The demonstration application mentioned earlier does this and it is a real fright. Tables 10.2 and 10.3 show how intimidating the situation can become.

Put most of the decision-making logic in the front-end transaction. This typically is the one in control of the user's terminal session and has the opportunity to communicate exigencies to the user. This enables a more usable and robust interface with the human user, who expects the computer to be a miraculously faithful servant.

Whereas the LU 6.1 and MRO flavors of DTP consume fewer cycles than LU 6.2, they may prove to be short-sighted investments. They incur the same data integrity logging as SYNCLEVEL(2), whether or not this is appropriate to the application's requirements. LU 6.1 is incompatible with most systems other than CICS and IMS/DC. MRO works only between CICS regions. Eventual labor to upgrade an LU 6.1 or MRO application to LU 6.2 is a distinct possibility. The VTAM path length is susceptible to having money thrown at it. Iron is cheaper than labor. Go for it.

Chapter

11

A Data Integrity Tutorial

Michael Snyder
Kaiser Health Foundation Plan, Inc.

Introduction

Data integrity means different things to different people, depending on their specialty. To an application programmer it means that the users' inputs are rigorously edited. To a database administrator it means that logical relationships among data are faithfully preserved. To a systems programmer it means that enqueues and commits are properly administered. To a production support person it means that backup and recovery are bulletproof.

These interests are illustrative and by no way exhaustive. For the purposes of this discussion, data integrity has the following properties:

- User input is edited for propriety and consistency.
- Business transactions are either applied completely or not at all.
- Users are prevented from inadvertently overlaying each other's updates.

- Program designs specifically address data integrity.
- Error recovery preserves the durability and completeness of business transactions.

The following is a survey of the elements of data integrity. The specifics are in terms of Multiple Virtual Storage (MVS), Customer Information Control System (CICS), Information Management System/Database (IMS/DB), and IBM Database 2 (DB2). The principles, however, are portable and implemented in varying degrees by other system software products. Being a survey, the discussion omits many details. The concepts of data integrity are fairly straightforward; the implementation and execution of the system software aspects in a large shop can be hair-raising indeed. (Things are never as easy as they look.)

To keep the narrative simple, the term *record* includes IMS segments and DB2 rows, and *database* includes DB2 tables.

Propriety and Consistency

The application program and sometimes the database management system (DBMS) are responsible for ensuring that the user cannot enter any data that violates the specifications of the database design. This is the realm of data editing.

There are several types of edit that can be applied to a single data field. The simplest is that it be non-null; it must have something (anything) in it. Next is must-fill; it must have something in it that fills the field to its full length.

Going up the complexity scale just a little, some fields must contain data matching some pattern. For instance, the requirement may be all numerics or a specific pattern of numbers and letters. Another type of single-field editing verifies that the field contains allowable values. For instance, a customer's credit code may be "A," "F," or "L," and nothing else but.

A data item in and of itself may appear valid but, when related to some other item, it may make no sense at all. For example, a birth date of 22Feb1992 is valid, and a medical visit date of 22Jan1991 is also valid, viewed in isolation. But a problem becomes obvious when the two dates are edited in context. A person cannot visit the doctor 13 months before being born. Opportunities for cross-field editing must be thoroughly explored during the design of a database.

IMS offers no help in the foregoing types of edits. DB2 offers a certain level of function, which needs to be judged in the context of the application.

An escalated version of the cross-field edit is referential integrity. The two realms often blend together; a dividing line may be impossible to find. And who cares what the edit is called, as long as it is faithfully done? Referential integrity means that a data item in one database record refers to the identifier of a record existing in the same or another database. A classic example is where a shipping order record contains the customer's identifying number. This number is used to access the customer database to verify that the order refers to an existing customer. The customer number in the order record is called a foreign key.

The customer database may be thought of as master data and the orders as transaction data. Transactions come and go but master data tends to stay. But what happens if a customer record is deleted? Referential integrity demands that the orders file be checked to ensure that there are none outstanding for this customer. If any exist, DB2 offers three alternatives: disallow the delete, nullify the customer number in the orders record, or delete the orders for that customer. No matter how much computer power is consumed in searching the orders file, if the company is serious about its data, the situation must be dealt with. A cheap and useful way to accomodate referential integrity is to redefine the requirement: Mark the customer record as inactive instead of deleting it. The application then must deal with orders pertaining to inactive customers.

With IMS, referential integrity is the responsibility of the application; it must be enforced procedurally. With DB2, the referential constraints can be recorded when the database is defined; DB2 will enforce them. One advantage of DB2 referential integrity is that it should run faster than if the application does it procedurally, since there are fewer calls to DB2.

A major disadvantage is that DB2 can be so rigid in its administration of the rules it has been given that it will not allow the database administrator (DBA) to do *anything* to violate them. For instance, consider a disaster that corrupts both the orders and customer databases in the earlier example. Whether the DBA (and the user) likes it or not, the customers must be recovered first and the orders second. Alternatively, the referential constraints could be dropped, the recovery accomplished, and the constraints defined again. There are scenarios where this can lengthen an outage. Application-implemented referential integrity may make DB2 easier to live with.

Commit and Backout

A prime aspect of data integrity is that of commit and backout. Consider a program that updates a database record and then abends. There is no reason to assume that the update was valid. Further imagine that it normally makes two database updates: a debit and a credit; it abends after posting the debit. The update is absolutely invalid because a debit with no credit throws the ledger out of balance.

Therefore, the rule is that database updates must either transform the data store from one internally consistent state to another consistent state, or be automatically rescinded as if they had never occurred at all. Committing an update makes it irrevocable. This means it is an error to commit the debit and the credit separately.

A program can explicitly request that an update be committed or, more commonly (especially in CICS programs), allow the commit to happen upon normal termination of the program. Closing an IMS program specification block (PSB) also commits the work.

Alternatively, if it has not yet caused commit, a program can request backout of the work it had accomplished up to that point. The updates are reversed by the system software as if they had never happened. The same action would result if the program were to abend before causing a commit.

The scope of commit or backout includes every recoverable resource updated by the task. In CICS this means IMS and DB2 databases, recoverable VSAM files, and recoverable Transient Data destinations. The program has no way to limit the scope to only some of the recoverable resources it has updated but not yet committed. The set of updates committed is called a logical unit of work (LUW).

When a CICS application updates both IMS and DB2 databases, CICS has an interesting job when commit is called for. If IMS Database Control (DBCTL) is not implemented, the IMS part of the commit is straightforward because that code is executing in the CICS address space. Because DB2 runs as its own subsystem, there is a window of exposure in coordinating the commit across the two address spaces. Because the commit is global, what would happen if the DB2 system were to fail? CICS needs a way to know if the DB2 crash was before the commit or after. This information would tell it whether the IMS work should be committed or backed out.

Data integrity across two address spaces is handled by two-phase commit. The sequence of events is as follows. CICS makes a note in its transaction journal that the commit is beginning. It then calls DB2 with the phase-one question, "Ready to commit?" DB2 annotates its journal and responds, "Ready." CICS then orders its local IMS code to commit that work and sends the phase-two commit order to DB2. DB2 responds, "Committed." If either CICS or DB2 crashes during this sequence, the notations (or lack of) in their respective journals will provide the information needed to assure commit or back-out of the LUW after the failed one is brought back up.

On the other hand, if DB2 responds, "Backed out" for some reason in phase one, CICS orders IMS to roll back its updates.

CICS is the coordinator of the LUW and takes the lead in recovering from a crash of itself or DB2. During the two-phase commit, if DB2 fails before responding "Ready," CICS can safely roll back the transaction's updates because the DB2 work was not committed. If DB2 crashes after saying "Ready" and before saying "Committed," CICS regards the LUW to be in doubt, and has to hold that transaction's data integrity locks until DB2 is back on the air. In any case, DB2 will back out its uncommitted updates when it restarts.

CICS also uses two-phase commit in its dealings with IMS DBCTL systems.

The two-phase commit also is supported by IBM's Systems Network Architecture Logical Unit 6.2 (SNA LU 6.2) in that it provides the multiple network flows required to accomplish the two phases. Applications in IBM and non-IBM systems can communicate via LU 6.2, and, if the participating system software supports it, implementation of two-phase commit will assure that related database updates in both computers are either committed or backed out as a unit.

Concurrency and Conflict

When more than one person is updating a database, the complexity goes up several notches; the challenge is to keep them from accidentally overlaying each other's work. For instance, if two people are updating an inventory with shipping and receiving data, there is always the chance that they will concurrently update the same record. If an item's quantity-on-hand is decreased by a shipment and increased by a receipt in an uncontrolled fashion, one transaction will overlay the other and the sum will come out wrong.

In a multiuser situation, integrity demands that attempts to update the same data be serialized through a locking mechanism. IMS and DB2 generally place data integrity locks on control intervals (blocks of data) rather than on individual records.

The concept is enqueuement: the orderly acquisition of temporary ownership of a resource. When a program attempts to read a database record with update intent, the DBMS checks to see if any other task currently holds the control interval containing that record. If so, the current task is made to wait politely in a single-file queue until all prior tasks needing that control interval have committed (or rolled back) their updates in turn. When there is no conflict, the current task becomes the owner of that control interval for the length of time it takes to commit its updates. Inserts and deletes also use this mechanism.

Enqueuement also is applied to reads. Under IMS read with integrity and DB2, any task attempting to read a record is queued if any other task has an update lock on the target control interval. This prevents reading uncommitted updates. Both DBMSs also provide that a program wishing to update a given record is queued if any other task currently is positioned on that control interval for read with integrity under IMS or any read under DB2. Further, a DB2 task using repeatable read places a read lock on every control interval that it touches, not just the one on which it is currently positioned. Repeatable read is discouraged for good reasons; it supports applications that need to browse a lot of records before deciding which ones to update.

IMS provides read without integrity to bypass read locking. The reading program is invisible to the data integrity software. This exposes it to the perils of accessing a database which may be in the process of splitting control intervals, adjusting pointers, taking secondary extents, and the like. IMS provides options to deal with this. A nice one is to retry the read once and return a status code to the application if it fails again.

When configured to support integrity among a mixture of batch and CICS regions, IMS uses Database Recovery Control (DBRC) and the IMS Resource Lock Manager (IRLM) to manage locking. This provides block-level data sharing, where multiple address spaces can read and update databases with full integrity. DB2 uses an IRLM at all times, achieving the same effect. An IRLM runs in its own address space. It accepts access requests from the DBMS and consults a dynamic list of integrity locks to determine if the requested operation can proceed or must wait in a queue.

IRLMs in two mainframes can make IMS databases subject to data sharing across both computers. This brings VTAM into the act, elongating response time. Integrity locks therefore last longer, which can cause the response time effects to ripple through the whole complex.

Abnormal events can cause data integrity locks to last for abnormal amounts of time. Consider a batch program in a data-sharing regime which does not commit its updates as it goes along. Assume that it abends after doing a few thousand; these uncommitted updates must be rolled back. This will take roughly as long as it did to make them in the first place. Meanwhile, all other tasks wishing to access the locked data are made to wait. This can totally disrupt a CICS system that uses that system, because the locks can hurt its response time.

A similar example is a data-sharing CICS region that crashes. Locks held by all its transactions at the time of the problem will persist until CICS comes back up and successfully backs out the incomplete updates. This is a compelling reason never to cold-start CICS, as this could result in a corrupted database.

These provisions apply both to IMS and DB2 databases. Data integrity demands that the locks be maintained, even though dozens of batch jobs and CICS regions might freeze in their tracks as a result. The situation may become unbearably tense; screaming and finger pointing is a traditional outlet activity while waiting for the restart to finish.

Locking can cause two tasks to run totally afoul of each other. Imagine task 1 which enqueues resource A, and task 2 which enqueues resource B. No problem yet. Then task 1 goes after resource B, which is held by task 2. Task 1 is made to wait. Then task 2 tries for resource A, held by task 1. Now each task is waiting on something the other holds and they are truly stuck. This is called a deadly embrace, or, more commonly, a deadlock.

Resolution is effected by the DBMS noting that each task has been in a wait state for some period of time. IMS will abend one of the tasks (whichever will take less time to back out, typically the one with fewer resource locks) and the other task is thus allowed to proceed unmolested. DB2 will roll back one task's updates and give a negative return code rather than an abend, so the application can retry the updates; this is kinder to the user.

If all programs access their databases and records within each database, in the same sequence, deadlock cannot happen.

Pseudo-Conversational Transactions

Most CICS transactions are designed to be pseudo-conversational. This means that each time a program sends a response to its user's terminal, it terminates. Before this, it saves (typically in COMMAREA or Temporary Storage) the data needed to re-establish the conversation with the user on the next transaction. This is called state data. After saving its state and telling CICS which transaction identifier (ID) to invoke upon the next input from that particular terminal, the task disappears. This way, during the user's think-time, the application is not tying up resources (memory, database threads, and integrity locks).

Updating a database usually requires at least two transactions from the user. In the first, the user sends a message identifying the record to be presented for update. The application receives the message, formats and transmits the record, saves its state, and ends. In the second transaction, the user sends a message consisting of updates to the data on the screen. The application receives that message, retrieves its state data, and processes the update.

Even though the user told the application (in the first transaction) which database record to display for further processing, the person has no claim on that record between the time of the first transaction's termination and the second transaction's startup; another user could be updating the record while the first user was looking at it on the terminal.

To enforce data integrity in this situation, when it rereads the record in the second transaction, the program must find out if it was updated by another user during the current user's think-time. If it was, the program might want to redisplay it to its current user and ask if it needs further work now that somebody else has stepped on it.

If a timestamp of last update is stored in the record, the application can save this as state data when it first displays the record to the user. When the person responds, the program compares the saved timestamp to the record's current one after it reads the record again. If the stamp is different, somebody has gotten in and updated it.

Storing an update counter in each record has the same integrity effect as a timestamp. The counter is incremented each time the record is updated, making the problem easy to detect.

If a timestamp or update counter is not stored in the record, the program must save the original record in its state data and compare that to the record's current contents in the second transaction.

Inserts or deletes in the database are a similar issue. While one user is viewing a record, another deletes it or inserts a new one that might affect a decision of the first person.

If it is absolutely necessary to lock data across pseudo-conversational transactions, an application can implement a lock table global to all involved CICS regions. Programs write in this table the keys of the records they wish to hold so others can avoid accessing them. All the programs must participate in order for the scheme to work. The lock table must involve little physical input/output (I/O) if the workload is at all heavy. This suggests a CICS data table, function shipped as necessary to make it global. Because the lock table need not exist between executions of CICS, the user-maintained type is an excellent candidate. Designing a lock table is a complicated exercise. For instance, users' locks must be timestamped and automatically overridden if the person does not respond in perhaps 30 seconds; otherwise there could be serious throughput problems on the database. Data-sharing batch programs, of course, would not participate in this design. To be global to CICS and batch, the lock table would have to be a shared database.

Pseudo-conversational dialogs pose a special problem in commit and backout. Consider an application that has to process several CICS transactions to capture all the data needed for one business transaction. It is usually a mistake to update the database during this dialog. To recover from an abend partway through the process, one might imagine that the work of the several foregoing transactions will need backout, rather than simply that of the one which failed. Yet backout cannot automatically be applied to work done in a prior transaction.

To make a business event span several pseudo-conversational transactions, the application must store the work-in-process data record(s) in its state data during the interactions needed to compose a complete update. When the user does the final one, the application must assure itself that no other person was updating the same or a related record, then apply the entire update.

The moral here is that only the last of a multitransaction series should be doing any database updates. With all these worries, it seems a miracle that pseudo-conversational programming ever made the big time, but it has been perforce the method of choice during the 25 years CICS has been around!

Multiple Update PSBs

The following is an example of a situation to avoid. If a program uses more than one update PSB, a data integrity exposure is assured. This is because only one PSB can be active at a time, and because a PSB's work will be committed when it is closed. Therefore, the task is committing multiple units of work, only one of which can be backed out if there is an abend.

An equally bad situation is that some CICS application designs require that a program issue an asynchronous START of a transaction (typically in a different CICS region) to complete a business event. The problem is that CICS cannot relate the two transactions to each other. If both the STARTing and the STARTed ones do database updates, there is an integrity exposure, because one of them might abend after the START is issued. One will have its work backed out and the other committed.

To avoid this problem, the first transaction must refrain from updating databases and instead send data for the record(s) to be updated to the second one. This way all the updates will be committed by a single task.

Common Work Area (CWA)

The CICS CWA is not usually a hot item in data integrity deliberations but it does present at least one opportunity for trouble. Relying on a CWA variable to remain unchanged during the duration of a task can be a mistake. For instance, a program sees the value "A" in a certain CWA field and makes a decision based on that. Then it issues a CICS command that causes the dispatcher to run a different task while the current one waits. When the current one resumes, the CWA field may now have some value other than "A" in it. To a given task, stability of the CWA is guaranteed only between CICS commands.

Journaling and Recovery

IMS and DB2 protect databases from disaster by journaling (logging) a before and after image of each record updated. The journals are used for error recovery in conjunction with a backup copy of the database. The backups are preferably the so-called image copies.

For instance, if a disk drive crashes, the most recent image copy of the database is restored to some other disk. Then the journal's after images of updated records are applied to the restored database to bring it up to the instant of failure. At the end of the journal there remains the problem of transactions that were in flight, updating the database at the moment of failure. Because they were unable to complete, their uncommitted updates must be backed out. The DBMS now reads the log backward and applies the before images of only these incomplete updates. The recovery is complete.

The frequency with which image copies are made has an obvious effect on the amount of journal data that must be applied to recover a database.

In IMS without DBCTL, every batch job and CICS region creates a separate journal. To recover, these must be collated according to the timestamps contained in them. The events in a single log are in ascending timestamp order because they were recorded in real time. The events in multiple journals must be merged into a single journal in timestamp sequence. This is the job of the change accumulation utility. It accepts multiple IMS logs created by batch and CICS address spaces and resolves them into a single one for recovery purposes.

Because IMS DBCTL and DB2 run as individual subsystems, each creates a single set of logs that does not need collating. The logs from these two subsystems, however, are not coordinated with each other.

Integrity management used to be a highly manual (error-prone) process before IMS DBRC and DB2 came along. For instance, when a database is reorganized, its previous image copy is no longer valid; a new one must be made before any update jobs run. If a batch update abends, leaving the database wanting backout, somebody has to ensure that this is done before running any more jobs against that database. If a database needs recovery, the pertinent backup and journals have to be identified and fed into the process.

DBRC and DB2 have equivalent functions to automate the solution to most of these problems. They use control files to make notes of databases that are in need of image copy or backout and to record the identities of journal tapes, among other things. DBRC implements the Recovery Control (RECON) dataset for this purpose; DB2 uses the Bootstrap Dataset (BSDS). They keep records regarding which databases' updates are present in the various journals. They automatically generate Job Control Language (JCL) to run a recovery job, applying the correct image copy and proper sequence of logs.

This control data is so crucial that it tends to exist in multiple copies on disks attached to separate I/O paths. For the same reason, some shops make duplicate image copies just in case a singleton turns out to be unusable. Likewise, some create dual logs. IMS and DB2 provide for the proper registration of the extra copies if the database administrator plays by all the rules.

Both DBMSs also provide for the retention of prior generations of image copies and journals. If the current image copy is unusable, the system will automatically look for the previous copy and all logs created since that one.

Logging to disk rather than tape adds interest to the DBRC area. If a CICS disk journal is archived to tape and DBRC not notified of this, it will be unable to perform a valid recovery.

This high level of automation makes it realistic to do all the tape tracking requisite to incremental image copy and image copy during update.

The former, a feature of DB2, backs up only those control intervals that have changed since the last backup. Recovery, of course, must be anchored to a full image copy. The incrementals are applied to the last full one, then the most recent log is used to complete the recovery.

IMS DBCTL and DB2 systems can take an image copy while the database is being updated by applications. This is called an on-line image copy. This copy plus the journal can reconstruct the data.

To this point the discussion has addressed only recovery up to the latest committed LUW. What about a rogue program that corrupts the database without abending? All its nasty work has been committed irrevocably; well, almost.

The drill is to fall back to the last full image copy, then forward recover to the point just before the program began execution. With IMS, this is done to the last log-ending timestamp before the rogue. DB2 views its logs as a single river of data anchored off the last image copy. The data is addressed by relative byte address (RBA) from beginning to end. Recovery is to the RBA of the first log record of the faulty program. In either case, all following updates from all sources are lost.

Point of Consistency

Think of a case where an application does referential integrity by verifying a foreign key in an IMS database with data from DB2, or vice versa, or imagine an application whose business event requires updating both IMS and DB2 databases. Then ponder the heartache of having either of the databases break. The IMS and DB2 journals are not integrated with each other. How to effect recovery? Related databases backed up by online image copy have the same problem.

The superficial answer is that the affected databases are restored to the last image copy and then forward recovered from the journals. The fact that there are relationships among multiple databases with separate integrity managements requires that the image copies be created during a period when all those databases are disabled for update. This is the only way to ensure that they are in a mutually consistent state when making the copies. It can take a long time and cause anguish in those who need high database availability. Data integrity demands that when IMS and DB2 databases are related and both updated, cutting these two subsystems off at a mutual commit point must be done on a regular schedule.

The alternative is corrupted or lost data when one of them takes a hit. It may be feasible to write a custom program to process the logs in order to resynchronize the databases, but it is a very risky business.

Data Conduits

Transferring data from the batch world to a running CICS system (or vice versa) is a promising area for data integrity offense.

Extrapartition Transient Data is an old technology deserving of neglect because it is not recoverable. VSAM entry-sequenced datasets are only a little better, but are not recoverable. Key-sequenced datasets, which are updated during the transfer, expose the reading task to the problems of splits, secondary extents, and the index not matching the data during some inserts and deletes.

A CICS journal can be used for output, but its data format is not simple to deal with.

The best way to maintain integrity in conduits between CICS and batch is to use a DB2 table or shared IMS database.

Conclusion

Data integrity is one long and twisty road. Understanding and cooperation among the many data processing disciplines can keep the data out of the ditch. Corrupted data annoys the customers and may cause them to shop elsewhere. In a hospital setting, the worst case is appalling to contemplate.

The principles are clear and airtight. Application development, being the most creative specialty, owns the widest opportunity for error. Implementing these principles conscientiously and thoroughly is the way for all parties to "keep to our knitting."

Chapter

12

Application Design for CICS/ESA Transaction Performance

James Peterson
Landmark Systems Corporation

The Problem

In the typical data processing department, a near total separation of goals exists between the application developers and the data center support staff. The application developer has the task of producing a program that accomplishes the desired result for the end user. The data center support staff is responsible for keeping Customer Information Control System (CICS) transaction response times within acceptable levels. Consequently, application design generally follows the end user's description of what he or she wants, and does not consider performance characteristics of the application programs during design phase.

Meanwhile, the data center personnel are busy reorganizaing tables in CICS, changing auxiliary storage definitions, altering transaction priorities, assigning transaction classes, setting operating system priorities, allocating real memory, creating separate application CICS regions, cacheing DASD, and buying more hardware. Such a CICS environment will frequently be characterized by relatively large variations in end-user response time, especially after the installation of new applications, during periods of heavy transaction activity, and at times without any outward indications of exactly why.

CICS transaction performance can suffer from the basic differences between the goals of the two data processing departments:

- Application development's goal is to produce code that meets the end users' requirements in a timely fashion, while
- Data center support's goal is to provide adequate resources for the end users' needs.

Because the data center staff has the primary responsibility for computer service levels, performance issues are generally addressed without the benefit of addressing the application code itself until most other resources are exhausted.

Granted, any application can probably be made to perform satisfactorily from a response time point of view by purchasing more and faster hardware and software for its operation. The decision to spend money, made at a business level, to achieve business goals is justifiable, but are we driven to make such decisions more often than we need? Can we adjust our approach to application design to conform to current data center resources and configuration? Performance-minded application design and development are required.

Let us go back to the data center technicians making changes to CICS to achieve response time goals. These technicians are almost assuredly using some form of performance and utilization measurement tool. The data center personnel have reviewed and evaluated the data from CICS system measurements. They have determined which application data sets to cache and which CICS regions need increased storage working set sizes. They have modified SRM parameters to distribute the processor resource effectively to the applications required. Why shouldn't the application developers benefit from effective performance measurements for the programs they write? Why shouldn't they be able to work toward a *homogeneous* program performance profile?

All CICS application code executes in the CICS region under one TCB or system task. Each transaction is given control by the CICS task dispatcher in turn and is expected by CICS to voluntarily return control to the CICS task dispatcher, probably via a resource request.

The resources requested may be:

- Input/output (I/O) resources such as transient data, temporary storage, VSAM files, database files, or journals
- External application resources such as interregion or intersystem communicated transactions, function shipped resource requests to another application region, or distributed processing transaction structures
- Internal application resources such as file strings, LSR buffers, database threads, record enqueues, or application-defined enqueues

Most of these resources can be tuned in some way without directly modifying the application. It is the responsibility of the data center staff to control CICS resources at a general level.

Whatever the reason the task originally began to wait, each transaction ultimately waits for its fellow application task to release control of the CICS application TCB, and, finally, for the CICS task dispatcher to give it control. This form of contention between CICS applications for the CICS application TCB cannot be tuned without addressing the applications involved.

An Approach

Let us discuss for a moment how CICS programs interact in CICS and how they become a source of resource contention to each other. In CICS, only one application task's program is active (dispatched) in the CICS region. All other tasks' application programs are waiting for CICS service module processing or for their turn to become the dispatched application task.

In a typical CICS test environment, a programmer has a nearly dedicated CICS region while he is verifying the execution of his new transaction. Even if multiple developers are using the same CICS region for testing it is unlikely that more than one, perhaps two, transactions will be concurrently active at any given time. In such an environment, even in a low-priority CICS region, all but the most resource-intensive transactions perform adequately. However, when some of these transactions are introduced into the production environment, they may perform erratically themselves or cause existing transactions to suddenly experience larger variances in response time. Can these changes be anticipated? Can program development time processing characteristics be defined that minimize these effects?

During development, each program accesses resources as required. This results in varying patterns of execution time to prepare for access to resources that may require a wait. CICS, as an application task dispatcher, depends on each application program to voluntarily give up control to the task dispatcher. Thus, the ability of one or more CICS tranactions to interleave their processing depends to a large degree on the original programming techniques used.

We know that our application code can dramatically affect both the application's own transaction and other transactions currently executing. But what do we measure? How do we evaluate a particular transaction or transaction's programs for performance? That effort begins with the data currently available in CICS transaction monitors. Regardless of vendor, we can generally tell how long a transaction was dispatched by CICS, how many times it was dispatched to accumulate this total, and the total wait time absorbed between the dispatches. Simple division results in an averagae time per dispatch and per wait for the transaction or group of transactions.

A serious problem can be easily hidden by an average calculation of dispatch timings. The smoothing of extreme values into the average will prevent us from identifying the transactions and programs which contribute to the problem.

Consider a program that executes in 50 discrete dispatch intervals totaling 2 seconds. A computed average dispatch time for this transaction would be .04 seconds. Let us assume that the distribution of dispatch time in the intervals is not uniform. In fact, let us assume that the largest dispatch intervals are 1 second in length and the shortest intervals are .01 seconds in length. We may now have a situation where 98 percent of the dispatches for this program average .02 seconds. Occasionally, under the conditions necessary to reach the particular routine, one dispatch interval in this program expands not only its own response times but *all concurrently executing transactions' response times* by a full second.

Keep in mind that we are talking about a single program in a CICS transaction and that the specific program involved is not available from the CICS monitor data. Several vendors may have a solution to this problem. Some of the sample analyses in this chapter are produced by a vendor product. However, we will use CICS AUX trace data to build an evaluation of task control and program control trace records. By processing data from the task control trace records we can determine the dispatch and wait time for each period of dispatch for a transaction.

Figure 12.1 is an example of an AUX trace listing from CICS. Only one page is displayed. The data represents .15 seconds of transaction activity. Although the data is extremely

```
1CICS/ESA  -  AUXILIARY TRACE FROM 08/05/92                                                                                PAGE 000002

AP 0501 APDS EXIT - FUNCTION(TASK_REPLY) RESPONSE(OK)

            TASK-AP    KE_NUM-000D TCB-007EB8E8 RET-84B0B67E TIME-18:04:35.3090718166 INTERVAL-00.0000146875    =000149=
              1-0000  00500000 00000003 00000001 00000000  A6000400 00000000 02000100 00000000  *.&..............w...............*
                0020  00000000 04C937B0 01090010 00000048  00000000 00000000 00000000 00000000  *.....I..........................*
                0040  00000000 00000000 0101000F 00000000                                         *................
*

DS 0013 DSKE  EXIT - FUNCTION(TASK_REPLY) RESPONSE(OK)

            TASK-AP    KE_NUM-000D TCB-007EB8E8 RET-84B01AE2 TIME-18:04:35.3090915041 INTERVAL-00.0000196875    =000150=
              1-0000  00480000 00000001 00000000 00000000  B8800000 00000000 02000100 04B81C70  *................................*
                0020  00000000 00000000 00000000 05F61698  00000000 00000000 00000000 00000000  *.............6.q................*
                0040  00000000 00000000                                                           *........
*

DS 0012 DSKE  ENTRY - FUNCTION(TASK_REPLY) TASK_TOKEN(04B81C70) ATTACH_TOKEN(05F61698)

            TASK-AP    KE_NUM-000D TCB-007EB8E8 RET-84B01AE2 TIME-18:04:37.8271976291 INTERVAL-00.0000555625    =000201=
              1-0000  00480000 00000001 00000000 00000000  B8800000 00000000 02000000 04B81C70  *................................*
                0020  00000000 00000000 00000000 05F61698  00000000 00000000 00000000 00000000  *.............6.q................*
                0040  00000000 00000000                                                           *........
*

AP 0500 APDS ENTRY - FUNCTION(TASK_REPLY) USER_TOKEN(04C937B0) TASK_TOKEN(01090011) SUSPEND_TOKEN(01010010)

            TASK-AP    KE_NUM-000D TCB-007EB8E8 RET-84B0B67E TIME-18:04:37.8272170041 INTERVAL-00.0000193750    =000202=
              1-0000  00500000 00000003 00000001 00000000  A6000400 00000000 02000100 00000000  *.&..............w...............*
                0020  00000000 04C937B0 01090011 00000048  00000000 00000000 00000000 00000000  *.....I..........................*
                0040  00000000 00000000 01010010 00000000                                         *................
*

SM 0B01 SMMC1 ENTRY - FUNCTION(GETMAIN_TCA) GET_LENGTH(5F8) TRANSACTION_NUMBER(2A) SUSPEND(YES) TCA_LOCATION(BELOW) TASK_DATA_KEY
                (USER) TWA_SIZE(0) LE_THREAD_SIZE(3C0)

            TASK-AP    KE_NUM-000D TCB-007EB8E8 RET-85C86160 TIME-18:04:37.8272480666 INTERVAL-00.0000310625    =000203=
              1-0000  00480000 00000011 00000000 00000000  B6C66000 00000000 03B90120 C4C6C8C5  *.................F-.........DFHE*
                0020  D4E3D740 05009600 000005F8 00000050  0000002A 0100060C 0111A264 00000000  *MTP ..o....8...&..........s.....*
                0040  000003C0 00000001                                                           *........
*

SM 0B02 SMMC1 EXIT  - FUNCTION(GETMAIN_TCA) RESPONSE(OK) ADDRESS(00069600)

            TASK-AP    KE_NUM-000D TCB-007EB8E8 RET-85C86160 TIME-18:04:37.8274397541 INTERVAL-00.0001916875    =000204=
```

Figure 12.1 AUX trace listing.

detailed, only a few events are required for effectvie analysis of program performance.

The first trace example was printed from a full AUX trace using the following trace print input parameters:

```
TASKID=(AP,00043)
```

The trace sample in Figure 12.1 illustrates the volume of detail information available from the trace. Fortunately, a significant degree of selectivity is available using the trace program. The next example of trace data (Figure 12.2) is for the same transaction, but here we are selecting only the trace events likely to be significant to the application's performance, which is either executing or waiting to execute, and identifying the application request resulting in the performance events. These events would be identified by EIP traces and ERM calls.

The following trace input parameters were used to create the listing in Figure 12.2.

```
TASKID=(AP,00044)
TYPETR=(DS0002-0005,DS0012-0013,AP00E1,AP00E7)
ABBREV
```

Unfortunately, the abbreviated trace sacrifices the time event and interval between events which are essential to our analysis process.

The key trace fields needed for a program performance analysis are:

TIME is the time of day of the event.
INTERVAL computes deltas between events.
FUNCTION determines the action required for this event.
DM and TRNM identify the domain and trace number of the event.

Sample CICS AUX Trace

The sample listing has been selectively printed to remove all *extraneous* trace calls. Unnecessary columns have also been removed from the trace. The selected events now represent a 3.40-second time period and contain representative dispatch

```
AP    1 DS 0013 DSKE  EXIT  TASK_REPLY/OK                                                                            =000150=
AP    1 DS 0012 DSKE  ENTRY TASK_REPLY               04B81C70,05F61698                                               =000201=
AP    1 DS 0013 DSKE  EXIT  TASK_REPLY/OK                                                                            =000364=
AP    1 DS 0012 DSKE  ENTRY TASK_REPLY               04B81C70,05F61698                                               =000398=
AP    1 DS 0013 DSKE  EXIT  TASK_REPLY/OK                                                                            =000780=
AP    1 DS 0012 DSKE  ENTRY TASK_REPLY               04B81C70,05F61698                                               =000806=
00044 1 AP 00E7 ERM   ENTRY TASK-CONTROL             ........           0304,A61958BA w...,2FDEA911 ..z.,........ =000817=
00044 1 AP 00E7 ERM   EVENT PASSING-CONTROL-TO-RM TX3TRUE               4004,A61958BA w...,2FDEA911 ..z.,TX3TRUE  =000820=
00044 1 AP 00E1 EIP   ENTRY INQUIRE-TERMINAL                            0004,05453018 ....,08005202 ....          =000825=
00044 1 AP 00E1 EIP   EXIT  INQUIRE-TERMINAL         OK                 00F4,00000000 ....,00005202 ....          =000840=
00044 1 AP 00E7 ERM   EVENT REGAINING-CONTROL-FROM-RM TX3TRUE           4104,A61958BA w...,2FDEA911 ..z.,TX3TRUE  =000843=
00044 1 AP 00E7 ERM   EXIT  TASK-CONTROL             ........           1304,A61958BA w...,2FDEA911 ..z.,........ =000844=
00044 1 AP 00E1 EIP   ENTRY RECEIVE-MAP                                 0004,00140528 ....,08001802 ....          =000856=
00044 1 AP 00E1 EIP   EXIT  RECEIVE-MAP              MAPFAIL            00F4,00000000 ....,00241802 ....          =000877=
00044 1 AP 00E1 EIP   ENTRY STARTBR                                     0004,00140528 ....,0800060C ....          =000880=
00044 1 DS 0002 DSAT  ENTRY CHANGE_MODE               CO,YES                                                         =000884=
00044 1 DS 0003 DSAT  EXIT  CHANGE_MODE/OK            QR                                                             =000885=
00044 1 DS 0002 DSAT  ENTRY CHANGE_MODE               QR                                                             =000886=
00044 1 DS 0003 DSAT  EXIT  CHANGE_MODE/OK            QR                                                             =000887=
00044 1 AP 00E1 EIP   EXIT  STARTBR                  OK                 00F4,00000000 ....,0000060C ....          =000891=
00044 1 AP 00E1 EIP   ENTRY READNEXT                                    0004,00140528 ....,0800060E ....          =000894=
00044 1 AP 00E1 EIP   EXIT  READNEXT                 OK                 00F4,00000000 ....,0000060E ....          =000899=
00044 1 AP 00E1 EIP   ENTRY READNEXT                                    0004,00140528 ....,0800060E ....          =000902=
00044 1 AP 00E1 EIP   EXIT  READNEXT                 OK                 00F4,00000000 ....,0000060E ....          =000907=
00044 1 AP 00E1 EIP   ENTRY READNEXT                                    0004,00140528 ....,0800060E ....          =000910=
00044 1 AP 00E1 EIP   EXIT  READNEXT                 OK                 00F4,00000000 ....,0000060E ....          =000915=
00044 1 AP 00E1 EIP   ENTRY READNEXT                                    0004,00140528 ....,0800060E ....          =000918=
00044 1 AP 00E1 EIP   EXIT  READNEXT                 OK                 00F4,00000000 ....,0000060E ....          =000923=
00044 1 AP 00E1 EIP   ENTRY READNEXT                                    0004,00140528 ....,0800060E ....          =000926=
00044 1 AP 00E1 EIP   EXIT  READNEXT                 OK                 00F4,00000000 ....,0000060E ....          =000931=
00044 1 AP 00E1 EIP   ENTRY SEND-MAP                                    0004,00140528 ....,08001804 ....          =000934=
00044 1 AP 00E1 EIP   EXIT  SEND-MAP                 OK                 00F4,00000000 ....,00001804 ....          =000948=
00044 1 AP 00E1 EIP   ENTRY RETURN                                      0004,00140528 ....,08000E08 ....          =000951=
00044 1 AP 00E7 ERM   ENTRY TASK-CONTROL             ........           0304,A61958BA w...,2FDEA911 ..z.,........ =000992=
00044 1 AP 00E7 ERM   EVENT PASSING-CONTROL-TO-RM TX3TRUE               4004,A61958BA w...,2FDEA911 ..z.,TX3TRUE  =000993=
00044 1 AP 00E7 ERM   EVENT REGAINING-CONTROL-FROM-RM TX3TRUE           4104,A61958BA w...,2FDEA911 ..z.,TX3TRUE  =000998=
00044 1 AP 00E7 ERM   EXIT  TASK-CONTROL             ........           1304,A61958BA w...,2FDEA911 ..z.,........ =001001=
AP    1 DS 0013 DSKE  EXIT  TASK_REPLY/OK                                                                            =001009=
AP    1 DS 0012 DSKE  ENTRY TASK_REPLY               04B81C70,05F61698                                               =001033=
AP    1 DS 0013 DSKE  EXIT  TASK_REPLY/OK                                                                            =001236=
AP    1 DS 0012 DSKE  ENTRY TASK_REPLY               04B81C70,05F61698                                               =001262=
AP    1 DS 0013 DSKE  EXIT  TASK_REPLY/OK                                                                            =001411=
AP    1 DS 0012 DSKE  ENTRY TASK_REPLY               04B81C70,05F61698                                               =001466=
```

Figure 12.2 AUX trace listing.

and wait events from task creation through initial display and termination for input for the ABRW sample transaction (Figure 12.3).

The DS domain traces are used to evaluate periods of processing and the state of the task. The following processing is required for each TRNM.

The traces from the DS domain of greatest interest are:

- The DS0012/DS0013 pair, which signal task start and end, respectively
- The DS0002/DS0003 pair, which signal a change of MODE (TCB affinity) or priority (wait) and subsequent completion (dispatch); these pairs are identified by the FUNCTION-(CHANGE_MODE) and FUNCTION(CHANGE_PRIORITY)
- The DS0004/DS0005 pair, which signal wait for and resources (ECBs) and subsequent dispatch
- 0004 trace entries

  Collect initial TIME for start of task WAIT. Resolve dispatch time for previous 0012 or 0005 04 0003.

```
DS 0012 DSKE  ENTRY - FUNCTION(TASK_REPLY) TASK_TOKEN(04B81C70) ATTACH_TOKEN(05F61698)
              TASK-AP    KE_NUM-000D TCB-007EB8E8 RET-84B01AE2 TIME-18:04:42.9490270666 INTERVAL-00.0000558750   =000398=

DS 0002 DSAT  ENTRY - FUNCTION(CHANGE_MODE) MODE(RO)
              TASK-00043 KE_NUM-000D TCB-007EB8E8 RET-84B10F72 TIME-18:04:42.9575901916 INTERVAL-00.0001150000   =000441=

DS 0003 DSAT  EXIT - FUNCTION(CHANGE_MODE) RESPONSE(OK) OLD_MODE(QR)
              TASK-00043 KE_NUM-000D TCB-007EBB80 RET-84B10F72 TIME-18:04:42.9586318166 INTERVAL-00.0008301250   =000444=

DS 0002 DSAT  ENTRY - FUNCTION(CHANGE_MODE) MODE(QR)
              TASK-00043 KE_NUM-000D TCB-007EBB80 RET-84B1070E TIME-18:04:43.1161466916 INTERVAL-00.0016608125   =000451=

DS 0003 DSAT  EXIT - FUNCTION(CHANGE_MODE) RESPONSE(OK) OLD_MODE(RO)
              TASK-00043 KE_NUM-000D TCB-007EB8E8 RET-84B1070E TIME-18:04:43.1194521916 INTERVAL-00.0001283125   =000454=

AP 00E1 EIP ENTRY RECEIVE-MAP                       REQ(0004) FIELD-A(00140508 ....) FIELD-B(08001802 ....)
              TASK-00043 KE_NUM-000D TCB-007EB8E8 RET-50141492 TIME-18:04:43.1197411916 INTERVAL-00.0000164375   =000462=

AP 00E1 EIP EXIT RECEIVE-MAP OK                     REQ(00F4) FIELD-A(00000000 ....) FIELD-B(00001802 ....)
              TASK-00043 KE_NUM-000D TCB-007EB8E8 RET-50141492 TIME-18:04:43.1207986291 INTERVAL-00.0000148750   =000483=

AP 00E1 EIP ENTRY STARTBR                           REQ(0004) FIELD-A(00140508 ....) FIELD-B(0800060C ....)
              TASK-00043 KE_NUM-000D TCB-007EB8E8 RET-50141528 TIME-18:04:43.1208886291 INTERVAL-00.0000146250   =000486=

DS 0004 DSSR  ENTRY - FUNCTION(WAIT_OLDW) RESOURCE_NAME(SINGLE) RESOURCE_TYPE(KCCOMPAT) ECB_ADDRESS(0005B734) PURGEABLE(NO)
              TASK-00043 KE_NUM-000D TCB-007EB8E8 RET-85C81EBC TIME-18:04:43.1243209416 INTERVAL-00.0001355000   =000504=

DS 0005 DSSR  EXIT - FUNCTION(WAIT_OLDW) RESPONSE(OK)
              TASK-00043 KE_NUM-000D TCB-007EB8E8 RET-85C81EBC TIME-18:04:43.1270678791 INTERVAL-00.0027469375   =000505=

DS 0004 DSSR  ENTRY - FUNCTION(WAIT_MVS) RESOURCE_NAME(ASYNRESP) RESOURCE_TYPE(CCVSAMWT) ECB_ADDRESS(05F7E5C4) PURGEABLE(NO)
              TASK-00043 KE_NUM-000D TCB-007EB8E8 RET-84B31E82 TIME-18:04:43.1276519416 INTERVAL-00.0004779375   =000510=

DS 0005 DSSR  EXIT - FUNCTION(WAIT_MVS) RESPONSE(OK)
              TASK-00043 KE_NUM-000D TCB-007EB8E8 RET-84B31E82 TIME-18:04:43.1842356916 INTERVAL-00.0565837500*  =000511=
       .
       .
       .
DS 0004 DSSR  ENTRY - FUNCTION(WAIT_MVS) RESOURCE_NAME(ASYNRESP) RESOURCE_TYPE(CCVSAMWT) ECB_ADDRESS(05F7E5C4) PURGEABLE(NO)
              TASK-00043 KE_NUM-000D TCB-007EB8E8 RET-84B31E82 TIME-18:04:46.2647155666 INTERVAL-00.0015480625   =000624=

DS 0005 DSSR  EXIT - FUNCTION(WAIT_MVS) RESPONSE(OK)
              TASK-00043 KE_NUM-000D TCB-007EB8E8 RET-84B31E82 TIME-18:04:46.2798250041 INTERVAL-00.0151094375*  =000625=

DS 0002 DSAT  ENTRY - FUNCTION(CHANGE MODE) MODE(CO) CONDITIONAL(YES)

              TASK-00043 KE_NUM-000D TCB-007EB8E8 RET-85D9AF16 TIME-18:04:46.2965438166 INTERVAL-00.0001285625   =000638=

DS 0003 DSAT  EXIT - FUNCTION(CHANGE_MODE) RESPONSE(OK) OLD_MODE(QR)
              TASK-00043 KE_NUM-000D TCB-007EB8E8 RET-85D9AF16 TIME-18:04:46.2979494416 INTERVAL-00.0014056250   =000639=

DS 0004 DSSR  ENTRY - FUNCTION(WAIT_MVS) RESOURCE_NAME(FILEA) RESOURCE_TYPE(FCIOWAIT) ECB_ADDRESS(04CBA520) PURGEABLE(NO)
              TASK-00043 KE_NUM-000D TCB-007EB8E8 RET-85D9B0AA TIME-18:04:46.2984004416 INTERVAL-00.0004510000   =000640=

DS 0005 DSSR  EXIT - FUNCTION(WAIT_MVS) RESPONSE(OK)
              TASK-00043 KE_NUM-000D TCB-007EB8E8 RET-85D9B0AA TIME-18:04:46.2999091916 INTERVAL-00.0013567500   =000643=

DS 0004 DSSR  ENTRY - FUNCTION(WAIT_MVS) RESOURCE_NAME(FILEA) RESOURCE_TYPE(FCIOWAIT) ECB_ADDRESS(04CBA520) PURGEABLE(NO)
              TASK-00043 KE_NUM-000D TCB-007EB8E8 RET-85D9B0AA TIME-18:04:46.3003291916 INTERVAL-00.0004200000   =000644=
DS 0002 DSAT  ENTRY - FUNCTION(CHANGE_MODE) MODE(QR)
              TASK-00043 KE_NUM-000D TCB-007EB8E8 RET-85D9AF16 TIME-18:04:46.3162604416 INTERVAL-00.0001420625   =000646=
DS 0003 DSAT  EXIT - FUNCTION(CHANGE_MODE) RESPONSE(OK) OLD_MODE(QR)
              TASK-00043 KE_NUM-000D TCB-007EB8E8 RET-85D9AF16 TIME-18:04:46.3163262541 INTERVAL-00.0000658125   =000647=

AP 00E1 EIP EXIT STARTBR OK                         REQ(00F4) FIELD-A(00000000 ....) FIELD-B(0000060C ....)
              TASK-00043 KE_NUM-000D TCB-007EB8E8 RET-50141528 TIME-18:04:46.3164914416 INTERVAL-00.0000151875   =000651=

AP 00E1 EIP ENTRY READNEXT                          REQ(0004) FIELD-A(00140508 ....) FIELD-B(0800060E ....)
              TASK-00043 KE_NUM-000D TCB-007EB8E8 RET-5014188C TIME-18:04:46.3165915666 INTERVAL-00.0000146875   =000654=

AP 00E1 EIP EXIT READNEXT OK                        REQ(00F4) FIELD-A(00000000 ....) FIELD-B(0000060E ....)
              TASK-00043 KE_NUM-000D TCB-007EB8E8 RET-5014188C TIME-18:04:46.3167918791 INTERVAL-00.0000142500   =000659=
              .
              .
              .
              .
AP 00E1 EIP ENTRY SEND-MAP                          REQ(0004) FIELD-A(00140508 ....) FIELD-B(08001804 ....)
              TASK-00043 KE_NUM-000D TCB-007EB8E8 RET-5014162E TIME-18:04:46.3175770666 INTERVAL-00.0000146875   =000686=

DS 0002 DSAT  ENTRY - FUNCTION(CHANGE_MODE) MODE(RO)
              TASK-00043 KE_NUM-000D TCB-007EB8E8 RET-84B10F72 TIME-18:04:46.3552843791 INTERVAL-00.0001196875   =000696=

DS 0003 DSAT  EXIT - FUNCTION(CHANGE_MODE) RESPONSE(OK) OLD_MODE(QR)
              TASK-00043 KE_NUM-000D TCB-007EBB80 RET-84B10F72 TIME-18:04:46.3555570041 INTERVAL-00.0002726250   =000697=

DS 0002 DSAT  ENTRY - FUNCTION(CHANGE_MODE) MODE(QR)
              TASK-00043 KE_NUM-000D TCB-007EBB80 RET-84B1070E TIME-18:04:46.5116658166 INTERVAL-00.0004512500   =000704=

DS 0003 DSAT  EXIT - FUNCTION(CHANGE_MODE) RESPONSE(OK) OLD_MODE(RO)
              TASK-00043 KE_NUM-000D TCB-007EB8E8 RET-84B1070E TIME-18:04:46.5119414416 INTERVAL-00.0002756250   =000705=

AP 00E1 EIP EXIT SEND-MAP OK                        REQ(00F4) FIELD-A(00000000 ....) FIELD-B(00001804 ....)
              TASK-00043 KE_NUM-000D TCB-007EB8E8 RET-5014162E TIME-18:04:46.5125375041 INTERVAL-00.0000153750   =000720=

AP 00E1 EIP ENTRY RETURN                            REQ(0004) FIELD-A(00140508 ....) FIELD-B(08000E08 ....)
              TASK-00043 KE_NUM-000D TCB-007EB8E8 RET-50141664 TIME-18:04:46.5126268166 INTERVAL-00.0000148125   =000723=

DS 0013 DSKE  EXIT - FUNCTION(TASK_REPLY) RESPONSE(OK)
              TASK-AP    KE_NUM-000D TCB 007EB8E8 RET-84B01AE2 TIME-18:04:46.5411931291 INTERVAL-00.0000315625   =000780=
```

Figure 12.3 Sample CICS AUX Trace

- 0005 trace entries

  Resolve WAIT time as the current TIME minus the time stored by the preceding 0004 trace entry. Start dispatch time by storing TIME as time of dispatch.

- 0002 trace entries

  Start the WAIT time by storing the time of the event. Resolve dispatch time by subtracting stored start of dispatch from current TIME.

  FUNCTION(CHANGE_MODE) implies redispatching the task on a different TCB; FUNCTION(CHANGE_PRIORITY) redispatches the task on the same TCB.

- 0003 trace entries

  Resolve the WAIT time from the previous DS0002. Start dispatch time by storing the current TIME as start of dispatch time.

- 0012 trace entries

  Start of execution for a task. KE_NUM should be used to identify traces for the same task. This trace provides the first indication of a new transaction to CICS. Store current TIME as start of dispatch.

- 0013 trace entries

  End execution time for the task. This is the last trace event for a task in CICS. Resolve dispatch time by subtracting current TIME from the stored start of dispatch.

AP events

- 00E1

  Pairs of EIP request traces indicate the times of events transitioning to and from the application program. The time from EIP ENTRY can be viewed as the SERVICE TIME for the command; the time between EIP EXIT and the next EIP ENTRY is the APPLICATION time.

Some other AP pairs of interest are 00E7, the ERM traces, and 00F8, the DLI traces.

By processing the program control events that are present in the AUX trace data at the same time, we can determine which of a transaction's programs is producing the respective dispatch intervals.

Program-Level Statistics Dump

Figure 12.4 is a sample of the detail data extracted from the trace events. The report illustrates the value of this analysis technique. One dispatch interval of the program TSTPROG1 was observed to be 270 milliseconds. The remaining dispatch intervals are less than 1 millisecond. The example is an extract of the detail data used to produce the summary reports later in this chapter.

The Application

All transactions have a base transaction reponse time for each unique function the transaction performs. The base transaction response time, in its simplest terms, is *when the transaction is isolated from all other transaction interference.* In this case, response time is:

(Dispatch Time + Wait Time)

Since most transactions will wait more than once during their execution, a transaction's response time becomes:

No. of Dispatches * (Mean Dispatch Interval + Mean Wait Interval)

TRAN ID	PROGRAM NAME	DATE	TIME HH:MM:SS.SSS	TASK NO	DISPATCH TIME	WAIT TIME
TST1	TSTPROG1	21 JUL 1988	11:09:45.071	0000103	0.0003	0.0163
TST1	TSTPROG1	21 JUL 1988	11:09:45.089	0000103	0.0004	0.0172
TST1	TSTPROG1	21 JUL 1988	11:09:45.106	0000103	0.0003	0.0168
TST1	TSTPROG1	21 JUL 1988	11:09:45.122	0000103	0.0003	0.0154
TST1	TSTPROG1	21 JUL 1988	11:09:45.143	0000103	0.0005	0.0203
TST1	TSTPROG1	21 JUL 1988	11:09:45.158	0000103	0.0003	0.0146
TST1	TSTPROG1	21 JUL 1988	11:09:45.174	0000103	0.0003	0.0158
TST1	TSTPROG1	21 JUL 1988	11:09:45.174	0000103	0.0001	0.0002
TST1	TSTPROG1	21 JUL 1988	11:09:45.448	0000103	0.2737	0.0004

Figure 12.4 Program-level statistics dump.

If we can collect our mean dispatch and wait intervals in an environment that supplies unlimited resources to the transaction (such as a dedicated CICS region) all wait times can be measured as the actual times required to provide the requested resources. With reliable values for the minimum waits required, and the fact that dispatch times for each transaction are relatively stable, we can compare the dispatch intervals to the wait intervals and establish a *concurrency level* (CL), that is, the number of additional concurrent transactions which can be active in the CICS region without significantly increasing response time. This value would be computed as:

CL = (Mean Dispatch Interval + Mean Wait Interval) / Mean Dispatch Interval

A CL value that is less than 2 implies that an increase in response time will occur as soon as more than one transaction is concurrently active. The higher the CL value, the more concurrent CICS tasks can be executing without affecting each other's response time. This does not mean all responses will be short, but rather response time will tend to remain uniform by transaction. The integer portion of the result represents the number of concurrent transactions that can be absorbed before a significant change to the base transaction response time is observed.

If all dispatch intervals are uniform within each application, the concurrency level provides the necessary information to determine the impact of each application in CICS on the total system. In reality, there will be some variance to the dispatch intervals for a given program or transaction (Figure 12.5). Figure 12.6 shows an example of a cross-tabluation report of wait intervals by program. Comparing the intervals observed for dispatch (Figure 12.5) with those collected for the corresponding waits (Figure 12.6) gives us an immediate sense for which application programs will most likely disrupt the smooth operation of the CICS application environment.

The combination of the wait distribution report and the dispatch time distribution report gives us an overview of application program performance. Programs with exceptional dispatch intervals are clearly apparent. Such a report indicates the

PROGRAM/NAME	DISP/TIME							
	0.01	0.02	0.04	0.08	0.16	0.32	0.64	TOTAL
CREATE	62							62
CONVPROG	109		1	1				111
DFH$AALL	22	1			1	1		25
DFH$ABARW	76							76
DFHACP			1					1
DFHAMP	36	1						37
DFHDMP	30							30
DFHECID	30							30
DFHCIP	17				2			19
DFHEDAD	37		1					38
DFHEDAP	12		1			1		14
DFHFCS	45	6						51
DFHPUP	10							10
TSTPROG2	76	8	1			7		92
TSTPROG1	215					23	2	240
TSTPROG3	8					1		9
TSTPROG4	94					1		95
TSTPROG5	3							3
TOTAL	882	16	5	1	3	34	2	943

Figure 12.5 Resource usage by program: dispatch time.

number of dispatches or waits that fall into specific time ranges. It allows you to quickly establish the general dispatch interval for the application mix and determine which programs are most frequently exceeding that value. A similar re-

PROGRAM/NAME	WAIT/TIME/RANGE									
	.01	.02	.04	.08	.16	.32	.64	1.28	2.56	TOTAL
CREATE	60			1	1					62
CONVPROG	45	9	3	13	21	1		5	14	111
DFH$AALL	6	12	4	2		1				25
DFH$ABRW	62			2				9	3	76
DFHACP						1				1
DFHAMP	4	23	10							37
DFHDMP	16	5	6	3						30
DFHECID	5	14	6	3				1	1	30
DFHECIP	4	9	3	3						19
DFHEDAD	9	12	10	4					3	38
DFHEDAP	4	5	5							14
DFHFCS	22	3	5	3	1	4	9	2	2	51
DFHPUP	4	2	2	2						10
TSTPROG2	17	29	20	24	1				1	92
TSTPROG1	63	104	19	39	14	1				240
TSTPROG3	2	6		1						9
TSTPROG4	70	9	6	8	2					95
TSTPROG5	3									3
TOTAL	396	242	99	108	40	8	9	17	24	943

Figure 12.6 Resource usage by program: wait intervals.

port of nonterminal wait distribution provides information to determine the level of multiprogramming that can be expected for the CICS region. Keep in mind that the wait time distributions already include the inflation, if any, caused by subsequently dispatched transactions during that data collection interval. Thus, you may want to establish the minimum wait values by analyzing the transactions in a single-user CICS. Comparison of the wait time distributions from the single-user and the active CICS region provides some indication of the amount to time each wait is being expanded by waiting for other transactions to give control back to the CICS task dispatcher.

If, after reviewing the dispatch intervals and wait intervals in the single-user CICS, you find that the dispatch intervals tend to exceed the wait intervals, you can infer that such transactions tend to increase in response time in a nearly direct relationship to the number of concurrent transactions. Whether or not this is a problem depends on how far below the target response time these transactions fall in the single-user CICS.

Conclusion

The CICS application transactions in a CICS region have a significant effect on each other. Most CICS regions operate without control over application program performance characteristics. The introduction of a new application whose performance profile is substantially different from the levels already present in the CICS region can and will produce erratic response time results for all of the transactions in the system.

This result can be minimized by implementing a measurement facility, especially for program modification testing and development use. This facility will assure that new and updated application code complies with CICS performance requirements of homogeneous task dispatch intervals as well as meeting the end-user functional requirements.

Once completed, a program-level analysis can identify candidate applications for migration to separate CICS regions to isolate them from the good mix applications. This allows us to convert an excessive dispatch in one CICS into a wait in that CICS, freeing up the critical dispatch time resource to other tasks.

Finally, with program performance reporting in place, application programmers can create or modify their programs for improved performance as well as function, increasing the reliability and serviceability of CICS.

About the Author

James Peterson is an employee of Landmark Systems Corporation, where he is involved in the design, development, and maintenance of the monitor for CICS/ESA performance monitoring software. He has 16 years data processing experience with the last 10 years in CICS performance measurement and resource accounting. Mr. Peterson has a strong personal interest in the development of object-oriented solutions to scheduling and capacity problems in client/server environments.

Part 5

Into the Future

Chapter

13

Database Gateways: The Impact of New Standards

Colin J. White
DataBase Associates

Introduction

The data processing industry is moving away from a centralized computing environment toward decentralized systems employing work-group computing. The workgroup environment is being used today to build both operational and informational applications that store and manage data on local workgroup database servers, but it is also often needed to access data in existing central databases. Interoperability between desktop computers and local and remote database servers is handled by a database gateway, and there is a significant amount of effort going on in the industry to try and standardize the interfaces and protocols used by these gateways. The objective of this chapter is to review architectures for building database gateways, and to discuss the current status of interoperability standards in this area. The chapter is divided into three parts:

- **The Technology** looks at the basic architecture of database gateways for providing interoperability between desktop applications and database servers.

- **Standards and Products** presents an overview of some of the main interoperability standards and products, and their status.
- **What Does All This Mean?** This section discusses the impact of new interoperability standards on vendor products and their users, by taking Gupta Technologies' products as an example.

The Technology

Desktop users need access to business data stored on a variety of hardware platforms and managed by various database and file systems. Access to data in such a mixed environment is done through what is commonly called a *gateway.* The objective of a gateway is to provide a common user interface to data, and to isolate users from the need to worry about where and how data is stored and managed. As shown in Figure 13.1, the key elements involved in gateway processing are:

- **Client Application.** Sends requests for data through the client application program interface (API) to a remote system for processing, and receives result data through the same API. Most gateways support data requests expressed in terms of the Structured Query Language (SQL). The SQL statements may be precoded in the client application, entered dynamically at run time by the user, or generated by a front-end user interface, for example, by a Windows-based

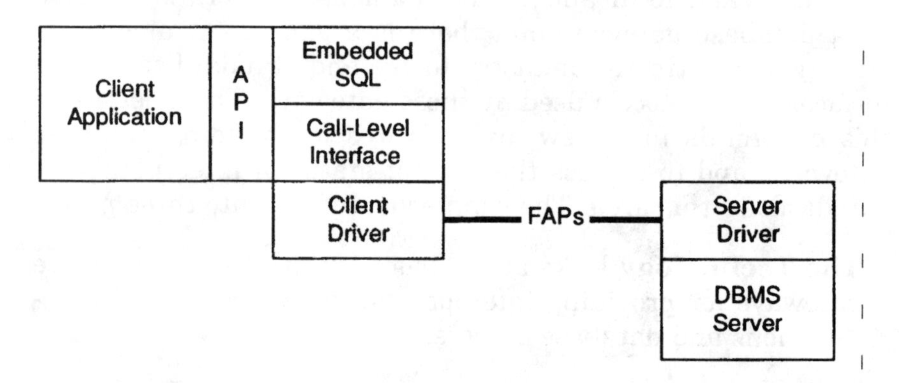

Figure 13.1 Gateway components.

end-user tool. Some gateways enforce a *common* SQL subset which will work with a variety of data management products; others require the application to use the *specific* SQL syntax of the target data management system. A variation on the common SQL approach is to provide a *passthrough* mechanism that allows the application to bypass common SQL enforcement, and use SQL statements that employ the syntax of a particular data management system. Each approach has its advantages and disadvantages. The main choice is between portability and functionality. Common SQL provides portability, but lacks functionality because the SQL syntax provided is the lowest common denominator of the various SQLs of the data management systems supported. The specific SQL approach provides functionality, but at the cost of portability.

In theory, a common SQL approach would work if there was a robust SQL standard that all vendors supported. The existing American National Standards Institute (ANSI) / International Standards Institute (ISO) standard (often called SQL89) could be used, but it is limited in function and not all vendors support the full standard. A new version of the standard (often called SQL2) is due to be released this year, and in the future could provide a sound basis for a common SQL approach.

Several gateway products allow client applications to issue *procedure calls,* which cause the execution of prewritten SQL procedures stored on the target Database Management System (DBMS). Stored procedures reduce network interaction and can, therefore, improve performance when accessing remote data. Some products support procedure calls that can be used to execute third-generation language programs stored on the target system. This facility not only improves performance, but also provides the capability to access data stored in nonrelational databases and file systems. No standard currently exists for caging stored procedures and programs in this manner; each vendor has its own proprietary approach.

- **Client Application Program Interface (API).** Provides a common interface to the client application for sending requests, and receiving results and return codes. Two types of interface exist: *embedded* and *call-level.* An embedded interface allows database requests (i.e., SQL statements) to be embedded in application program code. Before the program is compiled, it is passed through an SQL precompiler, which replaces the embedded SQL statements by host language call-level statements. Vendors must provide a precompiler for each programming language that could potentially be used. A call-level interface allows the application programmer to issue database requests and receive results using host language call statements. The interface is similar to that employed by the output of an SQL precompiler. A call-level interface is usually more complex to use, but frequently provides more functionality and eliminates the need for precompilers. Call-level interfaces are particularly useful for tools builders.

- **Client Driver.** Encodes a client request into a message and transmits the message across the network to the server driver. The client driver also receives and decodes messages containing result data sent from the server driver. In some gateways, the client driver is responsible for translating or converting (where required) data types and the character set of the incoming data. In other gateways these functions may be performed by the server driver prior to transmission of the results to the client driver.

  The client driver in Figure 13.1 handles a single client application, but most vendors also provide a multiuser client driver that acts as *gateway server* for multiple client applications (see Figure 13.2).

- **Server Driver.** Decodes a message sent by a client driver and extracts the client request. If the request is an SQL statement, it is passed to the underlying DBMS for execution. In some situations, the SQL statement may require translation or transformation before it can be processed. If, for example, the underlying DBMS is a nonrelational DBMS, or is a file system, the SQL request must be transformed into the data sublanguage of that DBMS or file system. If the underlying DBMS is a relational DBMS, the SQL request may require translation into the SQL dialect supported by that DBMS.

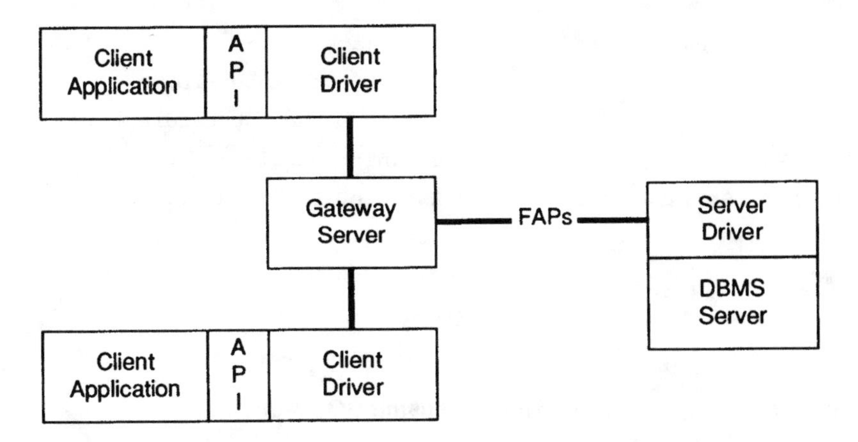

Figure 13.2 Multiclient gateway.

If the incoming request is for a stored program, the driver directly invokes the application program requested. In the case of a request for an SQL stored procedure, the driver passes the request to the underlying DBMS for execution.

Once a client request is processed, result data and return code information are encoded into a message by the server driver, and sent to the client driver. Data type and character set translation or conversion may be done by the driver during the encoding process. As mentioned earlier, this latter work may instead be done in some cases by the client driver.

- **Formats and Protocols (FAPs).** Used by client and server drivers to connect and communicate with each other. The FAPs handle messaging, support data, and character set encoding in messages, and handle network communications. The FAPs are used by the builders of the client and server drivers; they are transparent to the client applications. Potential gateway users, however, need to consider FAP issues like the network protocols supported, whether or not facilities for accounting or performance monitoring are provided, the facilities provided for character set handling, and the performance characteristics of the protocols. One big debate concerns the method used for encoding data and requests in messages. Some FAPs always encode information into a canonical form before sending it over the network. This makes the development of the client and server drivers easier, but

```
CONNECT TO db-name                 A-Associate <...>
                                   R-BeginDialog <user-ID,...>
                                   R-Open <db-name,db-handle,...>
BEGIN WORK                         R-BeginTransaction<...>
INSERT INTO S# VALUES (...)        R-ExecuteDBL<"INSERT ...">
COMMIT WORK                        R-Commit<...>
DISCONNECT                         R-Close<db-handle,...>
                                   R-EndDialog <...>
                                   A-Release <...>
```

Figure 13.3 Using ISO RDA FAPs to transmit SOL requests.

it has the performance overhead of conversion into and out of the canonical form. Other FAPs do not use a canonical form, which improves performance, but makes driver development more difficult because the driver must understand all the potential encoding formats it could be sent. Figure 13.3 shows an example of how FAPs (right side of Figure 13.3) are used to transmit SQL requests (left side of Figure 13.3). The FAPs shown in the figure are those provided by ISO Remote Database Access (RDA).

- **DBMS or File Server.** Executes data and stored procedure requests, and passes results to the server driver. Ad hoc SQL statements entered by the user or generated by end-user tools at run time are always optimized dynamically during execution. Prebuilt SQL statements embedded in client applications, stored procedures, or stored programs may be optimized dynamically at run time, or preoptimized (prebound) prior to execution. Different vendors use different approaches here. Preoptimization provides better control over end-user access to data, and has performance benefits for regular canned queries and transactions that have short execution times. The performance benefits are smaller for long-running queries and transactions.

Note: The discussion above assumes that the gateway is handling interoperability between a client application and a remote database or file management system. Gateways are also used to handle interoperability between DBMS products in a distributed database environment (see Figure 13.4). In

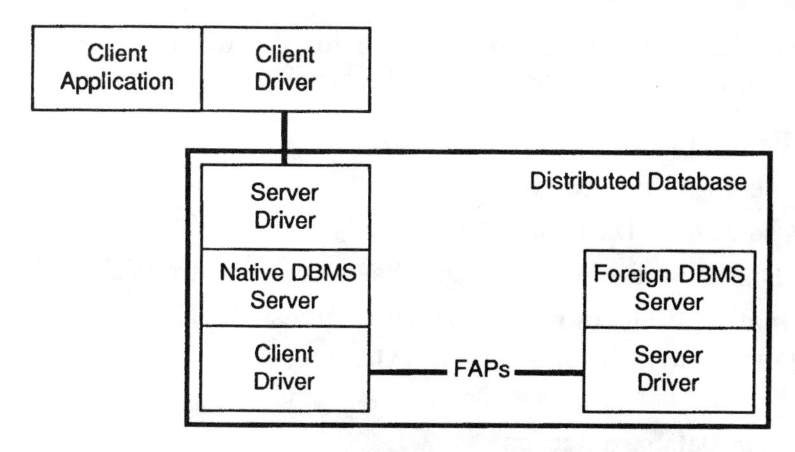

Figure 13.4 Gateways in a distributed database environment.

this chapter we concentrate primarily on client/server interoperability.

Vendors today employ a variety of proprietary, de facto, and de jure standards when building gateway products. When reviewing these architectures potential users should consider:

- The client application SQL syntax supported
- Whether SQL stored procedures or stored programs can be used
- The client application APIs provided
- Formats and protocols supported
- Driver data type and character set handling
- Driver multiuser capabilities
- Target File and DBMSs that can be accessed

There are many other facilities that should be considered when choosing a gateway. Several of these are performance related; for example, multitasking capabilities of the client and server drivers, result set handling and blocking, and monitoring tools. A detailed discussion of these considerations is beyond the scope of this chapter.

Standards and Products

Having looked at the basic technology of a gateway, we are now in a position to view some of the key gateway standards and products in use today or planned for the future. The following standards and products will be considered:

- ISO Remote Database Access (RDA)
- SQL Access Group (SAG)
- Microsoft Open Database Connectivity (ODBC)
- IBM Distributed Relational Database Architecture (DRDA)
- Information Builders Enterprise Data Access/SQL (EDA/SQL)
- Apple Data Access Language (E)AL)

ISO Remote Database Access

The ISO RDA service and protocol is the main de jure standardization effort for client/server interoperability. The standard being defined consists of the *generic* RDA standard, which defines a set of common core specifications, and a *specialization* standard for each type of database type to be accessed. At present, the only specialization standard being worked on is for SQL databases. In the United States, the ANSI committee has formed a task group (X3H2.1) to coordinate technical work with ISO.

RDA addresses the standardization of the client and server drivers and the FAPs for client/server interoperability. The client API is implementor defined, but it is assumed that the client application is using SQL. The key characteristics of RDA are (see Figure 13.5):

- The client application SQL syntax is assumed to conform with the ANSI/ISO SQL standard.
- The client API is implementor defined.
- The FAPs are an Open Systems Interconnection (OSI)–based (Application Layer 7) protocol that provides client and server drivers with the following services:
  - **Dialog management services.** Manage a client-to-server dialog or conversation (the version of SQL to be used can be negotiated using this service)
  - **Transaction management services.** Define transaction management for a one-phase commit protocol

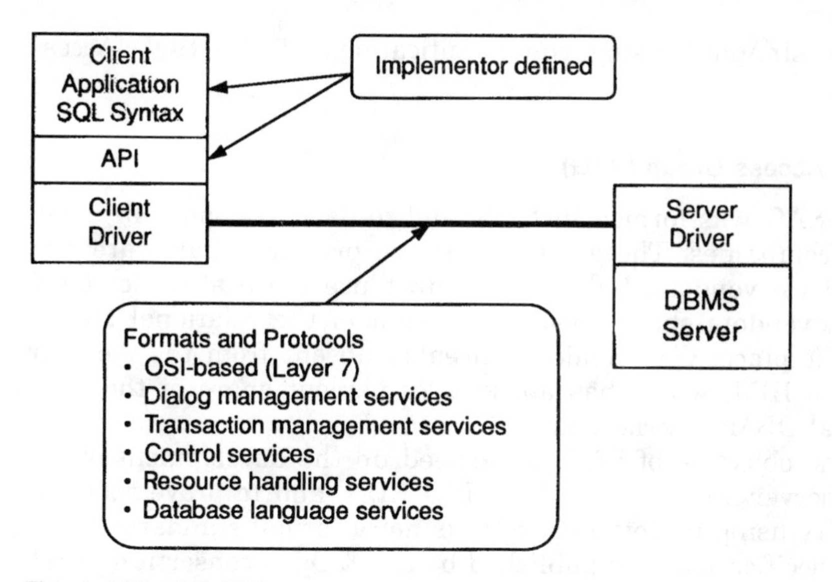

Figure 13.5 ISO RDA.

- **Control services.** Used to query and control the status of outstanding requests
- **Resource handling services.** Used to make a database resource available for use
- **Database language services.** Used to execute SQL statements

The FAPs employ several other ISO standards to define the messages used for communication between a client driver and a server driver, and for encoding protocol information and data values:

- **Message syntax:** ISO Abstract Syntax Notation (ASN.1)
- **Encoding syntax:** ISO Basic Encoding Rules (BER) for ASN.1; information inside an RDA message is encoded into a canonical form

ISO RDA Status At present RDA has a status of Draft International Standard, and is expected to become a formal standard by the end of this year. Most companies will implement the

RDA standard using the specifications of the SQL Access Group.

SQL Access Group (SAG)

The SAG was formed in 1989, and to date has some 45 member companies. These companies are primarily hardware and software vendors, but some product users are also members. SAG vendors share about 70 percent of the relational DBMS marketplace. One vendor noticeably absent from the member list is IBM, which has about a 20 percent share of the relational DBMS marketplace.

The objective of SAG is to speed up the development of client/server standards such as ISO RDA, and to prove their viability using prototyping. SAG is not a formal standards body; its specifications are published by the X/Open consortium.

Most of the SAG work to date has centered around ISO RDA and current SQL standards. Key characteristics of the SAG specifications are (see Figure 13.6):

- The SAG API enforces client application SQL syntax which conforms to the X/Open SQL standard (this is compatible with ANSI/ISO SQL89, but has some additional features) with certain extensions from ANSI/ISO SQL2 (for example,

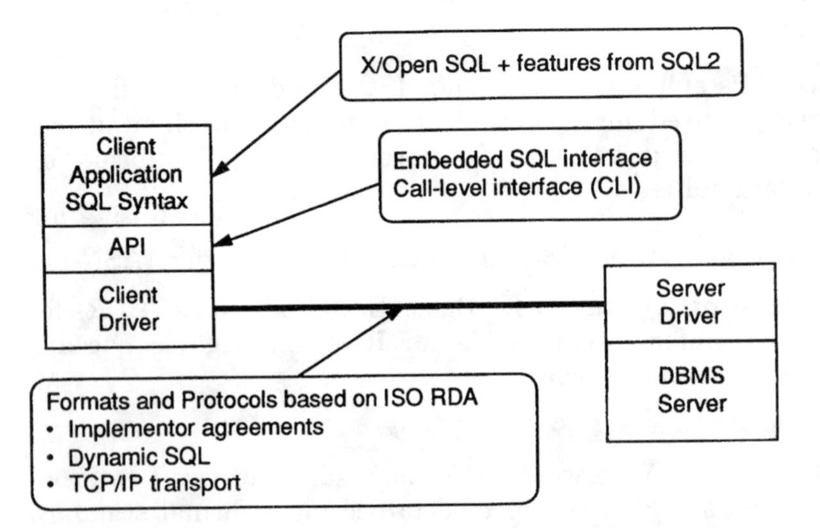

Figure 13.6 SQL Access Group specifications.

the CONNECT statement and schema information tables). Both static and dynamic SQL are supported. AH SQL is dynamically optimized.

- The client API supports embedded SQL in C programs. (A call-level API is also being developed; this is discussed below.)
- The FAP specification is based on ISO RDA. The specification clarifies certain aspects of RDA, contains implementor agreements, and contains proposed changes to RDA that for the most part have been accepted by the ISO RDA committee. Work done by SAG on ISO RDA includes mapping of SQL statements to RDA services (see Figure 13.3), encoding of SQL data, authentication and access control, diagnostic messages, and the inclusion of dynamic SQL.

At a media event in New York City in July 1991, some 16 SAG members demonstrated their products working together using prototype code that employed SAG specifications. The client API and FAP specifications were published in the 1991 edition of the X/Open portability guide.

SAG has now embarked on enhancing the specifications. Two more recent additions to the SAG specifications include a call-level client API (known as CLI; see Figure 13.6), and Transmission Control Protocol/Internet Protocol (TCP/IP) as an alternative communications transport to the OSI support in ISO RDA.

The SAG CLI supports dynamic SQL, and is designed to be compatible with the SAG-embedded SQL interface. X/Open published the CLI specifications. In addition, the CLI specifications have been submitted to the ANSI SQL committee for their consideration.

SAG Status Although over 40 SAG members are informally committed to developing and marketing products compliant with the SAG specifications, only a few have announced specific products. These companies include DEC, MUST Software, and Retix (for OEM use only). Microsoft has announced that it will support CLI through its Open Database Connectivity (ODBC) specifications. ODBC is discussed further below.

Microsoft ODBC

In March 1992, Microsoft announced that it intended to adopt the CLI of the SQL Access Group in the form of its Open Database Connectivity (ODBC) specifications. The key characteristics of ODBC (see Figure 13.7) are:

- Client applications typically use a *core* set of SQL statements based on the SAG CLI specification (i.e., X/Open SQL syntax). However, if the client driver provides access to non-relational data, only a subset of this core set of statements may be supported. ODBC also provides optional extensions that allow client applications to employ additional data types (e.g., data and time), use scrollable cursors, retrieve data dictionary information, and execute SQL requests asynchronously. These extensions may not be supported by a specific client driver. Only dynamic SQL is supported, which is dynamically optimized at run time.
- The client API is a C language call-level interface based on the SAG CLI.
- A Microsoft driver manager that loads client drivers provided by Microsoft or third-party vendors. These drivers process ODBC SQL statements, and either access data directly (for example, a local xBase file) or send requests to a server driver. When sending requests to a server driver, the

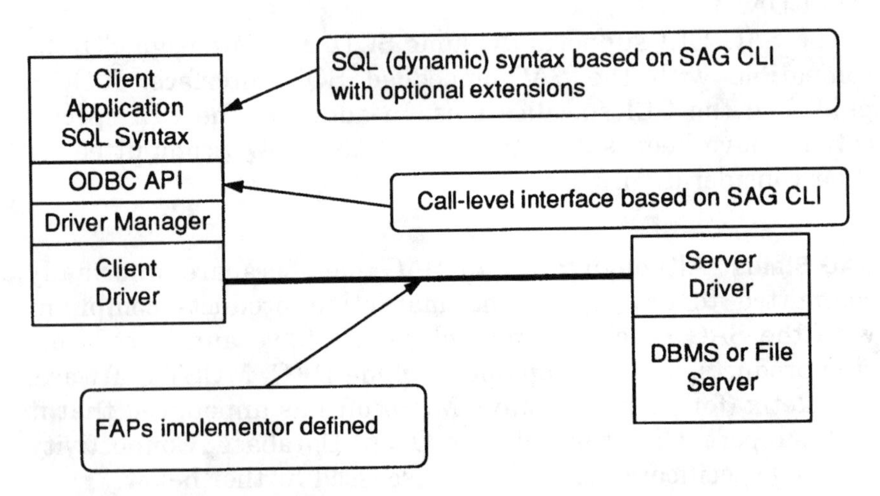

Figure 13.7 Microsoft ODBC.

client driver can use proprietary FAPs employed in products such as IBI EDA/SQL or Gupta SQLNetwork, or can use ISO RDA or IBM DRDA.

ODBC Status The specifications for ODBC can be found on Compuserve MSNETWORKS forum. Microsoft first shipped a prerelease version of the ODBC System Developer Kit (SDK) to developers in March, and released the final version soon after. It is expected that the ODBC interfaces and driver manager will be incorporated into a future release of Windows for DOS and Windows NT. Microsoft and its development partners have announced drivers for dBASE, DEC Rdb/VMS, Microsoft Excel, Oracle, Paradox, SQL Server, and ASCII files, for delivery in the third quarter of 1992. Independent software vendors that have announced support include Fox, Gupta Technologies, Information Builders (EDA/SQL bridge), Ingres, Micro DecisionWare, NCR/Teradata, Progress, and Pioneer.

IBM DRDA

IBM's Distributed Relational Database Architecture (DRDA) was designed originally to provide interoperability between its four relational DBMSs (DB2, SQL/DS, OS/400 Database Manager [DBM], and OS/2 DBM). IBM has now published the DRDA specifications and is encouraging vendors to adopt it for multivendor interoperability. DRDA is also a key component of IBM's Information Warehouse strategy. It is important to realize that DRDA is a set of FAP specifications; it does not address the client API. The importance of this point will become more apparent when we look at vendor support for DRDA.

The key characteristics of DRDA are (see Figure 13.8):

- Client applications use the specific SQL syntax of the target DBMS system. IBM's SAA SQL guidelines could assist developers in building applications that can run against different target DBMSs, but not even IBM's database products consistently implement SAA SQL. Both dynamic and static SQL are supported. Dynamic SQL is optimized dynamically at execution time, while static SQL is optimized into DRDA *packages* prior to execution.

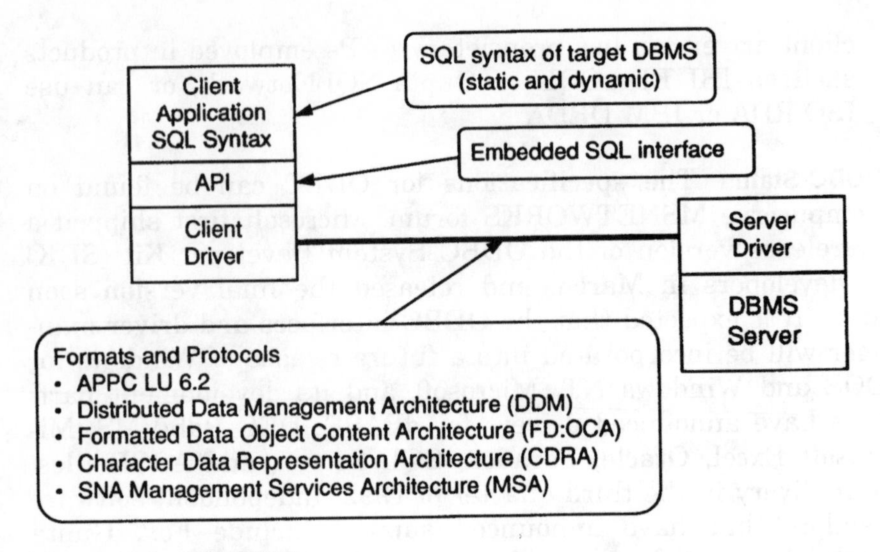

Figure 13.8 IBM DRDA.

- The client API is implementor defined. Most client products use the embedded SQL API provided by IBM's relational DBMSs.
- FAPs that use an APPC LU 6.2-based protocol. The FAPs employ several preexisting IBM architectures that have been extended to support DRDA. These architectures define the messages used for communication between a client driver and a server driver, and for encoding protocol information and data values:
  - **Message syntax:** Distributed Data Management Architecture (DDM) and Formatted Data Object Content Architecture (FD:OCA).
  - **Encoding syntax:** DDM and FD:OCA; DRDA does not use a canonical form. Client and server drivers can use either System/370, AS/400, or Intel encoding formats; it is up to the receiving driver to determine the format used and to decode appropriately.

DRDA Status The DRDA specifications have been published in IBM manuals, and IBM is running DRDA education classes. The company does not provide a developer's kit, and it is not a simple job for a vendor to build the client and server drivers.

IBM provides both client and server driver support in DB2, SQL/DS, and the OS/400 DBM. This eliminates the need to purchase the separate gateway software that is required with many other gateway solutions. Server driver support does not exist at present for the OS/2 DBM, but OS/2 client driver support is provided through IBM's Distributed Data Connection Services/2 (DDCS/2) product.

IBM has announced that many vendors support DRDA, but it is very important to understand what this means. IBM will say a vendor product supports DRDA if the product provides any one of the following:

1. A DRDA client driver that interoperates with an IBM or third-party DRDA server driver
2. A DRDA server driver for a third-party DBMS
3. A client product that uses DDCS/2 (see Figure 13.9) to access data from a DRDA server (i.e., DB2, SQL/DS, or OS/400 DBM)
4. A client product that uses a local DRDA DB2, SQL/DS, or OS/400 client driver (i.e., a client application that issues SQL using the standard IBM SQL API) to access remote data from a DRDA server (see Figure 13.9).

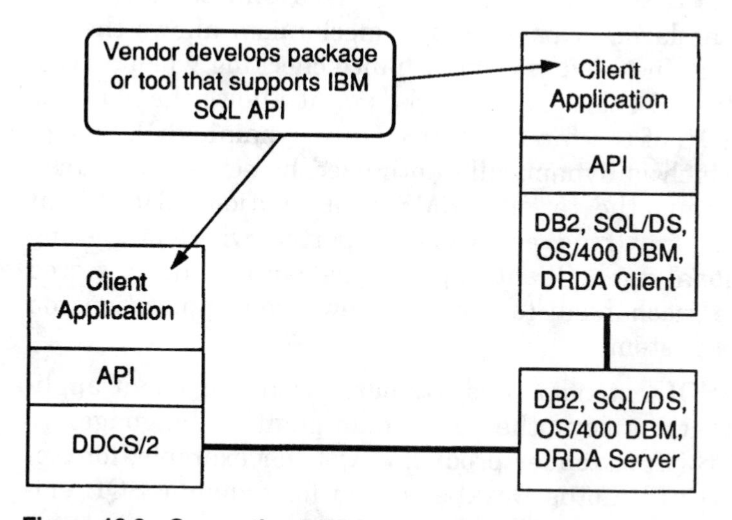

Figure 13.9 Supporting DRDA using IBM client drivers.

Strictly speaking, only items 1 and 2 above constitute DRDA support. Today, in reality, most of the support announced is based on items 3 and 4, and given the lack of sound DRDA expertise and knowledge, it will be some time before vendors are able to deliver their own client and server drivers.

IBI EDA/SQL

Information Builders Enterprise Data Access/SQL (EDA/SQL) product set provides client application access to both relational and nonrelational data. At present over 40 different files and database products are supported. EDA/SQL is a key component of IBM's Information Warehouse product. IBM positions EDA/SQL as being complementary to its DRDA strategy. DRDA is intended to be used to access IBM relational DBMSs, and EDA/SQL is intended for accessing data that is not stored in an IBM relational DBMS, or for accessing data in a mixture of different database and file systems. EDA/SQL is an outgrowth of IBI's Focus technology for accessing heterogeneous data.

The key characteristics of EDA/SQL are (see Figure 13.10):

- EDA/SQL enforces client application SQL syntax, which conforms to ANSI/ISO SQL89 Level 1 with some extensions and restrictions. (Note: Level 1 syntax is a subset of the full SQL89 standard.) A passthrough mechanism allows the client application to bypass conformance checking when accessing SQL-based relational DBMSs; i.e., it allows the client to use the SQL of the target DBMS. Only dynamic SQL is supported, which is dynamically optimized by server data drivers (assuming the target DBMS is a relational DBMS) at run time. Only read access is supported when processing nonrelational data. Client applications can also use a stored procedure mechanism to execute prewritten applications on the target system.
- IBI EDA/SQL extender products permit existing client applications that employ other data manipulation languages to use EDA/SQL. Extender products exist, for example, for Apple HyperCard, Lotus DataLens, and for dynamic SQL em-

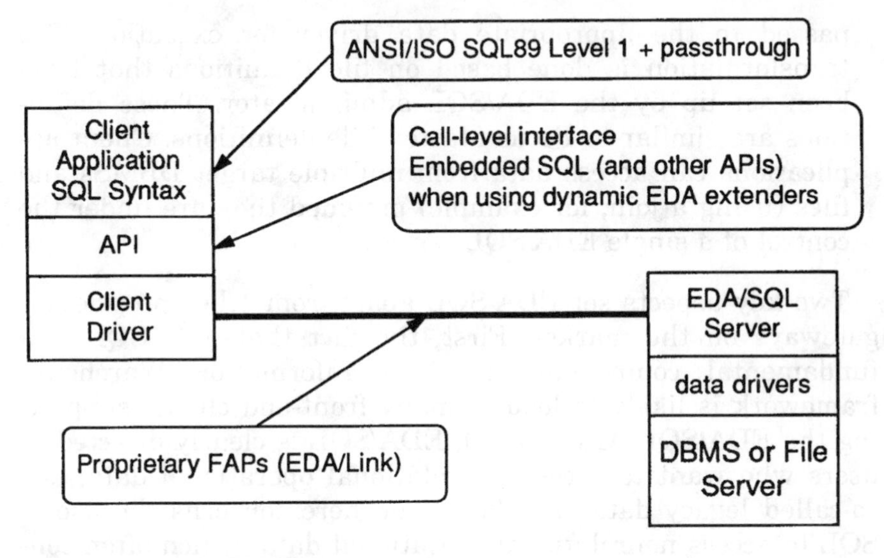

Figure 13.10 IBI EDA/SOL

bedded in DB2 and SQL/DS applications. The dynamic SQL in extender products must conform to ANSI/ISO SQL89 Level I syntax (with some extensions and restrictions). The extender translates or transforms native data manipulation requests into EDA/SQL calls. IBI is also developing a Microsoft ODBC client driver for EDA/SQL.

- The client API supports a nonstandard CLI.
- The FAPs are proprietary protocols provided by the EDA/Link component of EDA/SQL. These protocols are not documented and only IBI can, therefore, develop client and server drivers. Network protocols supported include LU 0, LU 2, LU 6.2, TCP/IP, and DECnet.
- IBI markets server data drivers for over 40 different files and databases (DB2, SQL/DS, VSAM, IMS, IDMS, etc.). These data drivers execute under the control of an EDA/SQL Server (see Figure 13.10) that validates the incoming SQL syntax. If passthrough mode is on, the SQL is passed directly to the underlying relational DBMS for execution. If the request is for nonrelational data, the request is transformed into a Focus-based intermediate language, which is

passed to the appropriate data driver for execution. The transformation is done based on file definitions that have been set up by the EDA/SQL administrator. These definitions are similar to Focus Master File definitions. Client applications can access data from multiple target DBMSs and files (using a join, for example) provided they are under the control of a single EDA/SQL server.

Two key aspects set EDA/SQL apart from other proprietary gateways on the market. First, the fact that EDA/SQL is a fundamental component of IBM's Information Warehouse framework is likely to lead to many front-end clients supporting the EDA/SQL API. Second, EDA/SQL is clearly directed at users who want to access nonrelational operational data, i.e., so-called legacy data. The key issue here concerns the use of SQL to access nonrelational operational data, which often contains embedded data processing codes, repeating groups, variable-length records, multirecord files, and so forth. This data is not usually in a suitable form for access by SQL or by end users. A better solution is to extract this data, clean it up, and load it into an informational relational database for end-user access. Preprogrammed access to nonrelational data could be done using stored procedure calls which execute third-generation language programs on the target system.

Apple DAL

The Apple Data Access Language (DAL) product set enables Macintosh client applications to access relational and nonrelational data stored on a variety of target systems. In many respects DAL is similar to IBI EDA/SQL; for example, it provides a call-level API that supports a common SQL subset which conforms to ANSI/ISO SQL89 Level 1 with some extensions. Unlike IBI, Apple licenses DAL to third-party vendors to allow them to develop their own DAL server drivers. The company also emphasizes access to relational data, rather than nonrelational data. At present, Apple provides access to data stored on DEC VAX systems and IBM mainframes. Third-party vendors, such as Pacer Software, provide access to data stored on several UNIX platforms. Apple recently announced that it will develop Microsoft ODBC client drivers for DAL. These drivers will support both Apple Macintosh and Microsoft Windows clients.

Conclusions on Standardization Efforts

We can see from the above discussion that the market is moving toward gateways that employ de jure standards and de facto standards, which are becoming established through the marketing momentum of certain vendors. If we review the status of the "standards" discussed, we see that:

1. The ISO RDA standard (the only de jure standard) is not yet a formal standard. RDA support is likely to appear in vendor products through the work of the SQL Access Group, but few products have yet been announced or shipped. RDA is likely to be more dominant in the UNIX marketplace than any other.
2. Microsoft ODBC will be the dominant API in the Windows (DOS and NT) arena, and is likely to be used in conjunction with a variety of FAPs, especially proprietary ones. Although many vendors have announced support for ODBC, products are not likely to be shipped before the end of 1992.
3. IBM DRDA will dominate the IBM marketplace, but it is likely to be some time before vendors are able to release their own DRDA drivers, and so, for the next few years, most DRDA support will be via vendor clients accessing IBM DBMSs through products such as DDCS/2.
4. IBI EDA/SQL will be used very much in the IBM marketplace, but mainly for accessing nonrelational legacy data. The issue here concerns whether or not it might be better to provide end-user access to this data by copying it to an informational relational database.

In summary, it is evident that these standards are still in their early stages, and the few products that are available have not been on the market long enough to get good experience with them. The other thing to note is that it is unlikely that a single standard will dominate; each platform will have its own preferred one.

What Does All This Mean?

The immaturity of the present interoperability standardization process creates problems for both vendors and users alike. Existing vendors who market proprietary gateways obviously need to move toward supporting these standards. The question is, which ones? Also, many of these vendors have spent considerable effort tailoring their gateways to exploit specific platforms. Making a gateway more open using some of the standards we have discussed may lead to a loss of functionality and may affect performance.

Gateway users are also faced with several problems. Should they wait for gateways that use industry standards to appear and mature? Or should they go with a proprietary gateway now and hope the vendor provides a migration path to the new world of interoperability standards? To help answer some of these questions, we will take an existing gateway product and look at the various options for potential users. The gateway we will use as an example is SQLNetwork from Gupta Technologies, Inc.

SQLNetwork

The main features and components of SQLNetwork are shown in Figure 13.11 and listed below:

- Client applications and Gupta tools such as SQLWindows and Quest use the SQL syntax of the target DBMS. Both dynamic and static SQL are supported. All SQL is dynamically optimized by target DBMSs. Applications can have multiple connections to multiple databases on multiple systems. Each connection runs as a separate *unit of work*, i.e., transaction. Client applications and tools run under DOS or OS/2.
- APIs provided include embedded SQL for COBOL programs and call-level interfaces for C and SQLWindows applica-

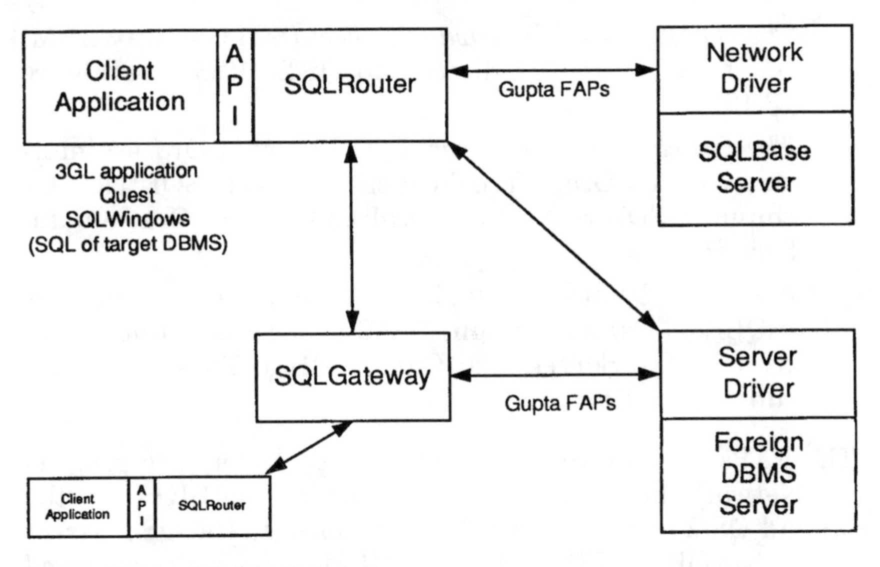

Figure 13.11 GTI SQLNetwork.

tions. The call-level interface provides many more functions than the embedded one.

- **SQLRouter** is a client driver that routes SQL requests to the appropriate server driver. Server drivers exist for:
  - **SQLBase:** A relational DBMS running on DOS, OS/2, Sun UNIX, and NetWare NLM.
  - **SQLNetwork:** Multiclient database gateways to foreign DBMSs such as DB2, OS/2 Database Manager (DBM), and Oracle. These gateways run under OS/2.

    The DB2 gateway driver (SQLGateway/APPC) interacts with a mainframe-based server driver (SQLHost) running under VTAM or CICS, which routes requests to DB2 (see Figure 13.12). The SQLHost *application services* facility allows client applications to execute host-based third-generation language programs. This facility can be used to reduce network interaction with the client application. It also allows client applications to access relational and nonrelational data, and to access DB2 databases using preoptimized SQL. The SQLGateway driver runs under OS/2 or as an NLM on a Novell NetWare server.

The OS/2 DBM gateway driver (SQLGateway/DBM) sends SQL requests directly to OS/2 DBM (see Figure 13.12).

The Oracle gateway driver (SQL Gateway/Oracle) interacts with an Oracle-provided client driver (SQL*Net) for shipping SQL requests to local and remote Oracle database servers.

Foreign DBMSs, single-user database gateways (SQLRouters) to foreign DBMSs such as Oracle, Microsoft SQL Server, and OS/400 DBM. These gateways run under DOS.

The FAPs used by the client and server drivers are proprietary. Network protocols supported include NetBIOS (to the DOS and OS/2 server driver), Named Pipes (to the OS/2 server driver), Novell SPX/IPX (to the NLM server driver), and TCP/IP (to the Sun UNIX and OS/2 server drivers). APPC is used for communication between the SQLNetwork server driver and the SQLHost server driver when accessing DB2 databases. The FAPs have been optimized for the handling and buffering of result sets sent to desktop clients from database servers.

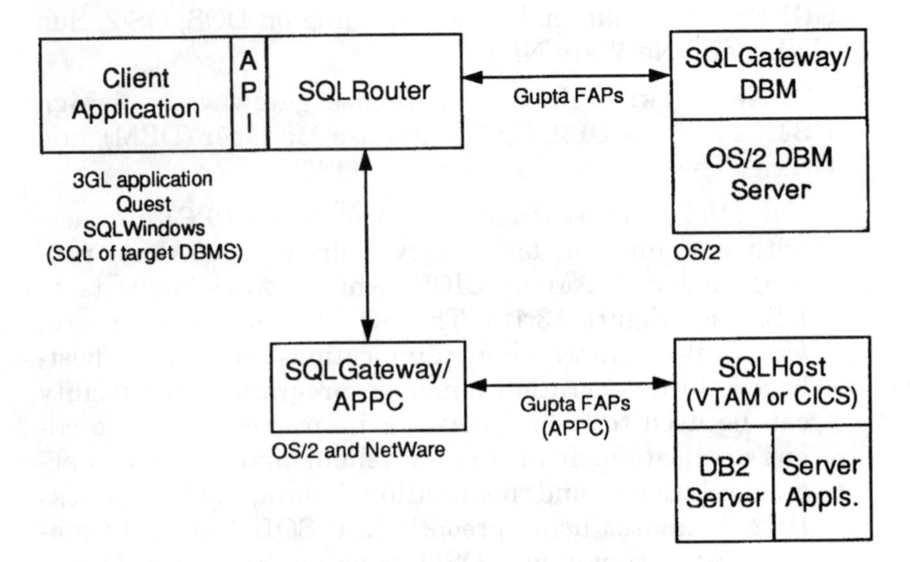

Figure 13.12 SQLNetwork IBM database support.

Gupta is planning to enhance SQLRouter to support IBM DRDA (through DDCS/2) and Microsoft ODBC. Access to Information Builders' EDA/SQL will be handled through the ODBC to EDA/SQL driver being developed by IBI. Gupta also intends to provide an ODBC driver that supports SQLBase. ODBC API support in SQLRouter will allow Gupta client applications to access any DBMS that provides an appropriate ODBC driver. An ODBC driver for SQLBase will allow third-party client tools to use the ODBC API to access SQLBase.

To see what the DRDA and ODBC support means for Gupta customers in IBM environments, we will consider users who need to access the following data using Gupta applications and tools:

Scenario Sl. DB2 databases
Scenario S2. DB2 and OS/2 DBM databases
Scenario S3. DB2 and SQLBase databases
Scenario S4. Nonrelational databases and SQLBase databases

Gupta support for IBM DRDA (through DDCS/2) and Microsoft ODBC provides the following options for the four scenarios detailed above:

SI. Access to DB2 databases can be done using Gupta SQLGateway for OS/2 DBM and IBM's DDCS/2 product (see Figure 13.13). The Gupta gateway converts calls from Gupta applications into calls to the OS/2 DBM. DDCS/2, which acts as a DRDA client driver, then translates these calls into calls to DB2. Using DDCS/2 in place of SQLGateway/APPC and SQLHost provides access to DB2 via DRDA, but it means that Gupta's application services cannot be used to access non-DB2 data. It is also important to note that the Gupta SQL API allows the switch from SQLGateway/APPC to DDCS/2 (via SQLGateway for OS/2) to be made without affecting the application. This approach may be preferred by users who wish to delay using DDCS/2 until it has a proven track record with respect to code stability and performance.

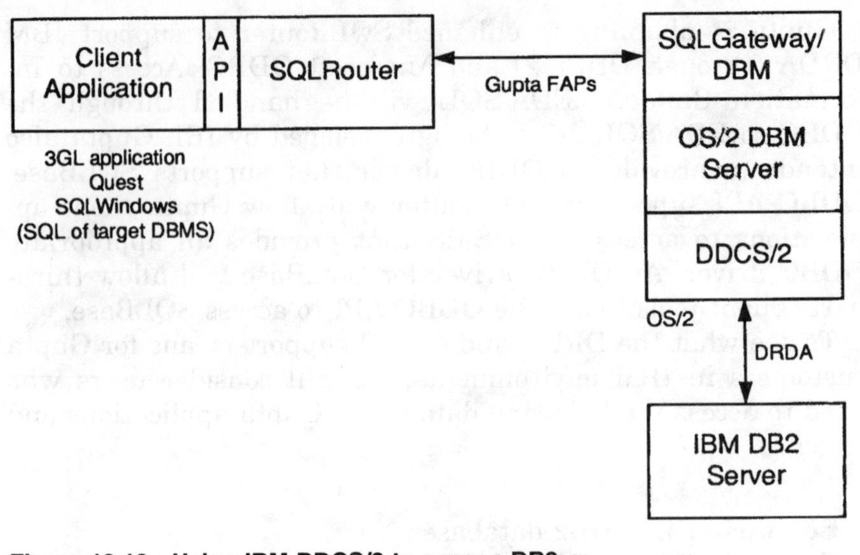

Figure 13.13 Using IBM DDCS/2 to access DB2.

S2. This solution is the same as solution S1, since SQLGateway for OS/2 DBM provides the access to OS/2 DBM databases (see Figure 13.13).

S3. There are two solutions to this scenario. In both cases SQLBase data is accessed through the standard Gupta APIs and SQLRouter. DB2 databases can be accessed through SQLGateway/APPC (see Figure 13.12) and SQLHost, or through DDCS/2 (see Figure 13.13), as in S1 and S2. The problem with the second solution is that it involves maintaining OS/2 DBM.

S4. SQLBase data is accessed through the standard Gupta APIs and SQLRouter. The nonrelational data can be accessed through ODBC and EDA/SQL, as shown in Figure 13.14. Note that this approach requires the use of the ODBC to EDA/SQL driver developed by IBI. As discussed earlier, it might be better to extract the nonrelational data into a relational database (DB2 on the mainframe or SQLBase on the work group) and access the cleaned data through an SQL database engine. Preprogrammed access to nonrelational data could be done using the application services facility of SQLGateway/APPC.

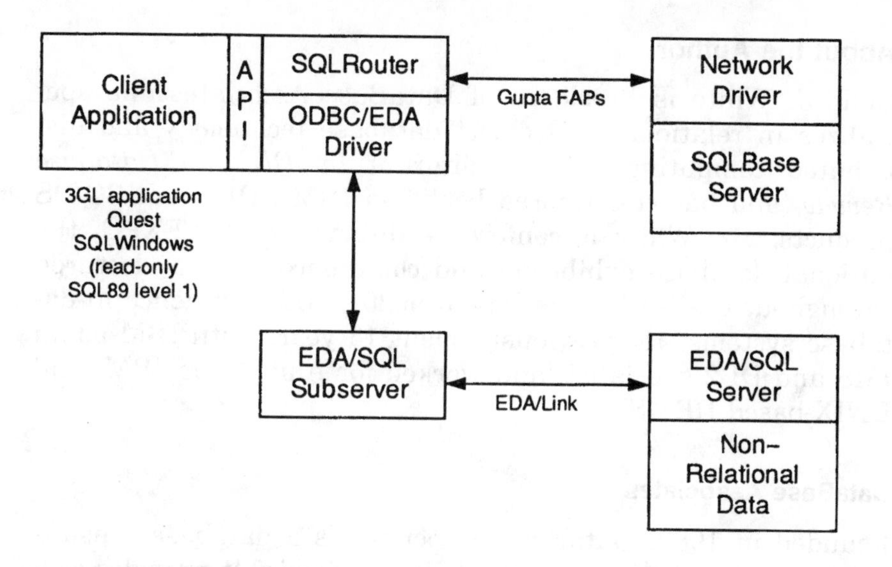

Figure 13.14 Using EDA/SQL to access nonrelational data.

Summary

In this chapter we looked at database interoperability, and the efforts to standardize interfaces between client applications and database servers. It is quite apparent from this discussion that we will not end up with one single standard that covers all environments, and that vendors are only now beginning to announce and ship products that support the various standards. Potential users who need database interoperability today should install and use existing products, keeping in mind standardization directions. They should only select gateways that have a clear migration path toward employing open standards, but should also be aware that in some situations the use of gateways based on open standards may lead to a loss of functionality and performance, compared with a proprietary solution that has been highly tuned for a specific environment.

About the Author

Colin J. White is President of DataBase Associates and specializes in relational and object database technology and distributed computing. He is editor of *InfoDB* and *Database Review,* and has co-authored books on IBM's DB2 and SQ/DS products. Mr. White is conference director for DB/EXPO, the national database exhibition and conference. He has lectured throughout the world, and has over 20 years experience in database systems. He previously spent 13 years with IBM as an IMS and DB2 specialist, and worked for Amdahl on IBM- and UNIX-based DBMSs.

DataBase Associates

Founded in 1989, DataBase Associates is a database consulting company based in Morgan Hill, California. It provides consulting and education in the areas of relational and object database, distributed computing, downsizing, CASE tools, and application development architectures.

This chapter was developed by DataBase Associates for Gupta Technologies, Inc. Material in the chapter is copyright of DataBase Associates. The chapter is reproduced by Gupta Technologies with permission from DataBase Associates.

Gupta Corporation

Gupta Corporation, founded in 1984 and based in Menlo Park, California, is the world's leading provider of client/server database systems for PC networks. Its mission is to enable the downsizing/rightsizing of corporate information systems to PC-LANs with client/server software solutions. Gupta's products have been instrumental in the fast growth of the emerging market for PC-based client/server software.

The complete Gupta SQL System consists of database servers (Gupta SQLBase), end-user and application development tools (Gupta SQLWindows and Gupta Quest), and SQL connectivity software (Gupta SQLNetwork) for connecting Gupta tools to a host of backends, including IBM DB2, Oracle, Sybase/Microsoft SQL Server, OS/2 Database Manager, Informix, AS/400, HP Allbase and TurboImage, Cincorn Supra Server and NetWare SQL.

Chapter

14

On-Line Complex Processing

The Database Solution for Complex Processing on the Desktop and in the MIS Environment

David McGoveran
Alternative Technologies

Introduction

Many companies need some form of OLTP and database management systems that can support it. Nonetheless, OLTP applications are only a special, albeit historically difficult, category of applications to support with a relational database management system (RDBMS). RDBMSs designed to support OLTP generally do not address the complex requirements of today's businesses.

As the business community moves to respond to a world market with needs that change in times as short as minutes, companies find it more and more difficult to compete. They must manipulate large databases in complex ways while continuing to support traditional day-to-day operations. Decision support, report generation, batch processing, and real-time data capture are no longer easily separated from OLTP systems.

In addition, the popularity of client/server architectures has made it increasingly likely that the desktop will be introduced into production and even mission-critical applications. Traditional desktop applications involve a way of working which is different from that found in larger multiuser systems. It is often difficult to change such work habits among desktop users; the result is that RDBMSs in production applications must support relatively unconstrained workloads.

Historical Perspective

Early commercial RDBMSs were designed to support ad-hoc query, decision support, and report writing requirements. These systems were tremendous improvements over existing, prerelational products. They were easier to use, easier to manage, and it was easier to develop applications using them. As the early successes accumulated, managers began to accept the new technology and encouraged the adoption of RDBMSs for more diverse applications. Like many successful technologies, the successes often led users to commit to projects without considering the potential risks.

Over time, the number of relation applications that ran into problems increased. There were a variety of reasons for this state of affairs. First, the technology was still new and vendors had not (and still have not) fully implemented the relational model. Second, the difficulties of managing and using large, shared databases efficiently were not well understood. Third, the user community had a lot of training which was not conducive to proper use of relational technology, and so often abused the technology through improper use.

In the early 1980s I recognized the need for supporting complex database processing; something beyond the capabilities offered by RDBMS vendors at the time. A series of requirements were identified, any one of which would stretch the current technology and products and which might warn of impending problems. This identification was based on years of experience with failed relational applications; my company was called upon frequently to perform postmortem audits and to redesign problem relational applications. An awareness of these requirements served as a successful guide to the company's consulting activities and our focus on difficult relational applications.

During the course of the 1980s, RDBMS vendors often heard complaints about limitations on the size of databases, the number of concurrent users, and transaction processing rates.

They interpreted this as a need to address a different area than complex database processing, namely that of on-line transaction processing or OLTP. OLTP characterized a certain type of application found in many larger firms. To many RDBMS vendors, OLTP support represented all the missing features that limited sales of their products to Fortune 500 firms. The term became an industry buzzword and many vendors introduced OLTP performance features at the expense of strong relational and large database capabilities.

In the meantime, a new, more marketing-oriented phrase was introduced to describe complex database processing: OLCP or on-line complex processing. Both of the business situations described above create a demand for OLCP support. Due to OLCP requirements, database management systems that support OLCP applications must be based on the relational model or some extension of it.

The Need for OLCP RDBMSs

As users demand the promised benefits of the relational model, OLCP may well replace the role played at the present time by OLTP in the relational database world. There are several reasons to think this is so. First, support for OLTP by RDBMSs does not meet the needs of many Management Information System (MIS) environments that claim to be doing OLTP. Part of the reason is that RDBMS vendors have attempted to provide OLTP features, but have ignored the cost to other kinds of features in their products.

Some of these neglected features conflict with vendor implementations of OLTP features. For example, many benefits of the relational model are attributable to the fact that requests involve high-level operations on many records at a time. Rather than spending research and development funds on making these set-processing operations more efficient and the DBMS more relational, vendors have focused on getting high marks in OLTP benchmarks such as TPC-A and TPC-B.

Such benchmarks test the ability of systems to perform simplified, OLTP, single-record operations. While there is no particular reason an RDBMS should not be able to perform well in such tasks, the vendors still had far to go in developing good relational systems.

Second, since the 1989 study by the Aberdeen Group (Boston, MA), it has often been pointed out that the performance needs of 90 percent of all OLTP applications could be met by an RDBMS delivering the equivalent of 12 DB/CR transactions per second. However, such studies neglect that fact that these applications do not run in isolation. Other applications with non-OLTP requirements must run at the same time. As a result, the total mix of transaction profiles in an MIS environment often places response-time, concurrency, and throughput demands on the RDBMS which it cannot meet because it has been too narrowly designed.

Third, the complexity of applications will continue to increase at a phenomenal rate over the coming decade. At the present time, the complexity of applications is limited by the capabilities and cost of the hardware and system software. Several trends suggest that the technology will not surpass the user demand:

- Users are becoming more familiar with the benefits of graphical user interfaces, artificial intelligence for query processing, and text/graphic/video databases.
- Businesses are attempting to integrate more and more of their operations into a common logical database, with applications being driven by the data.
- Design and development is becoming, with deployment and maintenance, integrated into a single environment.
- The development of reusable software driven by the applications backlog promotes data dictionary–driven software.
- The inability to train end users in a cost- and time-effective manner is promoting the use of smarter user interfaces and applications, which eliminate as much of the human involvement as possible.
- The increased popularity of client/server has introduced desktop processing habits into the MIS environment.

Each of these demands suggests that performance requirements, transaction volumes, transaction complexity, and very large database support will grow at phenomenal rates.

There are many examples of OLCP applications, including:

- Stock and bond trading systems
- Bill of materials explosion
- Dynamic scheduling and routing in flexible manufacturing
- Risk management
  - Portfolio analysis
  - Portfolio optimization
- CAD/CAM
- Elementary particle research
- Insurance policy maintenance
- Insurance claims adjustment/reconciliation
- Telecommunications provisioning

When Is It OLCP?

OLTP database environments can be characterized as including:

- Performance needs measured in 5–1,000 transactions/second
- Simple statements:
  - Few tables affected
  - Few columns updated
  - Few columns/table
  - Narrow columns
- Record-at-a-time updates/queries
- Thin transactions:
  - Few statements per transaction
- High availability essential
- Sophisticated recovery and tracking
- A few large (i.e., deep) volatile tables
- Batch reporting
- Optional batch updating

- Relatively straightforward integrity constraints
- Relatively stable schema and data model

For all the complexity that such business transactions introduce into RDBMS requirements, the high availability and performance requirements introduced by OLTP are not lessened in an OLCP environment. In fact, they may be increased over that of OLTP environments. Furthermore, there may also be purely OLTP, ad-hoc query, and decision-support applications within an OLCP environment, all using the same highly volatile data.

OLCP is not only more complicated than OLTP, it is somewhat more difficult to characterize. There are many requirements that can force an application to be considered OLCP. In this section we will examine a few of them. It is important to keep in mind that any one of these requirements can make an application complex.

Complex Statements

Complex statements are common in manner environments. Such statements often include mathematical computations, aggregate functions, and string functions, as well as access to multiple tables. Statement complexity is also affected by the number of columns that are referenced, the number of rows affected, and the fact that tables may consist of many columns, many rows, or "fat" columns. When a DBMS must process complex statements, it is essential that the DBMS optimizer be sophisticated.

Set Processing

Set processing involves accessing multiple rows in a single statement. Such processing is generally nonprocedural in the sense that the user does not determine the order in which the individual rows are processed. Nonprocedural or set processing in an on-line transaction-based environment introduces a need for efficiency that is seldom realized in a DBMS. This places serious demands on the DBMS optimizer. In one sense, these are exactly the sort of statements that relational DBMSs were designed to process in an ad-hoc query environment. If an optimizer can optimize complex selects, it can also optimize complex updates, inserts, and deletes, as these involve writing the result table back to the database rather than to the user process.

Fat Transactions

Transactions with a large number of statements in them are sometimes said to be fat. The number of statements in a transaction is a strong indication of the complexity of a relational application. First, the number of tables that a DBMS must manage tends to increase with the average number of statements in each transaction. Of course, one must be careful that record-at-a-time processing is not artificially increasing the number of statements per transaction. Second, larger numbers of statements in a transaction are often an indication that the data manipulation language is not handling application complexity well. For example, structured query language (SQL) does not provide a good method of computing the statistical mean or standard deviation. Third, this may indicate that the application is performing some intrinsically procedural processing—processing in which the order of operations is essential.

DBMSs can have difficulty handling such fat transactions in a multiuser environment, especially if the DBMS uses locks to manage concurrency. If locks are used, it becomes more important for the user to have control over the granularity of locking and over the degree of isolation enforced between transactions.

Long Transactions

Similar problems arise when transactions are long running. Highly interactive work is prone to such long transactions, although the more nonprocedural the request, the less likely that a transaction will run for a long time. An exception to this rule is the occurrence of batch processing. Some highly computational tasks are best run in batch (e.g., risk management, manufacturing, insurance reconciliation). In some cases, these have all-or-nothing transaction requirements simply because equivalent algorithms, which would permit the application to be run as a series of independent and iterative transactions, may not be known or may not exist.

Highly Active Database

Certain applications involve data that is frequently updated. Common examples include on-line database services, financial applications, flexible manufacturing, process control, near real-time data collection, and scientific research and development. As world dependence on information technology increases, the number of such applications will likewise increase. Such highly volatile databases stress the concurrency-handling capabilities of a DBMS and its update efficiency. If the DBMS is update intensive, maintenance utilities may have to compete with on-line users for resources. For example, it can be difficult to schedule backup operations or run report applications.

Logical Data Transparency

Many OLCP applications require frequent modifications to the database schema. For example, each new product in a manufacturing application may require a new table and it may be necessary to redesign the database by adding new columns, or either normalizing or denormalizing the database for performance reasons. Similarly, stock and bond trading databases often require a new table for each new type of security. These activities place above-average importance on support of logical data transparency.

The relational model traditionally emphasizes logical data transparency through views. In principle, views allow the database administration (DBA) to change the database design without impact on existing applications or users. Unfortunately, few DBMS vendors have implemented the ability to update views automatically, except for views that are extremely simple. In addition, even the best DBMS would not be able to update all views automatically.

There are several alternatives to automatic view updating which can also insulate the user from changes to the database design. For example, stored or database procedures can be used. However, this technique does not replace the user's view of the database. Instead, it can best be viewed as a means of creating, extending, and specializing DBMS operations. A second alternative is to allow the DBA to define view-update operations. One technique for accomplishing this is based on database triggers. Triggers are essentially stored procedures which are implicitly fired when a designated operation (e.g., insert, update, delete, or select) occurs against a designated table. If the designated table can be a view, triggers can be used to extend the view, updating capabilities of the DBMS. Of course, this assumes that the DBA can anticipate what is intended by view updates.

Special Characteristics

With the increasing popularity of graphical user interfaces such as Microsoft Windows and Motif, users are beginning to expect DBMS support for text and images. Low-cost workstations are generally capable of such support, but the data is generally stored locally in files. Although most RDBMSs now provide some support for text and image data under the name of BLOB support, few products provide integrated support for these types of data. One method of improving such support is through user-defined functions. User-defined functions can improve the RDBMS handling of text and image data types, make applications easier to develop, and improve integrity. The need to support text and image is, today, an OLCP application requirement.

Various applications involved in monitoring activities such as process control and programmed stock trading systems need to respond rapidly to changes in the database, called events. Sometimes, the application structure itself is event driven. Traditional RDBMSs required that each application poll the database, an expensive and inefficient technique. OLCP RDBMSs provide event management in which interested applications are automatically alerted to the occurrence of events.

Finally, OLCP applications may involve extremely large databases. In the 1980s, multiple gigabyte databases were considered large. By contrast, a recent elementary particle research program planned to collect terabytes of data each hour. Unfortunately, no one has been able to solve the complex database processing and management problems that multiple terabyte databases would introduce. OLTP RDBMSs usually are not designed to manage very large databases, unless the number of large tables is limited.

General Characterization

While OLTP can be characterized by the typical requirements for all OLTP applications, a database application is characterized by any of a number of requirements that stress the current RDBMS technology. In particular, OLCP applications are characterized as including any of the following:

- Many large volatile tables
- High availability
- On-line decision management (OLDM) requirement
- Unstable (time-dependent and unpredictable) schema and data model, possibly requiring multiple versions
- Complex integrity constraints
- Hybrid environment with:
  - Decision support
  - Interactive ad-hoc query
  - OLTP
  - Batch operational processing
  - Batch end-user processing

Conclusion

I believe that RDBMS vendors have been wrong about the importance of OLTP. To a large extent, both OLTP and OLCP represent different ways of solving business information processing problems. The distinction between the two in this regard is important. The user's need for an RDBMS that meets OLTP requirements is often driven by old, prerelational development methodologies. Similarly, the user's need for an RDBMS that meets OLCP requirements is often driven by relational development methodologies and client/server architectures.

About the Author

David McGoveran founded Alternative Technologies in 1976 and continues to serve as president of the firm. Mr. McGoveran is an Associate Editor of *InfoDB*, and has authored numerous technical articles and a book (with Chris Date) entitled *A Guide to SYBASE and SQL Server*. He has consulted for virtually every major relational database vendor and has made a number of contributions to theory and practice, including introducing and defining OLCP (on-line complex processing) and OLDM (on-line decision management). He often lectures and writes on topics such as OLTP and OLCP.

Mr. McGoveran designed and developed the first commercial computer integrated manufacturing (CIM) system using a relational DBMS. The client/server system also used custom knowledge-based technology. He has in-depth experience with a wide range of applications such as manufacturing, bond trading and portfolio management, health insurance, and telecommunications. He was the main architect of one of the first uses of object-oriented programming with RDBMSs and has taught workshops on the subject.

Mr. McGoveran has over 20 years experience in mission-critical applications and over 10 years experience consulting on RDBMS problems. He has broad experience with minicomputer systems (UNIX and VAX/VMS), fault tolerance, and client/server computing. He is knowledgeable with regard to PC and minicomputer database products and the key mainframe products. He is best known for his ability to blend practical solutions with a technical understanding, resulting in robust and flexible systems.

Alternative Technologies

Since 1981, Alternative Technologies has specialized in solving difficult relational database applications problems. The company provides strategic consulting, design/development services, and publishes the *Database Product Evaluation Report Series*. Alternative Technologies consults for RDBMS end users and vendors, covering needs such as database design, development methodology, design audits, application architecture, migration and integration (e.g., with object-oriented programming), performance tuning, database evaluation/selection, and deployment.

Questions and comments for Mr. McGoveran can be addressed to Alternative Technologies, 13150 Highway 9, Suite 123, Boulder Creek, CA 95006 (telephone 408-425-1859).

Chapter

15

Smartsizing

The Strategic Planning Group
Integris Corporation

How does one maximize the benefits of low-cost, high-performance open systems without also putting at risk critical mainframe-based corporate applications and without sacrificing substantial existing investments in mainframe application development and information system (IS) skills?

Certainly, each IS executive must answer these questions differently, responding to the particulars of his or her organization's needs, proficiencies, and culture.

The questions must be answered, however, for they signal transition from nearly exclusive IS use of large, proprietary, glass-house mainframes to increasing preference for distributed, nonproprietary, open systems. This transition has been variously dubbed "downsizing" and "rightsizing," but such terms offer little assurance to those caught in its benefit-versus-risk dilemma.

Fortunately, the dilemma does have a resolution, one that progresses beyond downsizing and even rightsizing. This resolution enables IS executives to enjoy the price/performance advantages of open systems without risk or sacrifice of current investments in mainframe applications.

Downsizing: Facing the Inevitable

There is nothing new about downsizing. At its heart is the idea that applications should be moved closer to the end user; this is the rationale behind terminals replacing punch cards as well as client/server networks replacing mainframes.

IS executives are finding that downsizing can be an effective response to the intensifying pressures of today's business environment, where the chief mandate is to boost profitability (Figure 15.1). That is why so many are embracing it:

- More than 70 percent of more than 300 U.S. companies surveyed recently by Dataquest are investigating or have already offloaded software from mainframes, and more than half regard their mainframe as a database or file server.
- Some 8 percent of 75 companies interviewed by Forrester Research report they are increasing downsizing efforts (Figure 15.2).

Pressure to Reduce Costs

Rarely is the IS budget not affected by financial constraints. Its forms vary—purchasing cuts, staff reductions, management "delayering," outsourcing—but all are effects of the pressure to cut IS costs. Often, the best an IS executive can hope for is a flat, no-growth budget.

Thus, mainframe-oriented IS business-as-usual is, in many organizations, simply no longer an affordable option.

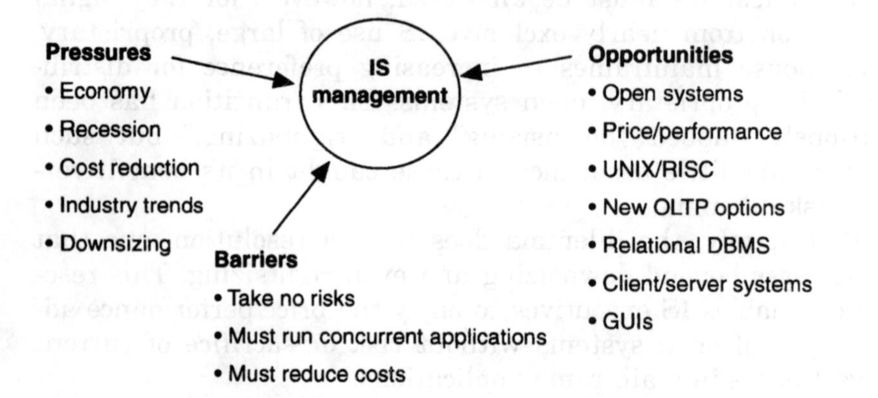

Figure 15.1 Today's business environment. (Source: Integris)

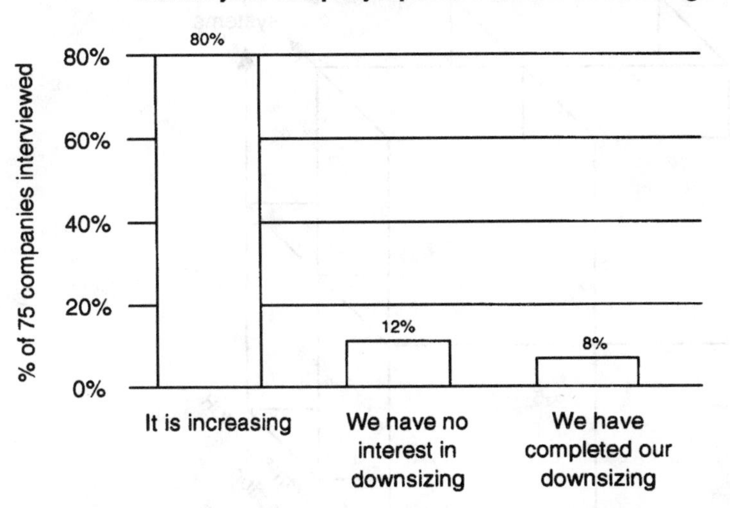

Figure 15.2 Downsizing trends. (Source: Forrester Research Inc.)

Meanwhile, an inversion of equipment and personnel costs over the last couple of decades is prompting IS decision makers to adopt new technologies.

Exploiting Open Systems

Today's open systems, particularly UNIX reduced instruction set computer (RISC) systems, turn in performance and value superior to that of mainframes by factors of 2 to 1, 4 to 1, and even 6 to 1 (Figure 15.3).

Moreover, UNIX RISC systems are improving their price/performance each year by almost 50 percent, while mainframes improve by only about 10 percent. So the gap between RISC system and mainframe performance continues to widen. Today's 6-to-1 RISC system price/performance edge over mainframes will be next year's 10-to-1 edge.

Essentially the same trend drives the evolution of software and peripherals, where open systems also are overtaking mainframes:

- UNIX high-volume on-line transaction processing (OLTP) and data center applications are run only by leading-edge users these days. But, believes the Gartner Group, UNIX

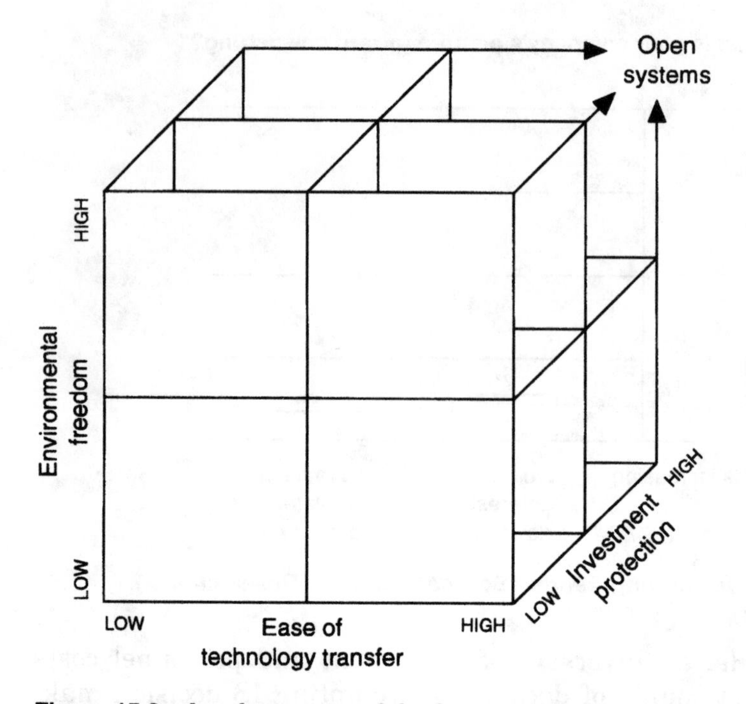

Figure 15.3 A reference model of open systems. (Source: International Data Corp.)

throughput is advancing so fast that by 1993 UNIX will be capable of high-volume OLTP (Figure 15.4). By 1996 UNIX will become a mainstream option for OLTP and data center applications.

- Both relational and object-oriented database management system (DBMS) products are much more widely available on UNIX open systems platforms than on mainframes.
- UNIX large disk subsystems have nearly a 10-to-1 cost advantage over their mainframe-based counterparts.

Twenty years ago, a mainframe price tag was roughly $1 million and the annual salaries of those who ran it stood at less than $10,000. Contrast that with the 1990s, when a fully burdened programmer year can cost a corporation $150,000, which is about the same amount as a typical business computer.

Meanwhile, top management wants to know why the organization should pay $3 million for the latest mainframe running

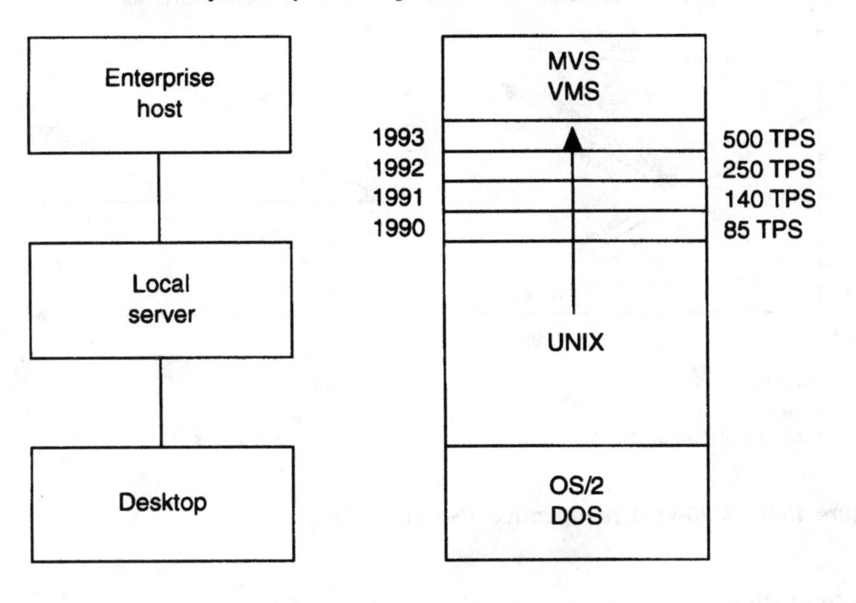

Figure 15.4 UNIX enters the mainstream. (Gartner Group/Source: SMS October 28, 1991)

at 30 million instructions per second (MIPS) when 70- or 80-MIPS desktop systems are advertised for $15,000. And why, IS executives are asked, does the organization continue to struggle with application development backlogs when IS staff spending is larger than it has ever been?

Clearly, lower-cost machines and more expensive people are dramatically changing IS dynamics (Figure 15.5). The inevitable result will be that:

- Fewer people must generate the applications an organization needs.
- More packaged software tools and solutions must be used more widely and more often.
- Fewer applications will stay on mainframes.
- Open networked systems must be mobilized by IS to meet organizational information needs.

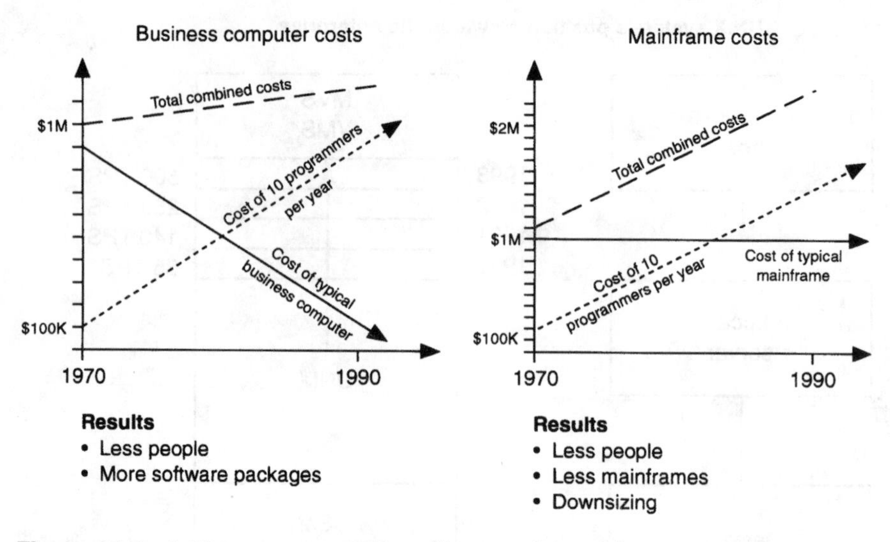

Figure 15.5 A 20-year perspective. (Source: Integris)

Minimal Risk

Because information has become an essential corporate resource, IS has become vital to the success of the enterprise, running mission-critical aplications that cannot be disrupted as new technologies are introduced, debugged, and adopted for daily use.

Important as the shift to open systems is, no organization can allow such a transition to provoke interruption or failure of its mission-critical computing operations.

Hence, a downsizing challenge faces IS executives—to implement a plan that takes advantage of today's open technologies but poses no risks to an enterprise's key applications.

Rightsizing: Making Downsizing Appropriate

If downsizing is about the migration of applications from mainframes to smaller systems, then rightsizing concerns the migration of those applications to the systems most suitable to an organization's needs. Rightsizing is possible thanks to:

- The freedom open systems grant, since they are nonproprietary and standards based, to choose among many products and vendors for the most appropriate implementation.

- The protection that open systems afford an organization's investment in current installations because open technologies can be integrated wth existing systems.
- The ease with which open technologies can be incorporated into both present and future systems, permitting IS decision makers to more effectively plan information technology growth.

Open Systems Price/Performance Plus Mainframe Application Breadth

Rightsizing is a first step toward combining the best of the mainframe with the best of desktop and UNIX open systems, without interfering with applications and end users.

IS decsion makers want to continue to benefit from the large and diverse family of mainframe applications even as they profit from the price/performance improvements offered by open systems.

The value-added that rightsizing provides—that is, focusing on the fit between an application and the system on which it is implemented—is pivotal, for not all applications should be offloaded from the mainframe. Some tasks, such as the processing of large volumes of transactions from thousands of concurrent users across hundreds of interdependent application platforms, are best left on the mainframe. Other tasks, however, like ones that can capitalize on point-and-click interfaces to hike end-user productivity, are ideally implemented in an open, desktop system environment.

Obviously, any rightsizing decision involves a judgment call. It requires that an IS executive understand not only the inner workings of an application but also the user environment that application serves.

Uses and Limits of Outsourcing

By contrast, with outsourcing, nothing is downsized or rightsized, so complete reliance on it can be dangerous. Because outsourcing is grounded in the principles of shared resources, it can reduce the size of an IS budget only through the leverage of economies of scale.

Of course, outsourcing may be a valuable transitional rightsizing strategy to ensure that current operations remain uninterrupted as new systems and processes are implemented. Or a set of tasks that are crippling an IS group's ability to undertake new endeavors can be outsourced, thus removing them from the critical path of change. Alternatively, since an IS group need not always own and operate all of its network elements, outsourcing may be the most effective way to deliver, for example, desktop/local area network (LAN) user help services or mainframe server functionality into a downsized environment.

By now, most enterprises have woven information technology into the very fabric of the organizational mission. Information technology can define a corporation's competitive advantage and differentiation. When key IS functions are outsourced, business processes themselves remain unchanged and information resources are not brought closer to users. Thus, tools that could be essential for responding to competitive escalation are surrendered.

Smartsizing: Making Rightsizing Most Advantageous

If rightsizing concerns the migration of applications to the most appropriate systems, then smartsizing is about what it takes to make rightsizing most advantageous, not only for the IS group but for the entire enterprise.

The following is a view of the benefits of smartsizing as conceived by Integris and its business partners.

Improving Return on Investment

An often forgotten element in most consideratons of downsizing, but a key to smartsizing, is the equation that calculates return on investment (ROI).

$$\text{ROI} = \frac{\text{Operations profits}}{\text{Operating investment (IS cost)}}$$

Often, downsizing is judged only in terms of reduced operating investment, that is, IS costs. And, indeed, it is not uncommon for a successful downsizing effort to lower IS costs by 25 to 30 percent; even 50 percent IS cost reductions are possible. But this alone is not smartsizing.

Integris understands that focusing on cost reduction alone will not maximize the ROI improvement potential.

Smartsizing focuses on boosting operational profits, which can result in more than 1,000 percent improvements in ROI. For those unaccustomed to such heady figures, a greater than 1,000 percent jump in ROI might sound hyperbolic. The majority of Japanese, American, and European firms that are leaders in their respective global industries have benefitted from just such improvements over the past decade in at least one aspect of their operations.

Smartsizing involves scrutinizing not only an organization's information systems, but also the business functions served by those systems. Smartsizing requires that IS be regarded as a corporate utility, a resource to be intelligently applied to the task of making the enterprise grow. There are many ways to use the Smartsizing process; three are listed below:

- **Do not allow downsizing decisions to be based on technology alone.** Information technology re-engineering must be accompanied by organizational re-engineering so that the power of new technologies can genuinely improve the business process. The value of downsizing will be limited if old business practices based on old technologies are re-emplemented on new systems. With re-examination of work flow, many tasks, from order entry to customer billing to product development, can be streamlined.
- **Get timely information to the people on the first line of customer contact.** Any time an organization cannot resolve a customer problem in a single contact, it risks a dissatisfied customer. Because the lowest cost of sales, by up to a 6-to-1 ratio, is achieved when selling to current customers, information systems that improve an organization's ability to please customers increase return on investment.

  Downsizing and distribution of data, decision-support systems, and even artificial intelligence–based problem solvers put at the fingertips of an organization's frontline troops can boost customer satisfaction and therefore the profitability of the enterprise.

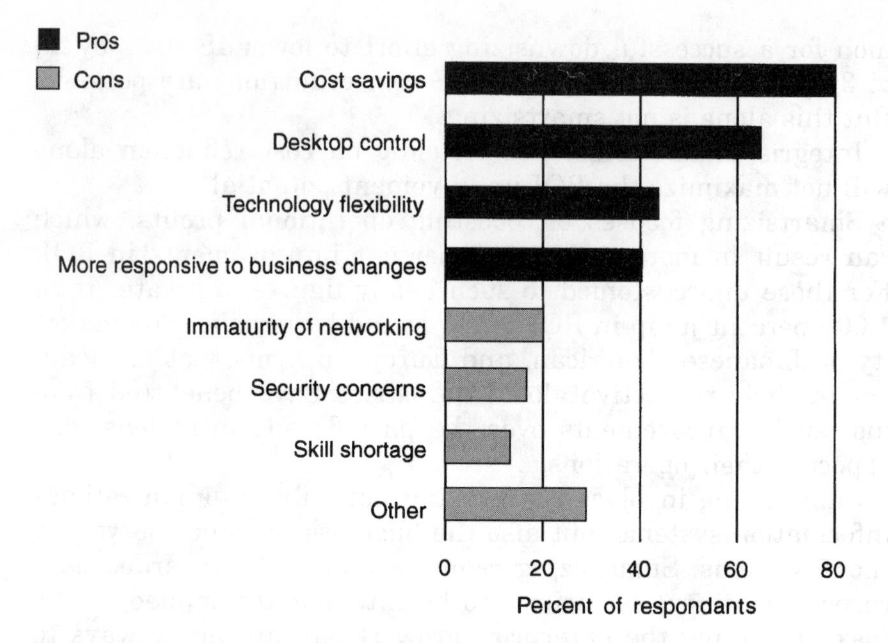

Figure 15.6 Scrapping the mainframe? (Source: Forrester Research)

- **Seek ways for information technologies to help get new products and services to market faster.** Distributing applications developed in powerful open systems environments can result in dramatically shorter organizational response times, since less time is needed to build the IS infrastructure supporting development, production, distribution, and sale of goods and services.

A well-designed distributed solution can contribute enormously to the advantages in margins and long-term profitability that accrue to those whose products get to market even 6 months before the competition.

Implementing More Productive Technology

Many IS executives feel the constraints of budgets that often must devote 60 percent—and sometimes as much as 90 percent—to maintenance of existing systems. That is why smartsizing can cut ongoing IS maintenance costs so funds can be reallocated to open systems that help the enterprise grow.

Among the ways smartsizing can loosen the maintenance stranglehold:

- **Putting existing applications on lower-cost platforms.** A number of studies have shown that the overall cost of client/server platforms is just one-seventh to one-tenth of the cost of mainframes. And the risk is minimal because, first, it is already clear that the applications work, and, second, the software tools are available.

  When expensive resources are reserved for only high-value-added applications while inexpensive resources deliver the more mundane applications, IS executives can discover that they may need less of those expensive resources. An example is forms management: personal computers (PCs) can be used for screen painting, while the mainframe or server can be reserved to drive the transaction and maintain data integrity.

- **Maximizing use of packaged software and fourth-generation language–based computer-aided software engineering** (4GL/CASE) tools based on structured development methodologies. Although CASE appears to confer little payback at first as staffers learn it, in the long term it will significantly reduce application maintenance and enhancement costs. Restructuring old COBOL code into a 4GL offers quick payback to organizations with frequent changes and high support demands.

- **Investigating the networks.** Many organizations are paying too much in maintenance, local area network (LAN) user support, and wide area network (WAN) transmission costs. Periodic looks at fast-growing networks can yield substantial savings as well as striking gains in user productivity and satisfaction. A centralized network and an application specialist "help desk," for example, might elevate IS efficiency and end-user satisfaction.

- **Checking the data.** Redundant copies of data should be eliminated whenever possible. Multiple copies waste storage resources, create unnecessary security risks, and make data synchronization difficult.

  An audit of user registrations and the applications library, meanwhile, might well reveal storage squandered on unused applications, or disproportionate spending on mainframe applications that are needed by few users and are ripe for offloading to inexpensive workstations.

Reducing Costs Permanently

By undertaking a gradual, planned shift to lower-cost hardware and software platforms that are selected based on their appropriateness for the applications they implement, an organization can liberate portions of its IS budget to fund the re-engineering of not only information systems, but also the business functions those systems serve.

Through this concentration on improving return on investment and making more productive use of information technologies, smartsizing can generate lasting cost reductions and help sharpen an organization's competitive posture (Figure 15.6).

Protecting Current Investments

Smartsizing will reshape an organization and change the ways its employees work. However, current investments in applications, in the skills of employees, and in currently installed systems and networks are protected and preserved. Smartsizing makes the use of open, standards-based systems that are designed to operate with older, proprietary computing platforms—no obsolescence, just enchancement.

Existing systems and staff skills are a bulwark against failure of the mission-critical applications on which the enterprise depends, but these investments must be tended if their value is to be sustained. Ultimately, the best hedge against risk is a vendor-independent, long-term plan that keeps the enterprise competitive by using open technologies as bridges from today's installed proprietary systems to the power and promise of tomorrow's leading edge.

About Integris Corporation

Integris, located in Billerica, MA, is a division of Bull HN Information Systems, Inc. Products from Integris include UniKix software tools, which provide a means of migrating CICS applications from the mainframe onto the UNIX platform. The company also provides imaging software, called IMAGEWorks, and a range of database tools based on a heterogeneous distributed database architecture, Integris' Distributed Data Access. Integris' core technical competencies are founded on key SmartSizing products and services the emphasize the use of open technologies.

Glossary

Note: Glossary terms are from Transarc Corporation.

ACID properties The four primary properties of transactions: atomicity, consistency, isolation, and durability.

AIX IBM's version of the UNIX operating system. IBM has developed specific AIX versions for its various hardware systems.

Application Programming Interface (API) A specification defining interfaces to make source code portable across different architectures.

Atomicity One of the ACID properties of transactions. Atomicity means that transactions are "all or nothing." In other words, transactions are either completely and accurately executed or they are fully "undone" in the event of a failure.

Client/server computing A data processing environment in which a program at one site sends a request to a program at another site and awaits a response. The requesting program is called a client, the answering program is called a server.

Consistency Data updates made by transactions preserve the integrity of data by mapping one consistent state to another.

Customer Information Control System (CICS) An IBM licensed program that enables transactions entered at remote terminals to be processed concurrently by user-written application programs. CICS includes facilities for building, using, and maintaining databases.

Distributed computing A computing environment where data, information, and other resources are spread throughout a network on a variety of different platforms (personal computers, minicomputers, workstations, mainframes, etc.).

Distributed Computing Environment (DCE) A comprehensive, integrated set of services that supports transparent communications and resource-sharing across heterogeneous networks. DCE was created by The Open Software Foundation and is licensed to systems vendors.

Distributed on-line transaction processing The collection and processing of business transactions across a network of platforms, and the immediate posting of resultant charges to an organization's database and files.

Durability Once committed, transactions are not "undone." Therefore, users and developers are assured that critical modifications to data will not be lost by subsequent system failures.

High availability The probability of a system's availability for operational work at any given time.

Institute of Electrical and Electronic Engineers (IEEE) A professional engineering organization that develops and publishes recognized standards for the computer industry. The most well know IEEE standard is called POSIX.

ISO (International Organization for Standardization) An international standards body that produces the OSI (open systems interconnection) reference model.

Isolation Concurrent transactions behave as if they were executed serially. The effects of a transaction on shared data are visible to other transactions only after that transaction is fully completed (committed).

Kernel The part of an operating system that performs basic functions such as allocating hardware resources.

LAN Local area network. A system for linking computer systems over a small geographic area, usually one building.

Monitor Software that observes, supervises, controls, or verifies operations of a system.

Motif A graphical user interface (GUI) for UNIX environments, developed by The Open Software Foundation.

Multithreading concurrent operation of more than one path of execution within a computer.

Nested transactions A group of transactions whose execution is conditional, based on the evaluation of a preceding or associated transaction.

On-line transaction processing (OLTP) Business transactions that are processed immediately, utilizing computer systems. Examples include point-of-sale applications in retail stores and automated-teller banking.

The Open Software Foundation A nonprofit consortium of worldwide systems and software vendors that creates and distributes "vendor-neutral" computer technologies.

Open systems Systems that comply with standards made available throughout the industry and that therefore can be connected to other systems complying with the same standards.

OSI (open systems interconnection) The interconnection of open systems in accordance with standards of the International Organization of Standardization (ISO) for the exchange of information.

Peer-to-peer Data communications between two nodes that have equal status in the interchange. Either node can begin the conversation.

POSIX (Portable Operating System Interface for Computer Environments) An important IEEE standard that defines services that an operating system must provide to C language applications in order to be considered vendor independent.

RDBMS Relational database management system.

Reduced Instruction Set Computer (RISC) A computer that uses a small, simplified set of frequently used instructions for rapid execution.

Remote Procedure Call (RPC) A client/server communication paradigm that offers location- and network-transparent communications.

SNA (Systems Network Architecture) The description of the logical structure, formats, protocols, and operations sequences for transmitting information units through, and controlling the configuration of, networks.

TCP/IP (Transmission control Protocol/Internet Protocol) A set of communications protocols that support peer-to-peer connectivity functions for both logical and wide area networks.

Two-phase commit A two-step process that permits updates to one or more protected resources to be committed or backed out as a unit.

UNIX A multiuser, multitasking operating system developed by AT&T Bell Laboratories.

VSAM (Virtual Storage Access Method) An access method for direct or sequential processing of fixed- and variable-length records on direct access devices.

WAN Wide area network. A network that provides communication services to a geographic area larger than that served by a local area network.

X/OPEN A standards organization that publishes portability guides for open systems, including programming interfaces and protocols.

List of Vendors

Note: Most of the entries in the following list were contributed by Tandem Corporation.

Aaron-Ross Corporation
1132 East Alosta Avenue
Glendora, CA 91740
United States
Tel: (818) 963-4119
Fax: (818) 963-8013

AD Technologie Inc.
4900 Jean-Talon West
Suite 220
Montreal, Quebec
Canada H4P 1W9
Tel: (514) 733-1377
Fax: (514) 737-3168

ADB Malmo/Malmator AB
ADB Malmo
Box 18600
S-200 32 Malmo
Sweden
Tel: 46-4034-1185
Fax: 46-4021-8569

Malmator AB
S-213 72 Malmo
Sweden
Tel: 46-4021-1560
Fax: 46-4021-8569

Admiral PLC
Admiral House
193-199 London Road
Camberley, Surrey
England GU15 3JT
United Kingdom
Tel: 44-276-692-269
Fax: 44-276-691-541

Aerie Development Corporation
25 Avila Road
Billerica, MA 01821
United States
Tel: (508) 663-9172

Allicance Systems, Incorporated
800-B Roosevelt Road
Suite 200
Glen Ellyn, IL 60137-5860
United States
Tel: (708) 858-8600
Fax: (708) 858-8603

Ameritech Services Inc. Telecom Industry Marketing
500 West Madison Street
Suite 2800
Chicago, Il 60661-2593
United States
Tel: (312) 906-4970
Fax: (312) 906-7990

Applied Communications, Inc. (ACI)
330 South 108th Avenue
Omaha, NE 68154-2684
United States
Tel: (402) 390-7600
Fax: (402) 330-1528

Automated Monitoring and Control International, Inc.
11819 Miami
Suite 200
Omaha, NE 68164
United States
Tel: (402) 496-5600

Baldwin Hackett & Meeks, Inc.
10855 West Dodge Road
Suite 220
Omaha, NE 68154
United States
Tel: (402) 333-3300
Fax: (402) 333-5770

Banksys C.V.
Chaussee de Haecht, 1442
B-1130 Brussels
Belgium
Tel: 32-2-727-6253
Telex: 21809

BCS Information Systems
10 Shenton Way
MAS Building #09-01/09
Singapore 0207
Tel: 65-221-8872
Fax: 65-222-7839
Telex: RS 43043 BCS

CACI Systems Integration, Inc.
One Lincoln Center
Suite 1460
Oakbrook Terrace, IL 60181
United States
Tel: (708) 916-2828
Fax: (708) 916-2830

CISCORP (Corporate Information Systems, Inc.)
Penn Center West Two
Suite 430
Pittsburgh, PA 15276
United States
Tel: (412) 787-9600
Fax: (412) 787-3070

CMG Information Services for Banks Ltd
Roman House
Wood Street
London
England EC2Y 5BA
United Kingdom
Tel: 44-71-628-4251
Fax: 44-71-374-2608

Commercial Data Corporation
3600 Regal Boulevard
Memphis, TN 38118
United States
Tel: (901) 375-1000
Fax: (901) 375-9197

Computer Associates
711 Stewart Avenue
Garden City, NY 11530-4787
United States
Tel: (516) 227-3300
Fax: (516) 227-3937

Computer-Integrated-Manufacturing America, Inc. (CIMA)
898 Airport Park Road
Suite 200
Glen Burnie, MD 21061
United States
Tel: (410) 760-8754
Fax: (410) 760-5829

COVIA Partnership
9700 West Higgins Road
Rosemont, IL 60018
United States
Tel: (708) 518-4500
Fax: (303) 397-5299

DACOS Software GMBH
Neue Bahnhofstrasse 21
D-6670 St. Ingbert
Germany
Tel: 49-6894-896-0
Fax: 49-6894-896-199

Dallas Systems Corporation
12740 Hillcrest Road
Suite 150
Dallas, TX 75230
United States
Tel: (214) 233-3761
Fax: (214) 788-4208
Telex: 73364

Data Design Systems
5915 Airport Road
Suite 625
Mississauga, Ontario
Canada L4V 1T1
Tel: (416) 677-6666
Fax: (416) 677-6671

Dataimage, Inc.
628 Hebron Avenue
Glastonbury, CT 06033
United States
Tel: (203) 659-3980
Fax: (203) 659-2216

Data Sciences
Meudon Avenue
Farnborough, Hampshire
England GU14 7NB
United Kingdom
Tel: 44-25-254-4321
Fax: 44-25-251-3739
Telex: 858228

Datatraffic BV
Jupiterstraat 48
2132 HD Hoofddorp
The Netherlands
Tel: 31-2503-71616
Fax: 31-2503-38794

Deluxe Data Systems, Inc.
400 West Deluxe Parkway
PO Box 12536
Milwaukee, WI 53212-0536
United States
Tel: (414) 963-5000
Fax: (414) 963-5099

Derieux
48 Rue des Vignerons
94205 Vincennes Cedex
France
Tel: 33-1-4365-0000
Fax: 33-1-4365-6062

D.E.S.
45 Rue du Fg Montmartre
75009 Paris
France
Tel: 33-1-4770-6560

Diebold, Incorporated
501 Madison Court
Canton, OH 44707
United States
Tel: (216) 489-4008
Fax: (216) 489-4140
Telex: 196115

Dornier GMBH
Postfach 14 20
D-7990 Friedrichshafen
Germany
Tel: 49-7-545-80
Fax: 49-7-545-84411
Telex: 734209-0

Early, Cloud & Company
Aquidneck Industrial Park
Newport, RI 02840
United States
Tel: (401) 849-0500
Tel: (800) 829-2050
Fax: (401) 849-1190

EDI, Inc.
19650 Club House Road
Gaithersburg, MD 20879
United States
Tel: (301) 670-0811
Fax: (301) 590-9284

Electronic Data Systems Corporation
7171 Forest Lane
Dallas, TX 75230-2399
United States
Tel: (214) 661-6000
Fax: (313) 265-2109

E.T.I.
180 Rene Levesque Blvd. East
Suite 410
Montreal, Quebec
Canada H2X 1N6
Tel: (514) 395-0595
Fax: (514) 395-8942

E.T.I. United States
66 Bovet Road
Suite 265
San Mateo, CA 94402
United States
Tel: (415) 345-9100
Fax: (415) 345-9322

Failsafe Computer Systems, Inc.
8303 West Higgins Road
6th Floor
Chicago, IL 60631
United States
Tel: (312) 693-1310
Fax: (312) 693-1315

Financial Automation Ltd
Tandem House
Level 7
18 St Martin's Lane
PO Box 8481
Auckland
New Zealand
Tel: 64-9-302-2551
Fax: 64-9-302-2650

Financial Systems Technology Pty.Ltd.
31 Coventry Street
South Melbourne, Victoria
Australia 3205
Tel: 61-3-690-0005
Fax: 61-3-690-6874

Fourth Dimension Software
999 Baker Way
2nd Floor
San Mateo, CA 94404-1579
United States
Tel: (415) 574-2666
Fax: (415) 574-3814

GCS Ltd
Strode House
4th Floor
50 Osnaburgh Street
London
England NW1 3ND
United Kingdom
Tel: 44-71-383-0505
Fax: 44-71-383-5808

GEC Computer Services Ltd
The Hollies
Newport Road
Stafford
England ST161BY
United Kingdom
Tel: 44-7-854-8131
Fax: 44-7-852-11148

GTI Informatique
80-82 Rue Gallieni
92100 Boulogne
France
Tel: 33-1-4712-4712
Fax: 33-1-4712-4799

Harbinger*EDI Services
1800 Century Place
Suite 340
Atlanta, GA 30345
United States
Tel: (404) 320-1636
Fax: (404) 320-6878

Icotech, Inc.
1800 McGill College
Suite 2420
Montreal, Quebec
Canada H3A 3J6
Tel: (514) 843-9077
Fax: (514) 843-9078

Immedia Infomatic Inc.
1155 West Rene-Levesque Boulevard
Suite 2250
Montreal, Quebec
Canada H3B 4T3
Tel: (514) 397-9747
Fax: (514) 398-0764

Information Builders, Inc. (IBI)
World Corporate Headquarters
1250 Broadway
New York, NY 10001
United States
Tel: (212) 736-4433
Fax: (212) 643-8105

Information Builders, Inc. (IBI)
European Headquarters
Station House
Harrow Road
Wembley, Middlesex
England HA9 6DE
Tel: 44-81-903-6111
Fax: 44-81-903-2191
Telex: 2959000

Information Processing Corporation
5930 LBJ Freeway
Suite 250
Dallas, TX 75240
United States
Tel: (214) 404-9244
Fax: (214) 404-9287

Innovative Electronics, Inc.
10110 USA Today Way
Miramar, FL 33025
United States
Tel: (305) 432-0300
Fax: (305) 432-0705

Insider Technologies Limited
Headquarters and Development Center
Spinnaker Court,
Chandlers Point
Salford Quays, Manchester
England M5 2UW
United Kingdom
Tel: 44-61-876-6606
Fax: 44-61-876-6607

Insider Technologies Limited
London Sales Office:
7 St Giles Court
26-28 Southampton Street
Reading, Berks
England
United Kingdom
Tel: 44-73-456-6377

Internet Systems Corporation
200 W Madison Street
Suite 1700
Chicago, IL 60606
United States
Tel: (312) 630-0050

ISM - Information System Management Inc.
393 University Avenue
Toronto, Ontario
Canada M5G 2H9
Tel: (416) 979-3900
Fax: (416) 596-4421

In Europe:
Rue Souveraine 97
1050 Brussels
Belgium
Tel: 32-2-506-4511
Fax: 32-2-511-4154

Key Base Development Corporation
PO Box 845
Danville, NJ 07834
United States
Tel: (201) 586-0797
Fax: (201) 586-0799

LeRoux, Pitts & Associates, Inc.
A NYNEX Company
5770 Roosevelt Boulevard
Suite 410
Clearwater, FL 34620
United States
Tel: (813) 531-3414
Fax: (813) 530-1096

Lighthouse Systems, Inc.
900 North Franklin Street
Suite 304
Chicago, IL 60610
United States
Tel: (312) 337-7708
Fax: (312) 337-3229

LOGFI
45 Rue de la Bienfaisance
75008 Paris
France
Tel: 33-1-4289-8319
Fax: 33-1-4561-1877

Logica Financial Systems Limited
68 Newman Street
London
England W1A 4SE
United Kingdom
Tel: 44-71-637-9111
Fax: 44-71-493-7075
Telex: 27200

Logica North America
950 Winter Street
Waltham, MA 02154
United States
Tel: (617) 890-7730
Fax: (617) 890-5034
Telex: 6817234

Magnum Communications, Limited
1600 Darkwood Circle
Suite 300
Atlanta, GA 30339
United States
Tel: (404) 952-4940
Fax: (404) 952-9534

Management Systems & Consultancy (M.S.A.C.)
PO Box 101
Weldon Road
Corby, Northants
England NN17 1UA
United Kingdom
Tel: 44-536-404-864
Fax: 44-536-404-063
Telex: 341561 BSTDHQ G

McComm International BV
Bergweg 25B
3701 JJ Zeist
The Netherlands
Tel: 31-3404-20828
Fax: 31-3404-21867

Menlo Business Systems, Inc.
201 Main Street
Los Altos, CA 94022
United States
Tel: (415) 948-7920
Fax: (415) 949-6655

MPact EDI Systems, Inc.
17197 North Laurel Park Drive
Suite 201
Livonia, MI 48152
United States
Tel: (313) 462-2244
Fax: (313) 462-9294

Muscato Corporation
225 South Westmonte Drive
Suite 3000
Altamonte Springs, FL 32714
United States
Tel: (407) 774-7800
Fax: (407) 774-7801

National Data Corporation
Two National Data Plaza
Corporate Square
Atlanta, GA 30329
United States
Tel: (404) 728-2000
Fax: (404) 728-2230

NETSYS
3 Rue Bellini
Paris la Defense
92086 Puteaux
France
Tel: 33-1-4900-8700
Fax: 33-1-4775-1067

Network Concepts, Inc.
201 Littleton Road
Morris Plains, NJ 07950-2932
United States
Tel: (201) 285-0202
Fax: (201) 285-1198

Neuron Data
156 University Avenue
Palo Alto, Ca 94301
United States
Tel: (415) 321-4488
Fax: (415) 321-3728

Oasis Technology
300 Winchester Drive
Oxnard, CA 93030
United States
Tel: (805) 988-1020
Fax: (805) 988-1020

OSIWARE Inc.
Suite 200
Burnaby, British Columbia
Canada V5G 4L7
Tel: (604) 436-2922
Fax: (604) 436-3192

Pace Systems Group, Inc.
Toronto, Ontario
Canada M4K 1T9
Tel: (416) 461-4920
Fax: (416) 469-9699

PBL Associates
10 Cottage Avenue
Point Richmond, CA 94801
United States
Tel: (510) 234-4338
Fax: (510) 234-6964

PCS Tehcnologies, Inc.
11800 Conrey Road
Cincinnati, OH 45249
United States
Tel; (513) 489-1191
Fax: (513) 489-1185

PHITECH, Inc.
220 Montgomery Street
Suite 845
San Francisco, CA 94104
United States
Tel: (415) 765-1700
Fax: (415) 765-1765

PSC Systems, Inc.
6100 Executive Boulevard
Rockville, MD 20852
United States
Tel: (301) 816-2555
Fax: (301) 816-2550

QPSX Communications Ltd
33 Richardson Street
West Perth, WA 6005
Australia
Tel: 61-9-324-1641
Fax: 61-9-324-1642

Qualitair Information Services Ltd.
Longstanton House
Longstanton, Cambridgeshire
England CB4 5BU
United Kingdom
Tel: 44-954-780-174
Fax: 44-954-782-903
Telex: 871438 QUALIT G

Return A/S
Fred Olsens Gate 1
Postboks 260 Sentrum
N-0103 Oslo
Norway
Tel: 47-2-426-110
Fax: 47-2-332-660
Telex: *RET01#

Rockwell International, Inc.
Switching Systems Division
1431 Opus Place
Downers Grove, IL 60515
United States
Tel: (708) 960-8000
Fax: (708) 960-8165
Telex: 910-695-4666

Rola GMBH
Duckerstrasse 2-4
D-4300 Essen 16
Germany
Tel: 49-201-49960
Fax: 49-201-49966

Saritel
Viale del Policlinico 147
00161 Rome
Italy
Tel: 39-6-849-41
Fax: 39-6-849-4481

SCC Inc
5710 Flatiron Parkway
Boulder, CO 80301
United States
Tel: (303) 447-8352
Fax: (303) 447-8446

Securities Industry Automation Corporation
Two Metrotech Center
Brooklyn, NY 11201
United States
Tel: (212) 383-6823
Fax: (212) 383-9084

Securities Industry Software Corporation (SIS)
4725 Independence Street
Wheat Ridge, CO 80033
United States
Tel: (303) 467-5050
Fax: (303) 467-1031

SEMA Group S.A.E.
Rosario Pino 14-16
28020 Madrid
Spain
Tel: 34-1-571-2444
Fax: 34-1-279-9378
Telex: 46739 Ginf-E

Transarc Corporation
707 Grant Street
Pittsburgh, PA 15219
Tel: (412) 338-4400

Twinsoft B.V.
Havenweg 24A
PO Box 76
4130 EB Vianen
The Netherlands
Tel: 31-3473-70164
Fax: 31-3473-70088
Telex: 40759

Twinsoft Limited
18 Hand Court
High Holborn
London
England WC1V 6JF
United Kingdom
Tel: 44-71-831-1788
Fax: 44-71-831-9693

Twintel N.V./S.A.
Chaussee de La Hulpe, 177 B14
1170 Brussels
Belgium
Tel: 32-2-675-3400
Fax: 32-2-672-2084
Telex: 20193

UNIX System Laboratories, Inc.
190 River Road
Summit, NJ 07901
Tel: 908-522-6000

VICORP
Vicorp Interactive Systems, Inc.
399 Boylston Street
Boston, MA 02116-3305
United States
Tel: 617-536-1200
Fax: 617-536-6647

Vicorp International Services
Group Marketing
Boulevard de la Cambre, 28-30
B-1050 Brussels
Belgium
Tel: 32-2-646-51-90
Fax: 32-2-646-59-64

VI Systems, Inc.
14755 Preston Road
Suite 200
Dallas, TX 75240
Tel: 214-960-8649

Volt Delta Resources, Inc.
1133 Avenue of the Americas
New York, NY 10036
United States
Tel: 212-827-2600
Fax: 212-944-1639

WM-Data Nordic AB
Sandhamnsgatan 61/71
Box 27030
S102 51 Stockholm
Sweden
Tel: 46-8-660-5200
Fax: 46-8-660-1013
Telex: 158337

XYPRO Technology Corporation
3325 Cochran Street
Suite 200
Simi Valley, CA 93063-2528
United States
Tel: 805-583-2874
Fax: 805-583-0124

SYSTEMS IMPLEMENTOR PROGRAM

Dataimage, Inc.
628 Hebron Avenue
Glastonbury, CT 06033
United States
Tel: 203-659-3980
Fax: 203-659-2216

Electronic Data Systems Corporation
7171 Forest Lane
Dallas, TX 75230-2399
United States
Tel: 214-661-6000
Fax: 313-265-2109

Rockwell International, Inc.
1431 Opus Place
Downers Grove, IL 60515
United States
Tel: 708-960-8000
Fax: 708-960-8165
Telex: 910-695-4666

Sierra Software, Inc.
6300 Montano Road Northwest
Suite G2
Albuquerque, NM 87120
United States
Tel: 505-899-0091

Smith, Dennis & Gaylord, Inc.
3211 Scott Boulevard
Santa Clara, CA 95054-3078
United States
Tel: 408-727-1870
Fax: 408-562-4246

Southwestern Bell Telephone Company
1010 Fine Street
Room 1212
St. Louis, MO 63101
United States
Tel: 314-235-3721
Fax: 314-331-9660

Sterling Software
5900 Canoga Avenue
Woodland Hills, CA 91367
United States
Tel: 818-716-1616
Fax: 818-716-5998

Sungard Financial Systems, Inc.
504 Totten Pond Road
Waltham, MA 02154
United States
Tel: 617-466-9800
Fax: 617-466-9829

System Integrators, Inc.
3755 North Freeway Boulevard
PO Box 13626
Sacramento, CA 95853
United States
Tel: 916-929-9481
Fax: 916-921-2145

System Strategies Inc.
225 West 34th Street
New York, NY 10122-0088
United States
Tel: 212-279-8400
Fax: 212-967-8368

Teknekron Communications Systems, Inc.
2121 Allston Way
Berkeley, CA 94704
United States
Tel: 510-649-3700
Fax: 510-848-8851

Teknekron Customer Information Solutions, Inc.
2150 Shattuch Avenue
3rd Floor
Berkeley, CA 94704
United States
Tel: 415-540-1110
Fax: 415-540-0808

Telcosolutions, Inc.
900 B Lake Street
Ramsey, NJ 07446
United States
Tel: 201-327-9300
Fax: 201-327-7508

Texas Instruments
PO Box 149149
Austin, TX 78714-9149
United States
Tel: 512-250-6809
Fax: 512-250-7104

Third Wave Systems, Ltd.
Sceptre House
75-81 Staines Road
Hounslow, Middlesex
England
United Kingdom
Tel: 44-81-569-5252
Fax: 44-81-569-5147

Transaction Innovation Corporation
109 Lafayette Street
Suite 802
New York, NY 10013
United States
Tel: 212-925-0821
Fax: 212-925-3666

Transaction Software, Inc.
2320 Santa Rita Drive
Las Vegas, NV 89104
United States
Tel: 702-737-8091
Fax: 702-737-6672

Transaction Software Technologies, Inc.
600 Pinnacle Court
Suite 655
Norcross, GA 30071
United States
Tel: 404-446-3211
Fax: 404-662-5577

Index

D